Learning Language Arts Through Literature

THE TAN
TEACHER BOOK

by

Debbie Strayer

and

Susan Simpson

Common Sense Press

The *Learning Language Arts Through Literature* series:

The Blue Book - 1st Grade Skills
The Red Book - 2nd Grade Skills
The Yellow Book - 3rd Grade Skills
The Orange Book - 4th Grade Skills
The Purple Book - 5th Grade Skills
The Tan Book - 6th Grade Skills
The Green Book - 7th Grade Skills
The Gray Book - 8th Grade Skills
The Gold Book - *American Literature* - High School Skills
The Gold Book - *British Literature* - High School Skills

Copyright ©1998 by:
Common Sense Press, Inc.
8786 Highway 21
Melrose, FL 32666
www.commonsensepress.com

Printed in the United States of America.

Rev. 08/11
Printed 08/11

ISBN 978-1-880892-86-2

Introduction

As parents we watched and marveled at the way our little ones learned to talk. By listening and responding to English spoken well, they were able to communicate quite clearly. The process was so gradual that they were not even aware it was taking place.

It is the belief of those associated with the *Learning Language Arts Through Literature* series that written language can best be learned in the same manner. By reading fine literature and working with good models of writing, children will receive a quality education in language arts. If you desire to teach using this integrated approach to language, this curriculum is for you.

In her books, Dr. Ruth Beechick has confirmed that this method of teaching is an appropriate and successful way to introduce our young students to the joys of reading, writing, and thinking. Our own experiences using these lessons have encouraged us to share them with you. Their enjoyment and enthusiasm for reading and writing is an unmatched recommendation for this method of teaching.

The **integrated language approach** has the benefits of all teaching methods. By working with pieces of literature, you focus on grammar, vocabulary, writing, reading, spelling, penmanship, and thinking skills. Your student has the best advantage for learning skills in this effective and lasting manner.

Grammar is taught in conjunction with writing, not as an isolated subject. Your student's **vocabulary** will be enhanced by reading the good literature selections which have been carefully chosen for his grade level. We realize that every student functions at a different reading level. For the more hesitant reader, we recommend you, the teacher, read aloud with your student. Grade appropriate **reading skills** are included. Helpful **Spelling Tips** are included to help your student develop his spelling skills. **Penmanship** skills may be developed as your student writes his dictation or any other writing assignment. Handwriting is influenced by maturity of fine motor ability so the goal is to improve from the point at which your student begins. **Thinking skills** are developed throughout the activities in this manual. Anytime a student is asked to respond to the literature with discussion, writing, drawing, or completing an activity, your student is developing higher order thinking skills.

How To Use This Book

This book provides materials, activities, and suggestions that will encourage and benefit you as you create a learning environment for your student. Since everyone is different, we suggest that you try our ideas and then freely experiment until you find patterns that work for you.

Let us first introduce *Learning Language Arts Through Literature*. After this introduction you will find the following:

Book Studies

The four *Book Studies* are provided for your student's enjoyment of good literature. Each story has a convenient summary, exciting activities, and vocabulary skills. Be flexible in how you use the book studies. If your student is a good reader and comprehends well, you may choose to ask only certain questions. For your hestitant reader, use the questions to help you discuss the book. Do not make this a tedious task, but rather use it as a springboard for your student to tell you about the story.

Dictation Lessons

Each lesson found in this section contains a passage of literature and learning activities. These activities are designed to help your student learn language skills in their context while developing writing and thinking skills. An emphasis is placed on grammar skills appropriate for sixth grade. Your student will write the passage from dictation.

Dictation is a very powerful learning activity which trains a student to look for details, strive for accuracy, and learn to write. After the student has made his first copy, ask him to check it with the model (also found in the *Student Activity Book*) and make any necessary corrections. When dictation is used in the lesson, the passage will need to be read clearly, sentence by sentence. It is also important to use your voice to stress pauses and indicate punctuation marks.

Since this method may be new for you, here are a few suggestions:

1. Before dictation, read the entire passage to your student.
2. Begin the dictation by reading one sentence at a time. If necessary, repeat the sentence, reading it one phrase at a time.
3. Instruct your student to leave a blank space between each line so that corrections are easy to make.
4. After dictation, allow your student to use the passage to edit the work. At first have the student check his work one line or phrase at a time. Asking the student to correct the work all at once may prove to be frustrating.

Review Activities

Review Activities are found directly after each lesson. New skills taught in each lesson are included in the *Review Activities*. It is not necessary to do each activity. Choose the skills your student needs.

Assessments

Six assessments are provided throughout the program.

An I C.A.N. Assessment has been created for each *Book Study*. At this grade level, you can expect your student to complete his work neatly with a good attitude. You may use these assessments to grade your student accordingly.

Skills Index

The *Language Arts Skills Index* is located in the back of the manual. To ensure that skills commonly held appropriate for sixth grade instruction were adequately covered, much research was involved in the writing of this book. This information was primarily gleaned from these sources:

You CAN Teach Your Child Successfully by Ruth Beechick
Teaching Children: A Curriculum Guide to What Children Need to Know at Each Level Through Sixth Grade by Diane Lopez

If your child has a particularly strong or weak area, you can easily locate lessons that will address specific skills using the skills index. If your child receives standardized testing, skills listed on the test may also be found in the skills index.

Enrichment Activities

In each lesson you will find the treasure chest icon for the *Enrichment Activities*. This is your cue to look for the activity located in the *Student Activity Book* where they are listed in full. Answers to these actitivities are found in the back of this manual. While optional, these acitivities develop thinking and reasoning skills necessary for higher level learning.

Bibliography

The Bibliography lists the information you need to locate the books quoted in the lessons. The selection includes wonderful books that we hope your family will read and enjoy.

Materials To Use

To use the manual you will need pencils, paper, colored pencils, drawing paper, a notebook, file folders, and construction paper. Additional materials are listed in the beginning of each lesson.

Previous lessons are sometimes used again, so keep all the student's work until the entire program is completed.

Reference books, such as a dictionary and thesaurus, will be used as well as encyclopedias. Availability of these materials in either the home or library is adequate.

Student Activity Books

*Student Activity Book*s are available for your student. Daily exercises corresponding to each lesson are included for easy use.

Table of Contents

Page

Book Study on *Carry On, Mr. Bowditch*   2

Dictation Lesson on Psalm 1:1-2   17

Dictation Lesson on *Carry On, Mr. Bowditch*   23

Dictation Lesson on *Bambi*   28

Dictation Lesson on *The Eagle*   34

Dictation Lesson on *Little House in the Big Woods*   42

Dictation Lesson on *The Story of a Bad Boy*   50

Assessment 1 (Lessons 1 - 6)   58

Book Study on *The Bronze Bow*   62

Dictation Lesson on *Prince Caspian*   69

Dictation Lesson on *The Bronze Bow*   78

Dictation Lesson on *King of the Wind*   86

Dictation Lesson on *The Wheel on the School*   94

Dictation Lesson on *The Wheel on the School*   101

Assessment 2 (Lessons 7 - 11)   109

How to Research   112

Dictation Lesson on *Jest 'Fore Christmas*   116

Dictation Lesson on *Swiss Family Robinson*   125

Dictation Lesson on *Swallows and Amazons*   133

Research Essay   144

Assessment 3 (Lessons 12 - 19)   162

Book Study on *Big Red* — 166

Dictation Lesson on *Kidnapped* — 173

Dictation Lesson on *Robinson Crusoe* — 180

Dictation Lesson on *Wind In The Willows* — 186

Dictation Lesson on *Caddie Woodlawn* — 192

Dictation Lesson on The Gettysburg Address — 200

Assessment 4 (Lessons 19 - 25) — 207

Dictation Lesson on *Where the Red Fern Grows* — 208

Dictation Lesson on *Where the Red Fern Grows* — 212

Dictation Lesson on *The Railway Children* — 224

Dictation Lesson on Psalm 136:1-5 — 231

Dictation Lesson on *Big Red* — 238

Assessment 5 (Lessons 25 - 30) — 247

Book Study on *The Horse and His Boy* — 250

Dictation Lesson on *The House at Pooh Corner* — 259

Dictation Lesson on *Anne of Green Gables* — 264

Dictation Lesson on *The Crow and the Pitcher* — 270

Dictation Lesson on *Little Women* — 276

Dictation Lesson on *Invincible Louisa* — 281

Dictation Lesson on Matthew 5:13-16 — 287

Assessment 6 (Lessons 31 - 36) — 293

Answers to the Enrichment Activities — 294

Prefixes/Suffixes — 299

Skills Index — 302

Bibliography — 306

BOOK STUDY

on
Carry On, Mr. Bowditch

Carry On, Mr. Bowditch by
Jean Latham
**Published by Houghton
Mifflin**

Readability level: 5th grade

Introducing
Carry On, Mr. Bowditch

Have you ever been tempted to give up because a task was difficult or seemed just impossible to do? Instead of getting frustrated, think about the life of Nathaniel Bowditch, a famous nineteenth century mathematician and navigator. When he met an obstacle in his life, he learned to "sail by an ash breeze," a shipping term that referred to using the oars for power when there was no wind to move the ship. For Nathaniel Bowditch this meant not allowing obstacles to keep him from pursuing his dreams.

Summary

Nathaniel Bowditch grew up in the shipping town of Salem, Massachusetts, in the late 1700's. Even at a young age he had an extraordinary understanding of mathematics and dreamed of one day attending Harvard College. Good fortune, however, seemed to elude the Bowditch family. After the deaths of his mother and grandmother, his father had trouble providing for the family and rather than being able to continue his education, Nathaniel was indentured at the age of twelve as bookkeeper at a ship chandlery for nine years.

Instead of giving up on his dream of getting an education, Nathaniel turned every situation into a learning opportunity, writing down everything he learned in notebooks. He first inquired and learned all he could about shipping, the items sold in the chandlery, how sails were made, and how chaulking on a ship was done. Soon his curiosity extended to surveying, navigation, algebra, astronomy, Latin, and French.

Eventually his time of indenture was finished, and he was free to pursue his dreams. After a brief time working as a surveyor, Nathaniel decided to go to sea, working as a ship's clerk and second mate. The ship was traveling to the Isle of Bourbon, also known as Reunion, off the east coast of Africa. Aboard ship he put his navigational knowledge to practical use and was soon teaching these skills to the other seamen. Often when he found an explanation that helped a man understand a skill, he would write it down in one of his notebooks so he would remember it. His mathematical calculations were so accurate that he found mistakes in the tables of Moore's *Practical Navigator*, considered to be the most accurate book of navigation available at that time.

Nathaniel's second voyage took him to Lisbon, Portugal, and on to Manila Harbor. Again, he taught navigation skills to the seamen, and to one man in particular, Lem Harvey, who became a lifelong friend. Nathaniel found that when the men realized they could learn, they had more pride in themselves and were a more cooperative crew.

Upon his return, Nathaniel married Elizabeth Boardman, a longtime friend. He was not married long before he took a voyage to Cadiz, Spain, and into the Mediterranean, to Alicante. However, before he returned, word came that his wife had died of consumption. Nathaniel found that keeping busy helped him deal with his grief, and he signed on for the position of supercargo with a ship headed for Batavia (now known as Djakarta, Indonesia) to buy coffee. When the ship arrived at Batavia, they found no coffee available to buy and traveled to Manila Harbor in the middle of monsoon season, an amazing feat of navigation. However, upon Nathaniel's return to Salem, he found that Lem Harvey's ship had sunk due to an error in Moore's navigation tables. Lem was believed drowned, however, he was later found to be alive. Then word came to him that his brothers, William and Hab, had died when their ships sunk, also due to errors in the navigation tables.

Nathaniel decided an accurate book on navigation and sailing needed to be written, and he was determined to write it. The book would contain three things: (1) correct navigation tables, (2) every sea term and maneuver would be explained in words that able seamen could understand, (3) mathematical tables that would allow any seaman to solve problems in navigation. He worked on his book day and night. The only interruptions he would tolerate were visits from Polly, Elizabeth's cousin, who he eventually married. Finally, his book, *New American Practical Navigator*, was finished. The book was immediately accepted in the United States and even in England.

Finally, Nathaniel Bowditch felt that in order for his book to be accepted by common seamen everywhere he must command his own ship on a voyage. He sailed to Sumatra, Indonesia, loaded a cargo of pepper, and returned home safely.

Nathaniel's philosophy of "sailing by an ash breeze" helped him to accomplish writing an accurate book of navigation to make sailing safer for all seamen. To honor his achievements, Harvard College awarded him the degree of Master of Arts, and he was elected a Fellow of the American Academy of Arts and Sciences.

1.

sextant - an instrument used by navigators for measuring the distance of the sun or a star from the horizon in order to fix the position of the ship

2.

ship log or chip log - an instrument used for measuring the speed of a vessel. It consists of a triangular piece of wood to which a line is attached that has knots that divide the line into lengths

3.

compass - an instrument with a rotating magnetized needle used for determining direction

4.

chronometer - a timepiece used in determining longitude at sea

5.

spyglass - a small telescope used to observe objects far away

Vocabulary

The following vocabulary words deal with some aspect of navigation. Look up the following words in the dictionary and write a clear definition for each word. Make sure your definition deals with navigation.

1. sextant - (Chapter 6)

2. ship log or chip log - (Chapter 6)

3. compass - (Chapter 12)

4. chronometer - (Chapter 12)

5. spyglass - (Chapter 15)

Use the definitions of your vocabulary words to help you match each word with the correct picture.

_____ _____ _____

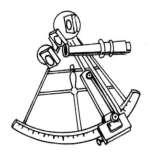 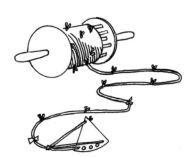

_____ _____

Discussion Questions

Chapters 1 - 2
1. Why did Nat use the shilling he found to buy an expectation?

Chapters 3 - 4
2. Why was Nat unable to continue going to school?

Chapters 5 - 6
3. What did Nat mean when he said that he was sailing by "an ash breeze"?

Chapters 7 - 8
4. Why did Nat decide to teach himself Latin?

Chapters 9 - 10
5. Why did Nat feel he was collecting his expectation from the *Pilgrim* when he was invited to join The Salem Philosophical Library?

Chapters 11 - 12
6. How did Nat apply Elizabeth Boardman's expression about "stumbling on people's dumbness" to teaching the seamen navigation?

---

1. Nat's family was poor and in financial trouble. His father told him that if he had a lot of money he would buy an expectation, so that is what Nat did with his shilling.

2. His father was unable to pay for him to go to school. Also, his older brother, Hab, had gone to sea, and he was needed in the cooperage to help his father.

3. He decided that he would not get discouraged even though he was indentured for nine years. He was determined to continue to learn even though he could not continue going to school.

4. Nat wanted to be able to read Isaac Newton's *Principia* so he could learn more about astronomy. However, since the book was written in Latin, he had to learn Latin in order to read it. Also, he was offered a tutoring position that would allow him to go to Harvard if he was released from his indenture; and he wanted to know Latin so he would be prepared if the chance came.

5. Many of the books in the library were cargo that was taken by the *Pilgrim*, the ship on which he had purchased an expectation when he was a young boy. He was now able to read those books.

6. Every time he would get impatient when it took the men so long to understand something he was teaching them, he would remember what she said and be more patient.

Chapters 13 - 14
7. Why was Nat so upset when he found a mistake in Moore's *Navigator*?

Chapters 15 - 16
8. How did Nat handle the troublemaker, Lem Harvey, aboard the *Astrea*?

Chapters 17 - 18
9. Who did Nat marry and why was it only for a short time?

Chapters 19 - 20
10. What three things did Nat did decide that his book of navigation would contain?

Chapters 21 - 22
11. What honor was awarded to Nat by Harvard College and why was it so important to him?

Chapters 23 - 24
12. Why was it so important to Nat to command a ship on a voyage?

---

7. First of all he felt that mathematics must be accurate if it was to be worth anything. Second, men's lives depended upon those tables being accurate. Mistakes could cause ships to sail off course and into danger.

8. He convinced him that he could learn navigational skills along with the other men if he could learn to control his temper and not get frustrated when it was hard for him. Soon Lem was so busy learning that he was no longer causing any problems.

9. Nat married Elizabeth Boardman, a longtime friend. However, their marriage did not last long because Elizabeth died of consumption while Nat was away on a voyage.

10. 1) correct navigation tables
   2) every sea term and maneuver a seaman needs to know in words any seaman can understand
   3) mathematical tables that would allow any seaman to solve problem in navigation

11. A Master of Arts degree was awarded to Nat by Harvard College. He had always wanted to attend Harvard College, so it was the fulfillment of a lifelong dream.

12. He felt his navigation book would never be accepted by the common seaman if he had never commanded a vessel. He felt he must prove that "book sailing" worked.

Activities

To help you continue your enjoyment of *Carry On, Mr. Bowditch*, choose any two of the following activities.

1. Journal Writing - pg. 7
2. Parts of a Ship - pg. 8
3. Mapping Skills - pg. 10

Journal Writing

After mapping on pages 11-12, create a journal entry as if you were Nat writing in one of his notebooks. Tell about the sights you would have seen on that journey. Refer to your book for the information you need.

Parts of a Ship

Answers to Parts of the Ship:

1. rigging - tackle, chains, and ropes used to support and control sails, masts and yards of a sailing vessel
2. mast - the long upright pole of wood or metal supporting sails and the rigging
3. quarterdeck - after part of the upper deck (usually reserved for officers)
4. capstan - vertical cylinder rotated to wind in the anchor cable. In the past, sailors hoisted the anchor or raised the heavy sails by turning the capstan
5. yard - long pole slung to mast to support head of sail
6. halyard - rope used to raise or lower sail or flag
7. poopdeck - deck at the stern (above ordinary deck); often forms the roof
8. stern - rear part of a ship
9. bow - front section of a ship
10. keel - strong beam (wood or metal) running along center line of a vessel from end to end
11. hull - framework or body
12. prow - forward part of a ship's hull; the bow
13. boom - long pole extending from the mast of a ship to secure or stretch out the bottom of a sail
14. bowsprit - long pole extending from front of ship to which lines are attached for securing sails
15. forecastle - section of the ship's upper deck; forward of the foremast

Look up the following words in a dictionary to find the part of the ship it identifies. Write the correct word in the space provided on the illustration of the ship (page 9).

1. rigging
2. mast
3. quarterdeck
4. capstan
5. yard
6. halyard
7. poopdeck
8. stern
9. bow
10. keel
11. hull
12. prow
13. boom
14. bowsprit
15. forecastle (also called fo'c'sle)

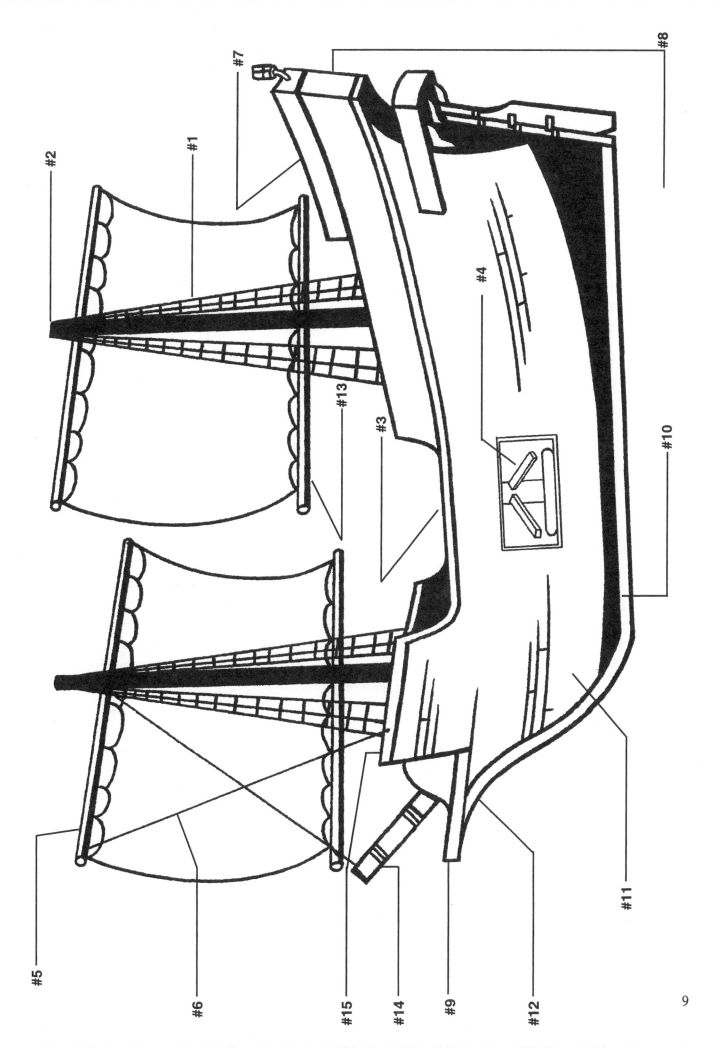

#8

#7

#1

#2

#4

#13

#3

#10

#5

#6

#15

#14

#9

#12

#11

9

Mapping Skills

Nathaniel Bowditch took a series of five voyages listed below. On the following map, draw the paths that the ship took using different colored pencils. Use a world atlas to help you locate the various seaports.

1. **Voyage 1** - (red pencil) Left Salem and sailed across the Atlantic Ocean and around Africa to the Isle of Bourbon also known as Reunion, a French-owned island off the east coast of Africa.

2. **Voyage 2** - (blue pencil) Left Salem and across the Atlantic Ocean, sailed to Lisbon, Portugal, then stopped over in Funchal in the Madeira Islands (off the northwest coast of Africa), sailed around Africa and through the Indian Ocean to Manila Harbor in what is now the Philippines.

3. **Voyage 3** - (green pencil) Left Salem and sailed across the Atlantic Ocean to Cadiz, Spain (a seaport in southwest Spain) and into the Mediterranean Sea to Alicante, Spain (a seaport in southeast Spain).

4. **Voyage 4** - (purple pencil) Left Boston and sailed across the Atlantic Ocean around Africa, through the Indian Ocean to Batavia (now known as Djakarta, a seaport of Indonesia on the northwest coast of Java) then sailed to Manila Harbor located in what is now the Philippines.

5. **Voyage 5** - (yellow pencil) Left Salem and sailed across the Atlantic Ocean, around Africa, across the Indian Ocean to Sumatra, a western island of Indonesia.

Journey 1

Journey 2

Journey 3

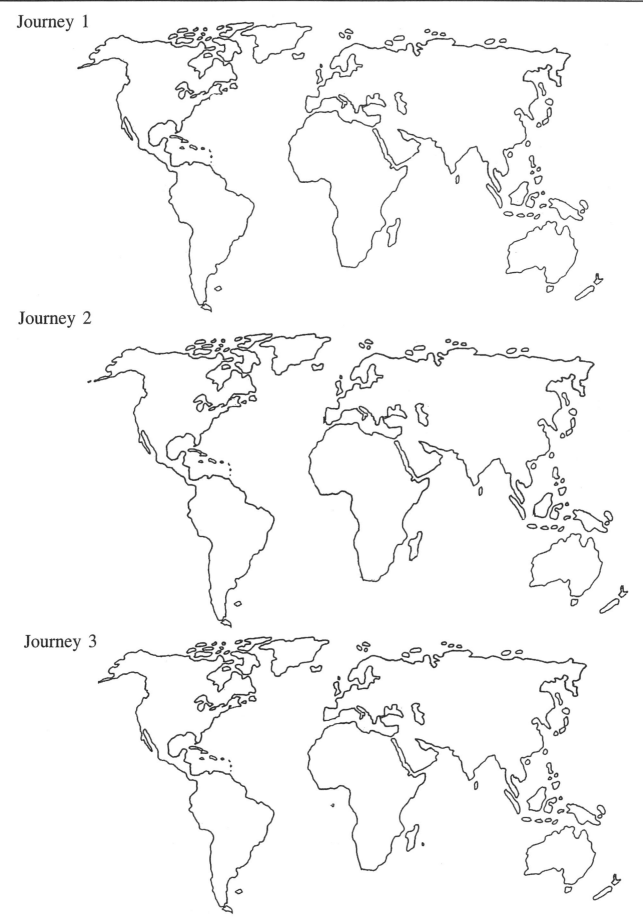

This page may be photocopied for student's use.

Journey 4

Journey 5

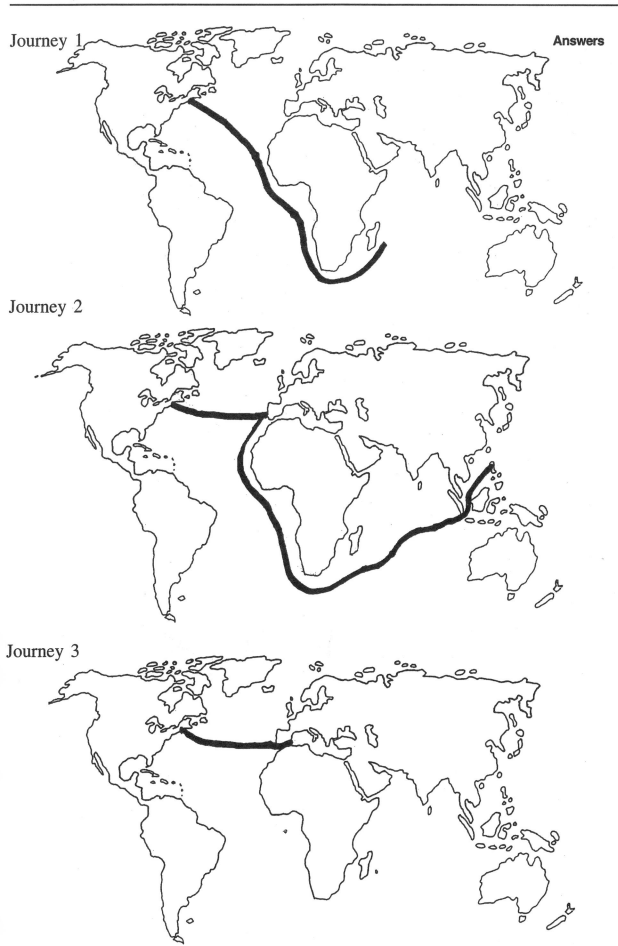

Journey 1

Answers

Journey 2

Journey 3

Answers

Journey 4

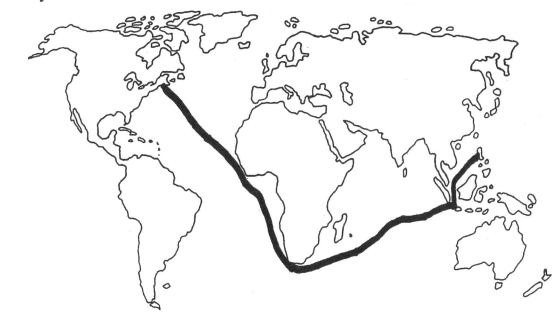

Journey 5

I C.A.N. Assessment

for

Carry On, Mr. Bowditch - Book Study A

After the *Book Study* is completed, check off each I C.A.N. objective with your teacher.

C   I can **complete** my work.

    I can be **creative**.

A   I can be **accurate**.

    I can do my work with a good **attitude**.

N   I can do my work **neatly**.

_____

_____

_____

_____

_____

Blessed is the man that walketh not in the counsel of the ungodly, nor standeth in the way of sinners, nor sitteth in the seat of the scornful. But his delight is in the law of the Lord; and in his law doth he meditate day and night.

Psalm 1:1-2 (KJV)

1. a. Listen as your teacher reads the literature passage. This passage was taken from the King James Version of the Bible. The King James Version was translated in 1611. You will notice that some of the words sound differently from the way we speak today. Circle these words. The reason we no longer use these words is because English is a *living language*. A living language is a language that is spoken and used in daily communication. The language changes as new words are added, words are changed, and certain words are no longer used. For example, fifty years ago words such as videotape, modem, and internet were not a part of our language. They are words that have been added. Can you think of any other new words that have been added to our language in the last fifty years?

   b. Write the literature passage from dictation. Compare your copy to the passage and check for mistakes. Make your own spelling list from any misspelled words or use the following list of suggested words:

   counsel   meditate   delight   ungodly

   c. Some of the words in the verses have prefixes. A **prefix** is a letter or group of letters which come before the main part, or **root** of the word. **Pre-** is a prefix which means *before*. Knowing the meaning of a prefix will help you understand the meaning of a word, as in *preview* which means *to view or show before*.

Teacher's Note: As your student completes each lesson, choose skills from the Review Activities that he needs. The Review Activities follow each lesson.

1.

a. **walketh, standeth, sitteth, doth**

Possible answers: microchip, fax, microwave, CD

1.
d. not godly

e. pre-; before; preview, precede
  un-; release; ungodly, unfair

d. Another prefix in the literature passage is **un-**. Underline the word in the literature passage that has this prefix. The prefix **un-** means *not* or *release*. Knowing the meaning of this prefix, how would you define the word *ungodly*?

e. Look at the prefix list on page 299. Find the prefix chart in the *Student Activity Book* and follow the instructions. If you are not using the *Student Activity Book*, set up a sheet of notebook papers like this example:

Prefix	Meaning	Word Examples
pre-	before	preview, precede

Write the prefixes **pre-** and **un-** in the spaces provided under the prefix heading. Add a definition and think of two word examples for each prefix. Refer to your dictionary if you need help. Keep this list available for easy reference as you will add to this list throughout the program.

2. a. In 1408 John Wycliffe was responsible for the first translation of the Latin Scriptures into the English language. The type of English used during this time period is called Middle English. Middle English was in use from the time of the Norman Conquest of 1066 to the introduction of printing in England in 1476. Many words of French origin became part of the English language at this time. Old English is the name given to the earliest English which was mostly Germanic in content. Modern English is the name given to the language from the time period extending from 1476 to present day.

b. The origin of a word is referred to as its **etymology.** Most dictionaries give the etymology of a word, as in the sample below:

counsel (koun's'l)n. [M.E.&OFr.]
1. a mutual exchange of ideas, opinions, etc. . . . .

Notice the abbreviations that appear in the brackets, [M.E.& OFr.]. These abbreviations stand for Middle English and Old French and tell us the origin of this word into the English language. Use your dictionary to look up a word from the literature passage. See if you can find the etymology for the word. (The meanings of the abbreviations used are usually found in the front section of the dictionary.)

c. Write the list of suggested spelling words from the literature passage. If any of them are in a form that is not longer in use today, write the word that would be the modern substitute for each. Using a thesaurus, write a synonym for each word. **Synonyms** are words which have the same or similar meaning. For example, a synonym for the word *blessed* would be *joyful*. Many of the words from the list can have different meanings. Be sure the word you choose can be substituted for the original word in the passage without changing the meaning.

3. a. Sometimes the best way to picture the order in which events happened is by creating a timeline. Using the following information about the history of Bible translation, make a timeline. The timeline should have the earliest translation date listed starting at the far left-hand side of the timeline with dates and names continuing in correct sequence up to the most current translation, which should appear at the far right-hand side. Only the information in bold print should be written on the time line, with the dates being written at the top of the line and list below it the corresponding translation or event.

✎ **Teacher's Note: Not all dictionaries have etymologies.**

2.
c. **Possible answers:**
   blessed - joyful
   walketh - walk - tread
   counsel - advice
   ungodly - wicked
   standeth - stand - abides
   sinners - wrongdoer
   sitteth -sit - squat
   scornful - mockers
   delight - happiness
   doth - does
   meditate - ponder

Student answers may vary, but meaning must remain the same.

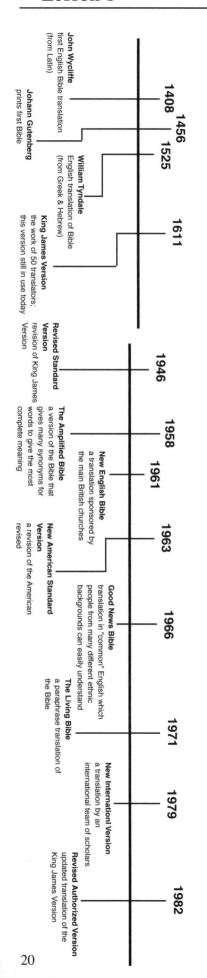

Ex:

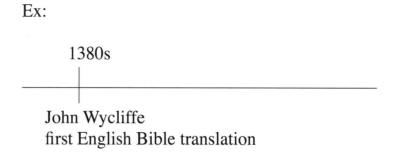

1380s

John Wycliffe
first English Bible translation

History of Bible Translation Information

John Wycliffe - first English Bible translation (translated from Latin) - **1408**

Johann Gutenberg - first prints Bible - **1456**

William Tyndale - English translation of the New Testament - **1525**

King James Version - the work of 50 translators; this version still in use today - **1611**

Revised Standard Version - revision of King James Version - **1946**

The Amplified Bible - a version of the Bible that gives many synonyms for words to give the most complete meaning - **1958**

New English Bible - a translation sponsored by the main British churches - **1961**

New American Standard Version - a revision of the American Revised - **1963**

Good News Bible - translation in "common" English which people from many different ethnic backgrounds can easily understand - **1966**

The Living Bible - a paraphrase translation of the Bible - **1971**

New International Version - a translation by an international team of scholars - **1979**

Revised Authorized Version - updated translation of the King James Version - **1982**

4. a. Bible translators follow three important rules in working on a translation.

1) Nothing must be added.
2) Nothing must be left out.
3) The original meaning must not be changed.

Read the passage again. Following the three rules of Bible translation, rewrite it as we might say it today. Use some of the synonyms you listed in **2c**. If you have a Living Bible, compare your translation to this version. Are they similar?

b. Discuss the literature passage with your teacher. How can you apply its principles to your own life?

c. Take a pretest of your spelling words. Review any words you found difficult to spell.

5. a. Choose one of the following activities.

1) Write the literature passage from dictation.

2) Read the remaining verses of Psalm 1. Tell your teacher what these verses mean to you. Rewrite verses 5 and 6 following the guidelines set forth in **4a**. Use your thesaurus to find synonyms to substitute for various words.

3) Psalms 1 compares a person who loves God's law to a well-watered tree. Draw a picture of the tree described in this verse. Underneath the picture write two of God's laws that will help you to grow strong in your Christian walk if you obey them.

4) Choose skills from the *Review Activities* on the next page.

4

a. **Possible answer: A man is happy if he doesn't listen to the advice of the wicked, or participate in sinful ways, or make friends with mockers. His joy is in the Lord's law, and he thinks about it all the time.**

b. **As Christians we want to be careful of the kind of friends we associate with and the advice we listen to. Our happiness comes from loving and obeying God's Word.**

5.

2) **Wicked people will not be able to last in the judgment and sinners will not be found amongst the godly people. The Lord protects those who are godly, but the path that ungodly people follow will be destroyed.**

3) **Possible answers: Love the Lord your God with all your heart and with all your soul and with all your strength. Deut. 6:5**

Fear the Lord and depart from evil. Prov. 3:7

Review Activities

Choose only the skills your student needs to review.

1.
a. pre
b. un

1. *Prefixes*
   Add the prefix that fits the definition in parentheses.

   a. The _____liminary (*before*) practice test will help you review for the final test.
   b. The materials are ____necessary (*not*) to finish the project.

2.
a. Latin
b. Middle English and Old English

2. *Etymology*
   Use your dictionary and find the etymology of the following words.

   a. dominant
   b. health

3. Possible answers:
a. sprint, scurry, race
b. discuss, confer, chat

3. *Synonyms*
   Use a thesaurus to find two synonyms for each of the following words.

   a. run
   b. talk

4. Answers will vary.

4. *Timeline*
   Write down important events that have occurred in your life and the year these events occurred. List the events in chronological order on a timeline. Remember to keep each entry as concise as possible.

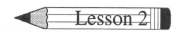

> *Nat shrugged and turned back to his bookkeeping. Even while he was still thinking of Sammy, his glance flicked down a column of figures and his fingers jotted the answer. He realized his mind was wandering. He jerked his thoughts back in line, and added the figures again. He'd been right the first time. For almost nine years now, he'd been right about figures. What would he do with the next nine years? Go on adding columns and columns of figures?*

Carry On, Mr. Bowditch, by Jean Lee Latham
© 1955, renewed 1983 by Jean Lee Latham

1. a. Write the literature passage from dictation. Proofread and correct any errors.

   b. Make a spelling list from any misspelled words or use the following list of suggested spelling words:

   bookkeeping   column   thoughts   realized

   c. Find the two words in the suggested spelling list that have the **/k/** sound. Note that one spells the **/k/** sound with the letter **k** and the other with the letter **c**.

> ### Spelling Tip
> To spell a word with a **/k/** sound, remember that **k** usually comes before **e** or **i**; **c** usually comes before **a**, **o**, or **u**.

✎ **Teacher's Note:** As your student completes each lesson, choose skills from the Review Activities that he needs. The Review Activities follow each lesson.

1.
d. 1) caught
    2) kitten
    3) kindle
    4) correspond
    5) kettle
    6) cubic
    7) keyboard
    8) carmel
    9) commission
    10) kitchen

2.
c. Common:
    1) bookkeeping
    2) glance
    3) column (used 3 times)
    4) figures (used 3 times)
    5) fingers
    6) answer
    7) mind
    8) thoughts
    9) time
    10) years

    Proper:
    1) Nat
    2) Sammy

---

d. Using this *Spelling Tip*, add the correct letter to the following words.

Ex: k̲ite; c̲ake

1) _____aught   6) _____ubic
2) _____itten   7) _____eyboard
3) _____indle   8) _____armel
4) _____orrespond   9) _____ommission
5) _____ettle   10) _____itchen

2. a. In the English language we identify words by placing them in one of eight different groups. These eight groups are called the **parts of speech.** The eight different parts of speech are nouns, pronouns, verbs, adjectives, adverbs, prepositions, conjunctions, and interjections. It is important to know the part each of these groups plays in a sentence and to know how to identify each of them.

b. A **noun** is a word that names a person, place, thing, or idea. If the word names a *general* person, place, thing, or idea then it is a **common noun** and is not capitalized. If a noun names a *specific* person, place, or thing, then it is a **proper noun** and the word begins with a capital letter.

Ex: Proper nouns: Jake, Mt. Rushmore, Florida, etc.
    Common nouns: father, mountain, state, etc.

c. Look over the literature passage and circle all the nouns you find. Above each noun write a **C** if it is a common noun and a **P** if it is a proper noun.

3. a. Verbs are words that show action or a state of being. They can also link a word to the subject or help another verb.

Ex: Jim *ran* all the way to the field. (action verb)
    We *are* here with the Brown family. (state of being verb)
    She *was thinking* about the answer. (helping verb)
    Jim *looks* handsome in his suit. (linking verb)

b. Often helping verbs and the main verb make up a **verb phrase**. Sometimes other words divide a verb phrase.

Ex: Many different hymns *were used* in the service.
       (undivided verb phrase)

The children *were* often *divided* into groups.
Could he *have* accomplished his goals with more determination? (divided verb phrases)

Look at the list of common helping verbs.

Common Helping Verbs				
have	do	shall	would	must
has	does	will	may	can
had	did	should	might	could

All forms of the verb *be* may also be used as helping verbs.

Being Verbs			
is	are	was	were
am	been	being	

c. Underline the verbs in the literature passage. Be sure to underline both parts of a verb phrase.

d. Examine the following sentences. Identify and underline the verb phrases and circle the helping verb.

Ex: The otter (could) not <u>slide</u> down the riverbank.

1) Would you run in the race on Saturday?
2) The computer has replaced the typewriter in the business office.
3) She has almost perfected that piece of music on the piano.
4) Goats were often used to graze areas of rough terrain.
5) Could you have avoided the accident?

3.
c. shrugged, turned, was thinking, flicked, jotted, realized, was wandering, jerked, added, had been, had been, would do, go

d. 1) (would) run
   2) (has) replaced
   3) (has) perfected
   4) (were) used
   5) (could have) avoided

e. He was not really bragging; he had a realistic view of his skills.

e. Nat knew what he could do well. Was he bragging? What are some things you can do well? Ask your teacher or friends what they think you do well. Are they the same things?

f. Review your spelling words.

4. a. A **biography** is a true story of a person's life. *Carry On, Mr. Bowditch* is a biography about Nathaniel Bowditch. Find out more about him. Look in an encyclopedia or research his name at the library. You may also want to check out this book from the library and read it.

b. A summary is a brief description covering the main points of a certain topic. Write a short summary, about one page, of Nathaniel Bowditch's life. Make sure you include when he was born, when he died, and what he did in his life that is important to history.

c. Take an oral or written spelling pretest.

5. a. Choose one of the following activities.

1) Write the literature passage from dictation. Compare your copy to the model and correct any mistakes you may have made.

2) Nat wonders what he will be doing in the future. What do you think you will be doing next year? Write a few paragraphs explaining what you feel you might be doing and give reasons for your predictions.

3) Choose skills from the *Review Activities* on the next page.

Review Activities

Choose only the skills your student needs to review.

1. *Parts of Speech*
   List the eight parts of speech. Give a definition for a noun and a verb.

2. *Nouns and Verbs*
   Circle the nouns and underline the verbs in the following sentences. Write a **C** above the common nouns and a **P** above the proper nouns. Be sure to underline all parts of a verb phrase.

   a. The monkeys swing from branch to branch.
   b. Ships will often sail through the Straits of Magellan.
   c. Children should learn to enjoy good literature.
   d. Mary teaches Bible to the children in her neighborhood.
   e. The car swerved on the slippery road.

3. *Literary Terms*
   Define a biography.

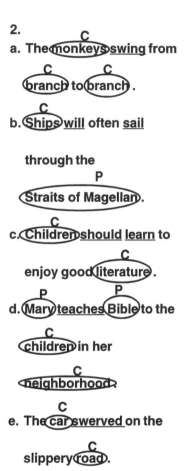

2.
a. The (monkeys) swing from (branch) to (branch).
b. (Ships) will often sail through the (Straits of Magellan).
c. (Children) should learn to enjoy good (literature).
d. (Mary) teaches (Bible) to the (children) in her (neighborhood).
e. The (car) swerved on the slippery (road).

Teacher's Note: As your student completes each lesson, choose skills from the Review Activities that he needs. The Review Activities follow each lesson.

Bambi walked under the great oak on the meadow. It sparkled like dew. It smelled of grass and flowers and moist earth, and whispered of a thousand living things. Friend Hare was there and seemed to be thinking over something important. A haughty pheasant strutted slowly by, nibbling at the grass seeds and peering cautiously in all directions. The dark, metallic blue of his neck gleamed in the sun.

Bambi by Felix Salten.
Used by permission, Simon and Schuster, Inc.

1. a. Just as an artist uses color to paint a picture, an author uses words to "paint" a word picture. Listen to the word picture the author "paints" as your teacher reads the literature passage aloud.

   b. Copy the literature passage from dictation. Proofread your copy for any mistakes. Make a spelling list from any misspelled words or use the following suggested list.

sparkled	whispered	gleamed
nibbling	peering	strutted

   c. The prefix **im-** means *into*. Find the word in the literature passage with this prefix and underline it. Add this prefix to your list of prefixes you started in Lesson 1. List the prefix, its meaning, and two examples of words that contain the prefix.

   d. A **suffix** is a letter or group of letters which comes at the end of the **base** or **root** of the word. While prefixes give you an understanding of the meaning of a word, suffixes can often help in determining the part of speech of a word, whether it is a verb, adjective, etc. Notice that all the words from your suggested spelling list end in **-ing** or **-ed**. These endings do not have specific meanings, but a word ending with these suffixes is usually a verb, a word that expresses action in the sentence. All the words in your spelling list are used as verbs in the literature passage.

1.

c. important

im-; into; Possible examples: important, imprison

e. Locate the suffix list on page 300. Find the suffix chart in the *Student Activity Book*. List the suffixes **-ed** and **-ing**. Write "no meaning" in the space for the definition, write "usually a verb" in the section for part of speech, and write example words from the spelling list in the space provided. If you are not using a *Student Activity Book*, set up a blank sheet of notebook paper as follows:

Suffix	Meaning	Part of Speech	Word Examples
-ed		usually a verb	sparkled, gleamed

You will be using this list throughout the program.

2. a. Writers often use figurative language to express thoughts. Sometimes it helps to produce a picture in your mind by using a comparison. When a comparison of two unrelated things is made using the words *as* or *like*, it is called a **simile**.

   Ex: smooth *as* silk   *like* a raging bull
        warm *as* toast   *like* the quiet after a storm
        sweet *as* honey   *like* a newborn babe

b. Finish the following expressions with words that create similes.

   1) as quiet as _____
   2) as light as _____
   3) as hungry as a _____
   4) sticky like _____
   5) sparkled like _____

c. Create two of your own similes. Remember to use the words *as* or *like* when you make your comparison.

1.
e. ed - usually a verb - sparkled, whispered, gleamed, strutted

ing - usually a verb - nibbling, peering

2.
b. Possible answers:
   1) as quiet as a mouse
   2) as light as a feather
   3) as hungry as a bear
   4) sticky like honey
   5) sparkled like diamonds

3.

a. spar-kled
   whis-pered
   gleamed
   nib-bling
   peer-ing
   strut-ted

b. (The meadow) whispered

c. The wind might howl,
   laugh, bite, etc.

d. Possible Answers:
  1) The (sun/plane) peeked
 through the clouds.
  2) The (donkey/stump)
 stubbornly refused to
 move.
  3) The (butterfly/bee)
 danced among the
 flowers.
  4) The (hole, ocean)
 swallowed him up.

---

3. a. Look at your spelling list from **1b**. One way to learn how to spell a word correctly is to divide the word into syllables. A **syllable** is a division of a word that contains a vowel sound. You can usually hear each syllable as you say the word slowly. It will help to clap each time your hear a syllable division in a word. The number of times you clap is the number of syllables the word contains. For example, the word *thinking* is divided into two syllables, *think* and *ing* because it has two vowel sounds. The word *walked* is only one syllable because it only contains one vowel sound; the suffix **-ed** has a /t/ sound. Write the words from your spelling list, dividing the words into syllables. If you are unsure how a word should be divided, check your dictionary.

   Ex: thou - sand

  b. **Personification** is a form of figurative language which gives human characteristics to an idea, object, or animal. Look at the third sentence of the literature passage. How did the meadow behave like a person?

  c. Read the following sentence:

   I heard the wind muttering through the trees.

   The wind does not literally mutter, but by giving the wind human qualities, it becomes vivid and alive. What else might the wind do like a person?

  d. Create a sentence using personification for each of the following phrases. Be sure to use your imagination!

   1) peeked through the clouds
   2) stubbornly refused to move
   3) danced among the flowers
   4) swallowed him up

4. a. A good author desires to keep the attention of the reader, their audience. Using colorful words will capture a mood or setting, allowing the reader to feel he is experiencing the scene. Often this is done through the use of adjectives. **Adjectives** are words that describe nouns, the words which name persons, places, things, or ideas. Adjectives answer the following questions: Which one? What kind? How many? How much? Whose?

b. Look at the first sentence of the literature passage. In this sentence the adjective, *great*, describes the noun, *oak*. Locate the other adjectives used in the literature passage and circle them. Now read the passage without these words. Do you notice how it is more difficult for you to picture the scene without these words?

c. Find a picture in a book or magazine of mountains, trees, clouds, animals, or anything you might want to describe using figurative language. Write a few sentences to describe the picture using similes and/or personification. Be sure to use adjectives to help you with your description. When you are finished, read your sentences aloud. Do they "paint" a good word picture of the scene you are describing?

d. Take an oral or written spelling pretest. Remember, sounding out the syllables as you write them will help you spell them correctly.

5. a. Choose one of the following activities.

   1) Write the literature passage from dictation.

   2) Choose a poem that offers a good descriptive image and read it to your teacher. After you have finished reading the poem, point out to the teacher any examples where the author used a simile or personification.

   3) How does the literature passage make you feel? Does it sound like a place you would like to be? Rewrite the literature passage and change the mood by describing the scene differently.

4.
b. great, moist, thousand, living, haughty, all, dark, metallic

5.
3) Possible answer: Bambi walked cautiously under the great oak tree at the edge of the meadow. Shadows danced across the grasses outlining strange shapes, and the wind whispered of a thousand living things. Suddenly Friend Hare and a haughty pheasant appeared out of the tall, green grasses, startling Bambi.

31

Review Activities

Choose only the skills your student needs to review.

1.
a. im-por-tant
b. pheas-ant
c. di-rec-tion
d. mead-ow
e. me-tal-lic

1. *Syllables*
   Divide the following words into syllables.

   a. important
   b. pheasant
   c. directions
   d. meadow
   e. metallic

2. *Prefixes*
   Add the correct prefix to the following words. Use the definition in the parentheses and your list of prefixes to help you choose the correct prefix.

2.
a. import
b. unthinkable
c. prelude

   a. The company wants to _____port (*into*) raw material for making the product.
   b. It would be _____thinkable (*not*) to be absent from the wedding.
   c. You are listening to the _____lude (*before*) of the musical symphony.

3. *Suffixes*
   Find the verbs in the following paragraph and circle them. Look for the suffixes **-ed** and **-ing** to help you identify the verbs. If there is a verb phrase, be sure to circle the full phrase.

3. loved
    seemed
    arrived
    are swimming
    announced
    are waiting

   Mary loved to visit her cousins at the farm. The car ride seemed to take forever, but they finally arrived. "All the children are swimming in the lake," her aunt announced. "The horses are also waiting in the barn for you to see."

4. *Similes*
   Write two similes. Be sure to use the words *like* or *as*.

4. Answers will vary.

5. *Personification*

Write a sentence using personification.

6. *Adjectives*

Underline the adjectives in the following sentences and circle
the noun each adjective describes.

a. The quiet, smooth water sparkled with cheerful sunlight.
b. Soft brown eyes peeked out from under the long, silky hair.
c. The sleek, shiny car sped down the busy street.
d. A gentle breeze swept through the tall trees.
e. The bright red apple crunched as the little girl bit into it.

5. Answers will vary.

6.
a. The <u>quiet, smooth</u> (water)
   sparkled with <u>cheerful</u>
   (sunlight).
b. <u>Soft brown</u> (eyes) peeked
   out from under the <u>long,</u>
   <u>silky</u> (hair).
c. The <u>sleek, shiny</u> (car)
   sped down the <u>busy</u>
   (street).
d. A <u>gentle</u> (breeze) swept
   through the <u>tall</u> (trees).
e. The <u>bright red</u> (apple)
   crunched as the <u>little</u> (girl)
   bit into it.

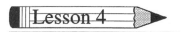

✎ **Teacher's Note:** As your student completes each lesson, choose skills from the Review Activities that he needs. The Review Activities follow each lesson.

The Eagle

He clasps the crag with crooked hands;
Close to the sun in lonely lands,
Ringed with the azure world, he stands.

The wrinkled sea beneath him crawls;
He watches from his mountain walls,
And like a thunderbolt he falls.

Lord Alfred Tennyson

1. a. Poems are divided into groups of lines called **stanzas.** This poem is written in two three-line stanzas called **triplets.** Close your eyes and imagine the eagle as your teacher reads the poem aloud. What kind of picture did you get as you listened? Now you read it aloud.

1.
b. of a sky blue color

b. Copy the poem from dictation. Look at the last line of the first stanza. What do you think *azure* means? Often if you do not know the meaning of a word, you can guess at its meaning by using context clues. **Context clues** are the other words that appear in the line or sentence that can help you to figure out the meaning of a difficult word. Read the first stanza of the poem again. Using context clues, decide what you think the meaning of *azure* might be. Look up the word in the dictionary to check its meaning.

c. beneath
   be-; on, away;
   Possible examples:
   beneath, bestow

c. Look in the first line of the second stanza. Locate the word with the prefix **be-**. The prefix **be-** means *on* or *away*. Find your prefix list and add this prefix to it. Write in the meaning and example words.

d. Make a spelling list from any words you misspelled in the dictation or use the following suggested spelling list:

| clasps | crawls | crooked |
| wrinkled | ringed | watches |

Look at the word *wrinkled.* The root of this word is *wrinkle.* Notice that the silent **e** was dropped before the suffix **-ed** was added.

> ## Spelling Tip
> Words that end in a silent *e* usually drop the silent *e* before adding a suffix beginning with a vowel.

e. Add the suffixes **-ed** and **-ing** to the following words. If the word ends in a silent **e**, be sure to drop the **e** before adding the suffix beginning with a vowel. The first one is done for you.

		-ed	-ing
Ex:	practice	practiced	practicing
1)	guide		
2)	escape		
3)	dictate		
4)	create		
5)	behave		
6)	believe		

2. a. In line 3 of the second stanza, what two things are said to be alike? These really aren't alike in most ways, but the poet shows us one way they are similar. The speed of the eagle falling is like the thunderbolt striking the earth. As we discussed in Lesson 3, when the words *like* or *as* are used to make a comparison, the writer is using a powerful writer's technique called *simile*.

b. The author also makes use of personification in this poem. Read the poem again, circling any words that give human qualities to animals and objects. In what ways are the eagle, lands, and sea given human qualities?

c. As well as the figurative language techniques of simile and personification, the author also makes use of adjectives to help create a picture in the reader's mind. Underline any adjectives you can identify in the poem.

1.
e. 1) guide, guided, guiding
   2) escape, escaped, escaping
   3) dictate, dictated, dictating
   4) create, created, creating
   5) behave, behaved, behaving
   6) believe, believed, believing

2.
a. the eagle falling and a thunderbolt

b. crooked hands - the eagle's talons are compared to hands

   lonely lands - the lands are given the quality loneliness

   wrinkled sea crawls - the sea's movement is compared to crawling

c. crooked, lonely, azure, wrinkled, mountain

3.
a. rest, best

d. Choose an animal and write a few sentences to describe it. Be sure to use adjectives and the technique of simile or personification.

3. a. In "The Eagle" the last word of each line rhymes with the other words in the stanza. Words that rhyme have similar sounds in the last syllable. For example, the words *hands, lands,* and *stands* from the first stanza all rhyme because they all have the same "*ands*" sound in the last syllable. The rhyming of words at the end of the line is called **end rhyme.** Complete the lines of the following stanza using end rhyme.

Nestled in her elaborate nest
The swallow laid her head to _____.
She knows she did her very _____.

b. The best way to write a poem with end rhyme is to write the first line of the poem about your subject and then write a list of words that rhyme with the end word that could be used in your poem. Make sure you do not choose a difficult word for your end word that would be hard to rhyme with. For example, if the first line of a poem is "He stalks the skink with spiteful eyes," then a list of words should be made that rhyme with eyes. It could include: spies, lies, cries.

c. Using "The Eagle" as a model, try writing a poem about the animal you chose in **2d**. Write two triplets (three-line stanzas) ending with rhyming words. Read "The Cat" as an example.

The Cat

He stalks the skink with spiteful eyes,
Close to the grass and dirt he lies,
And like a wraith, he sneaks and spies.

At night he curls by fire bright,
And in his eyes there gleams a light
Of pride's self-satisfied delight.

d. Practice writing your suggested spelling words, dividing them into syllables.

4. a. **Prose** is ordinary writing; the type of writing you would use in a report or story. If you were to rewrite the first stanza of "The Cat" from **3c** in prose form, it could read as follows:

The cat, with a spiteful look in his eyes, stalks the skink through the grass and dirt. Like a wraith he sneaks around and spies on everything.

b. Notice the meaning of the poem has not changed by rewriting it, just the form. Read over the poem, "The Eagle." Write this poem in prose form. After you have completed rewriting the poem, read both the original version and the prose version. Which do you prefer?

c. This poem is talking about an eagle, but notice that aside from the title of the poem, the noun eagle is never used. Instead pronouns have been used to identify the subject. **Pronouns** are words that take the place of nouns.

PERSONAL PRONOUNS		
Singular		
Subjective	**Possessive**	**Objective**
I	my, mine	me
you	your, yours	you
he, she, it	his, her, hers, its	it, him, her
Plural		
Subjective	**Possessive**	**Objective**
we	our, ours	us
you	your, yours	you
they	their, theirs	them

3.
d. clasps   crawls
crook-ed   wrin-kled
ringed   watch-es

4.
b. He holds onto the steep, rugged rock with his claws; beneath the blazing sun in a barren land amidst the blue sky. The waves below beckon him as he watches from the cliff, and with the speed of lightning he falls.

d. The noun which the pronoun takes the place of is called the **antecedent**. A pronoun must agree with the antecedent in number and gender.

> Ex: *Mary, Lois and Ginger* went to the mall where *they* shopped for new shoes. (Number - Since the antecedent is plural, the pronoun must be plural.)
>
> *John* will need to take the tent, and *he* will also need *his* fishing pole. (Gender - Since the antecedent is masculine, the pronouns also need to be masculine.)

4.
e. He, he, him, He, his, he

Without pronouns the poem sounds repetitive and is tiresome to read. It would be difficult to write without using pronouns.

e. In the poem, "The Eagle," the antecedent is the eagle. Underline the pronouns that appear in the poem. (The poet chose to give the eagle a masculine pronoun.) Try reading the poem using "the eagle" wherever a pronoun appears. How does this change the effect the poem? Do you think it would be difficult to write without pronouns? Why or why not?

f. Take an oral or written spelling pretest. Review any words you found difficult to spell.

5. a. Choose one of the following activities.

   1) Write the poem from dictation once more.

   2) A poem can create a world and bring an idea to life. Other forms of art can produce the same effect in a different way. Create a picture or clay sculpture to illustrate the poem, "The Eagle."

3) Take time to enjoy reading selections of poetry aloud. Look for examples of similes and personification in the poems you read. Have your teacher (or another student) read several poems aloud without reading the titles. Try to give them new titles and compare them to the original ones.

Suggested sources for selections:

A Child's Garden of Verses by Robert Louis Stevenson
When We Were Young, Now We Are Six by A. A. Milne
Oxford Book of Poetry for Children by Edward Blishen
Favorite Poems Old and New by Helen Ferris

4) Choose skills from the *Review Activities* on the next page.

Review Activities

Choose only the skills your student needs to review.

1. *Definitions*
   Refer to your lesson for the information to write the correct answer in the blank provided in the following sentences.

   a. Poetry written in ordinary language that does not rhyme is called _____.

   b. Words that take the place of nouns are called _____.

   c. The noun the pronoun takes the place of is called the _____.

   d. Poems are divided into groups of lines called _____.

   e. Poems written in groupings of three lines are called _____.

   f. Words that appear in a sentence that help you figure out the meaning of a word you do not know are called _____.

   g. The rhyming of words at the end of a line is called _____.

2. *Poetry*
   Write a poem in triplet form with end rhyme. Write the same poem in a prose form.

3. *Context Clues*
   Determine from the context clues the meaning of the underlined word in the following sentences.

   a. In order to avoid the traffic on the main highway, we decided to take a <u>byroad</u>.
   b. He was so impressed with his successful boss that he <u>emulated</u> his qualities.
   c. We are not sure, but he is <u>reputed</u> to be the leader of the neighborhood gang.

1.
a. prose
b. pronouns
c. antecedent
d. stanzas
e. triplets
f. context clues
g. end rhyme

2.
Answers will vary.

3.
a. a road that is not the main road
b. to copy
c. to regard or consider

4. *Prefixes*
Add the prefix **be-** to the following root words. Determine the definition of each word you create.

a. _____neath
b. _____side
c. _____siege

4.
a. **beneath - underneath**
b. **beside - at the side**
c. **besiege - to close in on**

5. *Suffixes*
Add the suffixes **-ed** and **-ing** to the following words.

Ex: love   loved   loving
a. skate _____ _____
b. smile _____ _____
c. chase _____ _____

5.
a. **skated, skating**
b. **smiled, smiling**
c. **chased, chasing**

6. *Figurative Language*
Read the sentences below. If the sentence contains an example of personification, write **P** in the space provided. If the sentence contains an example of a simile, write **S** in the space provided.

a. _____The birds chatted back and forth throughout the forest.
b. _____The eagle soared like a plane through the sky.
c. _____The picture was as refreshing as a garden on a spring day.
d. _____The brook laughed for joy as it cascaded over the rocks.
e. _____He ran as swiftly as a cheetah when he neared the finish of the race.

6.
a. **P**
b. **S**
c. **S**
d. **P**
e. **S**

7. *Pronouns and Antecedents*
Underline the pronouns and draw a line to its antecedent in the following sentences.

Ex: The fledglings were ready to leave their nest.

a. Jim was very proud of his new car.
b. Kelly went to the swimming pool this morning, and she was going to her friend's house this afternoon.
c. The bicycle damaged its wheel on the rough terrain.
d. The Wilsons are having their house painted.

7.
a. **Jim was very proud of his new car.**
b. **Kelly went to the swimming pool this morning, and she was going to her friend's house this afternoon.**
c. **The bicycle damaged its wheel on the rough terrain.**
d. **The Wilsons are having their house painted**

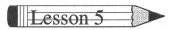

For breakfast there were pancakes, and Ma made a pancake man for each one of the children. Ma called each one in turn to bring her plate, and each could stand by the stove and watch, while with the spoonful of batter Ma put on the arms and the legs and the head. It was exciting to watch her turn the whole little man over, quickly and carefully, on a hot griddle. When it was done, she put it smoking hot on the plate.

Little House in the Big Woods by Laura Ingalls Wilder. Used by permission, Harper and Row.

1. a. Listen as your teacher reads the literature passage. Write the passage from dictation. Compare your copy with the model, correcting the spelling and punctuation.

   b. Using the description in the literature passage, draw a picture on a separate sheet of paper of the pancake man. Compare it to the description given. Do you feel you have drawn an accurate representation? With supervision, try cooking a pancake man.

   c. The prefix **ex-** appears in the literature passage. It means *forth* or *out*. Locate the word in the literature passage that has the prefix **ex-** . Add this prefix to your list along with the definition and word examples.

   d. Choose four to six words from the literature passage for your spelling list this week or use the following suggested list.

breakfast	pancake	exciting
griddle	smoking	children

   Notice that the words *breakfast* and *pancake* are nouns that are made up of two separate complete words. These are called **compound words**.

1.
c. exciting
   ex-; forth or out;
   Possible examples:
   exclaim, expel

> ### Spelling Tip
> It will be easier to remember how compound words are spelled if you recognize the two separate words it contains. For example, breakfast is made up of the words **break** and **fast**. Remembering the spelling of the two separate words is less difficult than trying to remember the spelling of the whole word.

e. Divide the following compound words into separate complete words.

1) smokehouse
2) peanuts
3) pancake
4) gingerbread
5) blackboard

2. a. Underline the two words in the literature passage that have the suffix **-ly**. The suffix **-ly** usually means *like* or *manner of* and often changes words into adverbs. Add this suffix to your list. Write "usually an adverb" under the part of speech, then fill in the definition and word examples.

b. **Adverbs** are words that describe a verb, an adjective, or another adverb.

Ex: He ran *swiftly*. - The adverb *swiftly* describes the verb *ran*.
The garden was *very* colorful. - The adverb *very* describes the adjective *colorful*.
She drives *too* slowly. - The adverb *too* describes the adverb *slowly*.

Adverbs answer the following questions:

How? When? Where? To what extent? How often?

Find the two adverbs you underlined. What do they describe? What question do they answer? Read the sentence from the literature passage without the adverbs. Notice how the adverbs help you to picture the action that is happening.

1.
e. 1) smoke - house
2) pea - nuts
3) pan - cake
4) ginger - bread
5) black - board

2.
a. quickly, carefully

-ly - like, manner of
Possible examples:
neatly, slowly

2.
b. how the pancake was turned

b. how the pancake was turned

c. The best way to locate adverbs is to first find the verb in the sentence and then find any words that answer the adverb questions.

Ex: The team screamed excitedly after they won.

The verb in this sentence is screamed. If you then ask the question, How did they scream?, you will find the word *excitedly* answers that question. It is an adverb describing how the team screamed.

d.
1) We (went) to the park yesterday. When?
2) They (are leaving) quickly. How?
3) The cats seldom (fight). How often?
4) The children (play) outside during recess. Where?
5) The play (is) almost finished. To what extent?

d. Circle the verb in each of the following sentences. Then find and underline the adverb that describes that verb. Remember, the suffix **-ly** often indicates the word is an adverb. What question does the adverb answer?

Ex: The horse (pranced) nervously.   how

1) We went to the park yesterday. _____
2) They are leaving quickly. _____
3) The cats seldom fight._____
4) The children play outside during recess. _____
5) The play is almost finished _____.

e. Add adverbs to the following sentences in order to better describe the action that is taking place. The word in parentheses following each sentence will tell you what question the adverb should answer.

Ex: The kitten purred softly. (How?)

e. Possible answers
1) brightly, brilliantly
2) tomorrow, tonight
3) often, seldom
4) nearby, away
5) very, scarcely, not

1) The diamond sparkled _____. (How?)
2) We will go to church _____. (When?)
3) We _____ miss a meeting. (How often?)
4) A school of fish swam _____. (Where?)
5) She was _____concerned about her grade. (To what extent?)

3. a. A group of sentences about one main idea is divided into paragraphs. A **paragraph** is a grouping of sentences about one specific part of the topic. The paragraph will include a sentence that expresses the main idea of the paragraph and sentences that support that main idea.

b. Read over the literature passage. Using your own words, tell your teacher what this paragraph is describing. Which sentence do you feel best expresses the main idea of the paragraph? This sentence is called the **topic sentence**. It is the sentence that tells what the paragraph is about. The first sentence of the paragraph is usually the topic sentence.

c. The rest of the sentences in the paragraph support or give more information about the topic. These are called **supporting sentences**. Supporting sentences make up the body of the paragraph. If a sentence in the paragraph does not support the main idea, it is not a supporting sentence and should not be in the paragraph.

Which sentences in the literature passage are supporting sentences?

d. Each paragraph should end with a **closing sentence** that summarizes or comments on the topic of the paragraph. Identify the closing sentence in the literature passage.

e. The literature passage paragraph explains how Ma made pancake men. Choose something you know how to do and write a topic sentence for a paragraph explaining how it is done. Keep your subject simple, such as how to wash the family car, set the table, or bake a cake.

f. Think about the activity you chose and the steps you take to complete it. You might want to act it out and write the steps in order as you go. For example, to bake a cake you might write:

3.

b. For breakfast there were pancakes, and Ma made a pancake man for each one of the children.

c. Except for the topic sentence, all the other sentences are supportive sentences. They all tell about Ma making pancakes.

d. When it was done, she put it smoking hot on the plate.

How to Bake a Cake
1) Preheat oven to 325°
2) Grease and flour two round cake pans.
3) Mix boxed cake mix with eggs, oil, and water according to the directions on the box.
4) Pour the mixture into cake pans, place in oven, and bake for 30 minutes.
5) Take the pans out of the oven and allow them to cool.
6) Remove cakes from pans and frost.

Be sure to write your steps in the correct sequence. Don't put the batter in the cake pan before you have given instructions to grease and flour the pans.

g. Review your spelling words. Remember to sound them out by syllables as you spell them. If a word is a compound word, be sure to break the word into separate words as you spell it.

4. a. Read the sample paragraphs below. Notice the step-by-step instructions for planting a garden.

> Planting a vegetable garden is a fun project that anyone can do with a little hard work and instruction. The first step to planting a garden is to choose a site for your garden. It should be a sunny location with good, rich soil, and a source of water nearby. Then you test your soil to determine what fertilizer you need to apply. Next, plan what types of vegetables you want to plant and draw out a diagram of how you want to arrange your garden.
>
> Be sure to run your rows north and south so more sunlight will reach the plants. Then prepare the soil by breaking up any sod and turning the soil. Also remove all woody weeds and trash from the garden plot. Rake and smooth out your planting surface. Next it is time to plant your seeds.
>
> Use a string with stakes at each end to help you to plant a straight row. Consult your seed package for information on planting depth and spacing and follow the instruction. Attach your seed package or other identification to the stake so you will know what you have planted in that row.
>
> Finally, keep your garden well watered, free from weeds, and apply the proper fertilizers. Now that you have learned how to plant a vegetable garden, enjoy the harvest!

b. The topic sentence tells what the paragraphs are about. The topic sentence is often the first sentence. Underline the topic sentence. All the other sentences must support the main idea.

Transitional words help tie thoughts together. They can show time or order throughout the paragraphs. Some transitional words are *first*, *then*, *next*, and *finally*. Underline the transitional words.

4.
b. Topic Sentence:
Planting a vegetable garden is a fun project that anyone can do with a little hard work and instruction.

Transitional words:
The first step
Then
Next
Then
Next
Finally

c. Now using the steps you listed in **3f** write sentences to form your paragraphs. Begin with your topic sentence.

d. Read your paragraph. Does the topic sentence tell what the paragraph is about? Are the steps in the explanation written in order? Does each sentence support the topic? Does the closing sentence summarize or comment on the topic of the paragraph?

e. Give your paragraph to someone and ask him to follow the directions. Can he understand them? Do any changes need to be made to make the directions easier to follow? Make any corrections and complete your final copy.

f. Take an oral or written spelling pretest. Review any words you had trouble spelling.

5. a. Choose one of the following activities.

1) Write your literature passage from dictation, paying special attention to spelling.

2) Ma took the extra time to make the pancake men because she knew it was special for the children. Think of someone in your life who takes time to do special things for you. Write a letter thanking him. A friendly letter should include a **date**, **salutation**, **body**, **closing**, and **your signature**. Follow the format below for your letter. (The words in parentheses identify the parts of the letter and are not to be written as part of the letter.)

(Date)
June 30, 1996

(Salutation or Greeting - remember the comma)
Dear Susan,

*Indent*_____*(Body)*_____

_____

(Closing - comma)
Your friend,
(Signature - no period)
Kathy

3) Choose skills from the *Review Activities* on the next page.

Review Activities

Choose only the skills your student needs to review.

1. *Prefixes and Suffixes*
   Use your prefix and suffix list to fill in the correct prefix or suffix in the space provided to complete the word. The definition of the prefix or suffix is in parenthesis. Check to see how many you get correct. Using context clues and prefix or suffix definitions, see if you can accurately guess the meanings of the words.

   a. I believe I ____cede you in line. (*before*)
   b. The boy grinned sly___ at his friend with a water balloon hidden behind his back. (*like, manner of*)
   c. Mary was mirth_____ when she discovered the joke had been played on her. (*full of*)
   d. His warnings went ____heeded by the sailors. (*not*)
   e. He ____pounded upon the reasons for his belief. (*forth, out*)

2. *Compound words*
   Create five compound words from the following words.

wood	rain	foot	pecker	room
son	bow	grand	ball	class

3. *Adverbs*
   Underline the adverbs in the following sentences. What question does the adverb answer?

   Ex: We walked <u>quickly</u> to the class.   How?

   a. I will write you a letter soon.
   b. I could hardly see the road through the fog.
   c. I have always completed the assignment.
   d. I searched everywhere for the perfect gift.
   e. We must be sure to leave quietly for the early morning trip.

1. a. pre(cede)
  b. (sly)ly
  c. (mirth)ful
  d. un(heeded)
  e. ex(pounded)

2. woodpecker, rainbow, football, classroom, grandson

3. a. <u>soon</u> When?
  b. <u>hardly</u> To what extent?
  c. <u>always</u> How often?
  d. <u>everywhere</u> Where?
  e. <u>quietly</u> How?

4. *Paragraphs*
Read the following paragraph and underline the topic sentence. There is one sentence in the paragraph that does not support the topic sentence. Cross out that sentence.

Many animals have unique techniques for escaping from their enemies. The opossum fools its enemies by rolling over, lying very still, and pretending to be dead. The armadillo protects itself from attack by rolling itself into a tight ball with only its bony plates exposed. The armadillo feeds at night on insects, birds' eggs, roots, and fruit. When a skunk is attacked it squirts a terrible-smelling liquid from under its tail at its enemy. Many attackers are defeated by these escape techniques and move on to find easier prey.

5. *Letters*
Add the correct punctuation to the following letter.

June 19 1997

Dear Mary

I really miss you, and I wish you were here with us on our family vacation. The mountains are beautiful. We have enjoyed fishing, hiking, and sightseeing. Our vacation ends next week, so I should be home soon.

Your friend

Jan

4. **Topic sentence: Many animals have unique techniques for escaping from their enemies.**

Cross Out: The armadillo feeds at night on insects, birds' eggs, roots, and fruit.

5.
June 19, 1997

Dear Mary,

Your friend,

There was very little hard study done in the Temple Grammar School the week preceding the Fourth of July. For my part, my heart and brain were so full of fire-crackers, Roman-candles, rockets, pin-wheels, squibs, and gunpowder in various seductive forms, that I wonder I didn't explode under Mr. Grimshaw's very nose. I couldn't do a sum to save me. I couldn't tell, for love or money, whether Tallahassee was the capital of Tennessee or of Florida. The present and the pluperfect tenses were inextricably mixed in my memory, and I didn't know a verb from an adjective when I met one.

The Story of a Bad Boy by Thomas Bailey Aldrich

1. a. Listen to your teacher as she reads the literature passage. Write the passage from dictation. Carefully proofread and correct any errors. Pay close attention to the words which are capitalized.

   b. Is Tallahassee the capital of Tennessee or Florida? If you don't know, look in an atlas, encyclopedia, or on a map to find out.

   c. Locate the word *inextricably* in the literature passage. The prefix **in-** means *not* or *into*. Try to guess the meaning of inextricably using prefix meaning and context clues. Check your definition with the dictionary. Add the prefix **in-** to your prefix list, along with its definition and word examples.

   d. Some compound words are joined together by a hyphen. Find the compound words in the literature passage that have hyphens. Locate the one compound word in the passage that is not joined together by a hyphen. What two words make up that compound? It is hard to know whether a compound is joined together with or without a hyphen. If you are unsure of the correct way to write a compound word, check with a dictionary.

1.
b. Tallahassee, Florida

c. in-; not or into
    Possible examples:
    incorrect, inside

d. fire-crackers, Roman-candles, pin-wheels

   gunpowder

e. Make a spelling list from words you misspelled or use the following suggested list:

preceding   gunpowder   whether
memory   couldn't   didn't

Two of the suggested spelling words are contractions. **Contractions** are words formed by joining two words and leaving out one or more letters. An **apostrophe** (') shows where the letter(s) have been left out.

> **Spelling Tip**
> It will help in the spelling of contractions to remember that the apostrophe is always placed at the exact point where letters are omitted.

f. Underline the four contractions used in the paragraph. What two words does each represent? Some contractions are formed by joining a verb to the word *not*, while others are formed by joining a pronoun and verb. Write the following words as contractions. Be sure to place the apostrophe in the correct position.

Ex: could not - couldn't

1) did not
2) have not
3) she will
4) let us
5) we have

f.
<u>didn't</u> - did not (used twice)
<u>couldn't</u> - could not (used twice)

1) didn't
2) haven't
3) she'll
4) let's
5) we've

2.
a. Mr. Grimshaw's

2. a. In **1d**, we used the apostrophe in contractions to show where letter(s) had been omitted. An apostrophe can also be used to show possession. The possessive form of a singular noun is made when an apostrophe **s** (**'s**) is added to the noun. This is called a **singular possessive noun**.

   Ex: the horse belonging to Joanna - Joanna's horse

   Locate an example of a singular possessive noun in the literature passage.

   b. The plural possessive form of a noun is formed by placing the apostrophe after ending **s**. If a plural noun is irregular and does not end in **s**, then an apostrophe **s** (**'s**) is used to form the possessive. This is called a **plural possessive noun**.

   Ex: the room belonging to the girls - girls' room
       the cars belonging to the men - men's cars

   Write each of the following nouns as a singular and plural possessive. Remember, if the plural of the noun is irregular, then an apostrophe **s** (**'s**) is used to form the plural possessive.

Noun	Singular Possessive	Plural Possessive
Ex: dog	dog's	dogs'

b. 1) kitten's - kittens'
2) teacher's - teachers'
3) mouse's - mice's
4) girl's - girls'
5) goose's - geese's

   1) kitten
   2) teacher
   3) mouse
   4) girl
   5) goose

c. very little
   so full
   (did)n't
   (could)n't
   (could)n't
   inextricably
   (did)n't

   c. Read the literature passage once more. Locate the adverbs used in the literature passage and circle them. Remember, adverbs answer the questions: Where? When? How? How often? To what extent? Since adverbs describe verbs most of the time, first find the verb, then ask the questions that adverbs answer. The word **not** is a frequently used adverb. It is often in the contraction form, **n't**. Notice how the author's use of adverbs helps to convey a mood of excitement.

d. Have you ever been so excited over an upcoming event you couldn't concentrate on anything? Share about the event with your teacher or other students.

3. a. Reread the literature passage paying special attention to the capitalization. Capitalization is used in three main ways:

1) to indicate the beginning of a sentence
2) to help the reader quickly identify proper names and titles
3) to show respect, such as references to God and the Bible

Although there are many specific capitalization rules, most rules fall under one of the three main categories listed above. The one rule that does not fall under one of these categories is the capitalization of the letter **i** when it is used as a word. The letter **i** is always capitalized when it is used as the word I.

b. Circle all the words in the paragraph that begin with a capital letter. Write each of the words under the correct category which the capitalization rule would fall under. The category for showing respect has been omitted since there are no references to God in the literature passage. The first one is done for you as an example.

Beginning of Sentence	Proper Name	Title
There		

c. Pretend you are this boy's friend. Briefly write a few sentences explaining to him the difference between a verb and an adjective. Refer to the definitions for a verb and an adjective in Lessons 2 and 3 if you need help.

d. Review your spelling words.

3.
b. Beginning of Sentence:
There, For, I, I, I, I, The, I, I

Proper Name or Title:
Temple Grammar School, Fourth of July, Roman-candles, Mr. Grimshaw's, Tallahassee, Tennessee, Florida

c. Verbs show action or state of being. Adjectives describe nouns.

4. a. The boy in the literature passage describes his excitement concerning a holiday. What is your favorite holiday? Today you are going to write a paragraph describing your favorite holiday.

   b. Before you begin writing your paragraph, it is a good idea to think about what you want to write and organize your thoughts. One of the best methods for doing this is to use a "circle word picture." Find the circle word picture in Lesson 6 of the *Student Activity Book* or draw the following diagram on a sheet of paper.

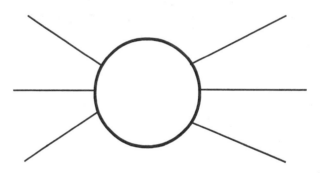

   c. Look at the following circle word picture about the Fourth of July as it was described in the literature passage. After you have reviewed the example, choose your favorite holiday and write it in the center circle of the diagram. Now brainstorm. Why do you like the holiday? What special things happen? What makes it special? Put your ideas on the lines extending from the center circle.

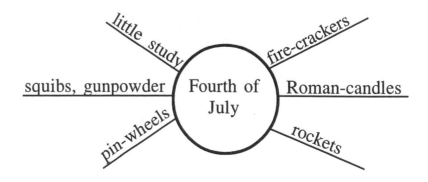

d. Look over your completed diagram. Begin writing your paragraph by starting with a good topic sentence. All the other sentences you write should tell about and support the topic sentence. Then end your paragraph with a closing sentence. Be sure to use adjectives and adverbs to help convey your excitement about the holiday.

e. Look over your paragraph for any mistakes in punctuation, spelling, and capitalization. Once you are satisfied, write the paragraph neatly for your teacher to review.

f. Take an oral or written spelling pretest.

5. a. Choose one of the following activities.

   1) Write the literature passage from dictation.

   2) A caricature is a cartoon type drawing used to stretch the imagination. Can you envision this boy with his heart and brain full of firecrackers, Roman-candles, etc. right under his teacher's nose? Close your eyes and think how this would look. Draw a caricature of this scene. You don't have to be an artist to draw a caricature. There's no right or wrong way. Draw it the way you "see" it. Have fun!

   3) Choose skills from the *Review Activities* on the next page.

Review Activities

Choose only the skills your student needs to review.

1. *Prefixes*
Look in your dictionary and find three words with the prefix **in-**. How does the prefix **in-** change the meaning of the root word?

2. *Contractions*
Write the contractions for the following words.

    a. should not
    b. she will
    c. are not
    d. they have
    e. we would

3. *Use of Hyphens in Compound Nouns and Number Words*
Identify the compound words in the following sentences and add hyphens.

    a. I have saved forty five dollars.
    b. Jim is his brother in law and good friend.
    c. Being the youngest, she always wore hand me downs.
    d. She was the runner up in the contest.

4. *Possessives*
Write each of the following expressions as a possessive.

    Ex: the earrings of the girl - the girl's earrings

    a. the tails of the dogs
    b. leaves of the trees
    c. prints of the deer
    d. the cars belonging to the ladies
    e. the motorcycle belonging to Larry

---

1. Answers will vary:
   in- means not or into

2. a. shouldn't
   b. she'll
   c. aren't
   d. they've
   e. we'd

3. a. forty-five
   b. brother-in-law
   c. hand-me-downs
   d. runner-up

4. a. dogs' tails
   b. trees' leaves
   c. deer's prints
   d. ladies' cars
   e. Larry's motorcycle

5. *Capitalization*

The following paragraph is written without capitalization.
Circle the words that need to be capitalized and explain why.

our trip to washington, d.c. was so exciting. there was so much there to see and do. the first stop on our tour was the lincoln memorial. made out of white colorado-yule marble, the memorial is similar in shape to the greek parthenon. it took over six years to complete and was dedicated on memorial day, may 30, 1922. abraham lincoln's statue is located in the center of the memorial and the gettysburg address is etched in marble on the south wall.

6. *Writing Skills*

Choose a writing topic of your choice. Draw a circle word picture and brainstorm, writing down your ideas on the lines extending from the main circle. Write a paragraph about your topic using the ideas you have written down.

5. **Beginning of a sentence:**
   Our, There, The, Made, It

   Proper Name or Title:
   Washington, D.C.,
   Lincoln Memorial,
   Colorado, Greek
   Parthenon, Memorial Day,
   May, Abraham Lincoln's,
   Gettysburg Address

Assessment 1
(Lessons 1 - 6)

1. like a lightning bolt
   (The two things being
   compared are *invaders*
   and *like a lightning bolt*.)

2. Answers will vary.

3. The sun sighed.

4. Answers will vary.

5. a. un-
   b. -ly

6. Possible answers:
   careful, joyful, etc.

7. Possible answers:
   example, exchange, etc.

8. Adjectives are words
   that describe nouns,
   the words which name
   persons, places, things,
   or ideas. Adjectives
   answer the following
   questions: Which one?
   What kind? How many?
   How much? Whose?

9. Possible answer:
   Has anyone seen the
   wind? You haven't; I
   haven't. But the wind
   makes the leaves move.
   Has anyone seen the
   wind? You haven't; I
   haven't. But the wind
   makes the trees bend.

---

1. A simile is a form of figurative language. It compares two different things using the words **like** or **as**. Find the simile in the following sentence:

   The invaders struck like a lightning bolt.

2. Using the words **as** or **like**, write a simile.

3. Personification is a form of figurative language. It gives a thing or idea human characteristics. What is the personification used in the following sentence:

   The sun sighed as it set in the west.

4. Give an example of personification about the wind.

5. a. What is the prefix in the word ungodly?
   b. What is the suffix?

6. Write a word with the suffix **-ful**.

7. Write a word with the prefix **ex-**.

8. Tell your teacher what an adjective does.

9. Read the following poem and rewrite it in prose.

   "Who Has Seen the Wind?"
   by Christina Rossetti

   Who has seen the wind?
   Neither I nor you:
   But when the leaves hang trembling
   The wind is passing thro'.

   Who has seen the wind?
   Neither you nor I:
   But when the trees bow down their heads
   The wind is passing by.

10. Look at the literature passage in Lesson 5. What is the topic sentence?

11. Write the following phrases as contractions.

    a. he is
    b. they are
    c. we will

12. Rewrite the following holidays using correct punctuation.

    a. columbus day
    b. fourth of july
    c. new year's day

13. Use your thesaurus to find three synonyms for each of the following words.

    a. good
    b. say
    c. nice
    d. cold

14. Complete the following sentences by adding the correct ending to the adjectives.

    a. You are tall_ than he.
    b. Which of the three boys is the strong_?
    c. Bring me the long_ of the two ropes.
    d. I know which of the two children is the young_.
    e. Which of the four rooms is the warm_?

10. **For breakfast there were pancakes, and Ma made a pancake man for each one of the children.**

11. **a. he's**
    b. they're
    c. we'll

12. **a. Columbus Day**
    b. Fourth of July
    c. New Year's Day

13. **Possible answers:**
    a. kind, excellent, fair
    b. speak, utter, declare
    c. pleasant, delightful, fine
    d. chilly, icy, shivering

14.
    a. taller
    b. strongest
    c. longer
    d. younger
    e. warmest

BOOK STUDY

on

The Bronze Bow

The Bronze Bow by
Elizabeth George Speare
Published by Houghton
Mifflin

Readability level: 6th grade

Introducing
The Bronze Bow

Elizabeth George Speare began writing after spending most of her years being a wife, mother, and teacher. Her first novel, *Calico Captive*, was based on the actual captivity of Susanna Johnson. It was recognized by the Children's Services Division of the American Library Association as a Notable Book in 1957. The following year, her second book, *The Witch of Blackbird Pond*, won the ALA's Newbery Medal as the most distinguished contribution to American literature for boys and girls. In 1961, she was once again honored with this award for *The Bronze Bow*.

Summary

Young Daniel Bar Jamin is driven by one passion: his hatred for the Romans who occupy his homeland. This hatred has grown steadily since the Romans executed his father and uncle and brought about the early death of his mother. His happy home life shattered, Daniel is apprenticed to a harsh master to train to be a blacksmith. He finally runs away to the mountains outside his village, leaving behind his elderly grandmother and deeply troubled younger sister, Leah.

On the mountain, Daniel is befriended by the outlaw, Rosh, who styles himself as a commander amassing a band of men who will one day overthrow the Romans. Daniel eagerly joins them until one day he meets Joel and his sister Malthace, twins who have come up on the mountain for a picnic. This meeting opens up a whole new world for Daniel. He realizes his longing for a home and friends. When his grandmother dies, Daniel must come down off the mountain and take care of his sister, Leah, who has never left the house since her father's death. She has lived in a world tormented by fear. Before Daniel can help his sister conquer her fears, he must first conquer the bitterness and hatred that controls him.

As Daniel enters into the world once again, he has several encounters with a Rabbi whose teaching is very hard for Daniel to understand. He speaks of liberty for the oppressed but doesn't call for the picking up of arms. Is he a Zealot? Is he the one they have been waiting for? The one who will lead them to freedom? In the end, Jesus gives Daniel the key that sets him free.

Vocabulary

Find each of the following words in the chapters indicated and use context clues to decide the meaning of each word. Then, look up each word in the dictionary and write a definition.

1. synagogue - (Chapter 1)

2. Rabbi - (Chapter 1)

3. Zealot - (Chapter 1)

4. Sabbath - (Chapter 3)

5. mezuzah (Chapter 24)

Choose the correct word from the words listed above to complete the following sentences.

6. The _____ was teaching from the book of Genesis and discussing the law.

7. He touched the _____ at the doorway as he entered their home.

8. All work must be finished before the _____ begins.

9. We must meet at the _____ for worship.

10. Simon is known as a _____ because he is determined to rid his city of the Romans.

1. synagogue - a Jewish place of worship and religious instruction
2. Sabbath - the seventh day of the week (Saturday). It is observed as a day of rest and worship by the Jews and some Christians.
3. rabbi - the Jewish spiritual leader and interpreter of Jewish laws
4. mezuzah - a piece of parchment that has God's word written on it. The parchment is rolled up, placed in a container, and attached to the door frame of a Jewish home.
5. Zealot - a Jew who is intensely devoted to the cause of freeing the Jewish people from Roman rule

6. rabbi
7. mezuzah
8. Sabbath
9. synagogue
10. Zealot

1. While *The Bronze Bow* does show conflict between man and man, conflict between man and society, and perhaps even conflict between man and fate, the main conflict in the story takes place within Daniel himself.

2. Love is stronger than hate.
   Love your enemy.
   Perfect love casts out fear.

3. Answers will vary.

4. In approaching the Roman soldier, Daniel was actually following Jesus in a truer sense than if he had physically walked after him. His gratitude to Jesus caused the hate to leave his heart and caused him to reach out to his enemy.

5. traitor - one who betrays his country by violating his allegiance
   rebel - one who refuses allegiance to, resists, or rises in arms against the established or rightful government or ruler
   patriot - one who loves his country zealously, supporting and defending it
   Depending upon the viewpoint of the people making the judgment, a person could be perceived as all three of these at the same time by three different people. Rosh was viewed as a rebel by the Romans and as a patriot by most of his countrymen.

Discussion Questions

1. The conflict of a story is the problem that triggers the action. There are five basic types of conflict:

   1) **Man versus Man** - problems between characters in the story
   2) **Man versus Society** - problems with society
   3) **Man versus Himself** - problems with himself
   4) **Man versus Nature** - problems with natural happenings in nature
   5) **Man versus Fate (God)** - problems with strange or unbelievable coincidences

   What is the type of conflict in *The Bronze Bow*?

2. The **theme** of a story is the statement about life which the writer is trying to get across to the reader. It is sometimes called "the **moral** of the story." What would you say the theme is of *The Bronze Bow*?

3. What character do you most identify with in the book? Why?

4. At the end of the story Daniel doesn't follow Jesus but walks across the street to the Roman soldier. In what way does this show how Daniel has changed?

5. Discuss with your teacher the meaning of the words *traitor*, *rebel*, and *patriot*. Could one person be viewed by different people as each one of these? Was Rosh a rebel or a patriot?

6. *"It's just that I don't want to face Jesus with a lie. I couldn't bear the way his eyes would look at me."*

   "If he understood the reason he wouldn't blame you."

   "Yes, I think he would," she said thoughtfully. "I think that for Jesus a lie is impossible, no matter what the reason."

   "In war a lie is a weapon," said Daniel. "We have to use what weapons we have. Even Jesus must see that."

   What do you think Jesus would think about Daniel's conclusion about lying?

7. *"Rosh is no bandit," he said. "When he robs it is for a good purpose."*

   "So, I've heard. Rob the rich to feed the poor. I'll be glad to see the poor that gets one penny of what he took last night."

   "There may be more important needs," said Daniel.

   Is there ever a good reason for stealing? Would it make a difference if the poor did receive what Rosh's band had stolen?

8. Who did Daniel think was his enemy? Who did Jesus say was Daniel's enemy? Why?

9. Discuss Daniel's reaction to discovering Marcus had been visiting his sister? Do you think he was justified? Can you understand why he felt the way he did? What reaction did it cause in Leah?

10. As the story ends, both Daniel and Leah have greatly changed. In what ways do you think their lives will be different now? In what ways will things still be the same?

6. Allow time for discussion.

7. Allow time for discussion.

8. Daniel thought the Romans were his enemies because they had destroyed his family and ruined his sister's life.
   Jesus told him that hate was his enemy.
   He told him that hate is never satisfied and will destroy the person harboring it.

9. Allow for discussion.

10. Daniel and Leah have both experienced healing. They have both been set free: Daniel from hate; and Leah from fear.
    This does not change the fact that their nation is under Roman rule and their lives will still be physically very hard, but they both can now continue on with their lives. Daniel will probably marry Malthace.

Activities

The following activities are intended to help you explore Daniel's world and better understand his experience. Choose one or two activities to complete your study.

1. Stories can be set in many different places and times. Read about the world at the time Daniel lived. You may use your history book, an encyclopedia, or books from the library that will give you a picture of the times.

2. The setting of this story is Galilee at the time of Christ. Find a map of the area and locate the places mentioned in the story such as Capernaum, Tiberias, Jerusalem, etc.

3. Whenever an author chooses to write a fictional work that includes Jesus, he must treat the subject carefully. Do you think Mrs. Speare's portrayal of Jesus accurate to His character? Use passages from the book to support your argument.

4. Daniel was trained as a blacksmith. Research this skill. Are there still blacksmiths today?

5. In chapter 15, the author recounts the story of Jairus and his daughter. Read the account as recorded in Scripture (Luke 8:40-56). Do they agree? What information did the author add?

6. What do you think it was like to be a Roman soldier during this time? Research and write a short report.

7. One of the most compelling characters in the book is Samson. Although not much is told of him, his example of loyalty to Daniel is very moving. Using information provided, and filling in the missing details using your imagination, write a story around Samson.

8. Read *Calico Captive* or *The Witch of Blackbird Pond.*

I C.A.N. Assessment

for

The Bronze Bow – Book Study B

After the *Book Study* is completed, check off each I C.A.N. objective with your teacher.

C   I can **complete** my work.

_____

_____   I can be **creative**.

A   I can be **accurate**.

_____

_____   I can do my work with a good **attitude**.

N   I can do my work **neatly**.

_____

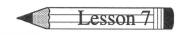

After that they went on till they came among tall beech trees and Trufflehunter called out, "Pattertwig! Pattertwig! Pattertwig!" and almost at once, bounding down from branch to branch till he was just above their heads, came the most magnificent red squirrel that Caspian had ever seen. It was far bigger than the ordinary dumb squirrels which he had sometimes seen in the castle gardens; indeed it was nearly the size of a terrier and the moment you looked in its face you saw that it could talk. Indeed the difficulty was to get it to stop talking for, like all squirrels, it was a chatterer.

Prince Caspian by C.S. Lewis.
Used by permission, Wm. Collins & Sons, Inc.

✎ **Teacher's Note:**
As your student completes each lesson, choose skills from the Review Activities that he needs. The Review Activities follow each lesson.

1. a. Copy the literature passage from dictation. Proofread and correct any errors.

   b. Find the word *indeed* in the literature passage. What prefix does this word contain? You know from Lesson 6 that the prefix **in-** means *not* or *into*. The root word is *deed*. The root or base of a word can be free or bound. A root word that is **free** is a word that can stand by itself, such as deed. If the root is not a word by itself, then the root is said to be **bound**. For example, the root in the word *presume* is *sume*. Since there is no such word in the English language, the root is considered bound.

   c. Find the word *almost* in the literature passage. This word has the prefix **al-** which means *to* or *towards*. Look at the root or base part of the word. Is it free or bound? Add the prefix **al-** to your list and be sure to write the definition and word examples.

1.
b. the prefix in-

c. free
   al-; to or towards
   Possible examples:
   almost, always

d. Unlike the prefix, the suffix is always added to an existing word. The suffix **-er** means *one who* or *that which*. The suffix **-er** usually changes the word into a noun or adjective. Find the word *chatterer* in the literature passage. Identify whether the word is an adjective or noun from the way it is used in the sentence. Add the suffix **-er** to your list of suffixes and write the definition along with word examples. Under the part of speech section include the information, noun or adjective.

Now find the word *bigger* in the literature passage. The suffix **-er** in this word is used to compare two things.

e. Make a list of spelling words from any words you misspelled or use the following suggested list:

bigger	chatterer	ordinary
sometimes	difficulty	magnificent

Look over the suggested spelling list. The word *bigger* has the suffix **-er**. The root of this word is *big*. When a one-syllable word ends with a short vowel and a consonant, double the last consonant before adding a suffix beginning with a vowel. Therefore, when the suffix **-er** is added to the word big, the **g** is doubled, forming the word *bigger*.

> ### Spelling Tip
> When a one-syllable word ends with a short vowel and a consonant, the final consonant must be doubled before adding a suffix beginning with a vowel.

f. Add suffixes to the following words. The first one is done for you as an example:

Root Word	Add Suffix	New Word
Ex: swim	**-ing**	swimming
1) mop	**-ed**	
2) bat	**-er**	
3) get	**-ing**	
4) run	**-er**	
5) dig	**-ing**	

2. a. Adjectives are words that describe nouns. Adjectives often show how one person or thing compares to another. There are three degrees of comparison in adjectives: positive, comparative, and superlative.

b. Circle the word in the first sentence of the literature passage that describes the beech trees. This is an adjective in the **positive form**. It only describes the noun; it does not compare the noun to anything else.

Ex: Joan is tall. (positive form)

c. Find the phrases that describe Pattertwig. Underline the word that compares the size of the squirrel with other squirrels. When comparing two objects or people, the suffix **-er** is added to most one-syllable adjectives and many two-syllable adjectives. Use the word *more* with adjectives of three or more syllables. This is the **comparative form** of an adjective.

Ex: Joan is taller than Mary.
     The berries are more plentiful on this bush.
     (comparative form)

1.
f. 1) mopped
    2) batter
    3) getting
    4) runner
    5) digging

2.
b. tall

c. bigger

71

2.

d. the most magnificent red squirrel

f. 1) wiser, wisest
   2) more dangerous, most dangerous
   3) worse, worst
   4) faster, fastest
   5) better, best

d. When three or more objects or people are being compared, the suffix **-est** is added to most one-syllable adjectives and many two-syllable adjectives. Use the word *most* with adjectives of three or more syllables. This is the **superlative form** of the adjective.

> Ex: Joan is the tallest of all the girls.
> She is the most cooperative student in class.
> (superlative form)

Find the example in the literature passage where a superlative form is used to describe Pattertwig.

e. The comparative and superlative forms of some adjectives are formed irregularly. The most commonly used forms of irregular comparisons are listed below:

Positive	Comparative	Superlative
good, well	better	best
much, many	more	most
bad, ill	worse	worst
far	farther, further	farthest, furthest

f. Fill in the following chart with the comparative and superlative forms of each of the positive forms of adjectives listed below. The first one is done for you as an example. Watch for irregular forms.

Positive	Comparative	Superlative
Ex: small	smaller	smallest
1) wise		
2) dangerous		
3) bad		
4) fast		
5) good		

g. Read the literature passage once more. Draw a sketch or describe what you think Pattertwig looks like.

3. a. In this story the animals talk and have very distinct personalities. Mr. Lewis describes the squirrels as "chatterers." Think about other stories you have read in which animals have personalities. As we learned in Lesson 2, anytime an animal or object is given human qualities, the writing technique of personification is being used.

   b. Choose four of the animals listed below and decide what personality traits would best suit them. List words beside each name that you feel would describe that animal.

      bear   deer   lion   dog   mouse
      tiger   cat   eagle   horse   dolphin
      an animal of your choice

      Ex: horse: stubborn, intelligent

   c. Next choose two of the animals you wrote personality traits for and write one or two sentences about each animal describing the animal in a way that gives him at least one of the personality traits you chose.

      Ex: horse - Lucky shook his head angrily at Vanessa when he found no treat in her pocket. Then, like a spoiled child, he refused to cooperate.

   d. Practice writing your spelling words, sounding out the words by syllables.

4. a. Stories often contain parts in which the characters are speaking to one another. This is called **dialogue**. Dialogue is used to help the story seem more real and alive. Whenever dialogue is used, the actual words spoken by the characters in the story are called **direct quotations**. Direct quotations are surrounded by **quotation marks** (" ") to set them apart. Examine the literature passage and underline the direct quotation. The person speaking is referred to as a **speech tag**.

4.
a. "Patterwig! Patterwig! Patterwig!"

✏ **Teacher's Note:** Your student will learn more about direct quotations in later lessons.

Quotation Rules

Direct Quotations

1. Be sure to capitalize the first word of a direct quotation.

2. When the speech tag comes before the direct quotation, place a comma before the direct quotation.

   Ex: Jim asked, "Can you come with us tonight?"

3. When the speech tag comes after the direct quotations, place the punctuation after the direct quotation inside the closing quotation marks.

   Ex: "We will go to the movies together," announced Sarah.
   "When does the movie start?" asked Tim.
   "You went without me!" gasped Luke.

4. Whenever punctuation is a part of the direct quotation, it appears inside the quotation marks. Punctuation goes outside the closing quotation mark if it applies to the whole sentence instead of just the direct quotation.

   Ex: The team exclaimed, "We will win this game!"
   (punctuation is part of the direct quotation)

   Who said, "Give me liberty or give me death"?
   (punctuation applies to the whole sentence)

5. When writing dialogue be sure to indent and start a new paragraph each time the speaker changes.

6. When direct quotation is more than one sentence and is not divided, then quotation marks should be used at the beginning of the quote and the end of the quote. Quotation marks should not enclose each sentence separately.

7. In a split quotation, the second part of the direct quotation does <u>not</u> begin with a capital letter.

   Ex: "Yesterday," said Amy, "we went to the beach."

b. Look over the quotation rules listed in this lesson. Add correct punctuation to the following sentences. Be sure to enclose all direct quotations with quotation marks and capitalize the first word of a direct quotation. Note the use of the comma.

Ex: Jean said we cannot all fit in the car
     Jean said, "We cannot all fit in the car."

1) The ringmaster cried welcome to the circus
2) There are many formulas used in solving this equation the teacher announced
3) Is there only one doughnut left asked Sue
4) Touchdown yelled the announcer
5) Did Mrs. Scott say "Matthew cannot go"

c. Write a short conversation between the two animals you described in **3b** and **3c**. The conversation should reflect the personality traits you have assigned to each animal. Be sure to set off each speaker's words with quotation marks, and follow the rules for direct quotations. When writing your conversation, indent and begin a new paragraph each time the speaker changes.

d. Take an oral or written spelling pretest.

5. a. Choose one of the following activities.

1) Take the literature passage from dictation paying careful attention to spelling and punctuation.

2) Examine your work from **4c** and make any edits. Use your thesaurus to improve your writing by substituting synonyms that add more description. For example, instead of saying the dog said, substitute a more descriptive word such as exclaimed, growled, or questioned. When you have done your best and are pleased with your work, make a neat copy to give to your teacher.

3) Choose skills from the *Review Activities* on the next page.

4.
b. 1) The ringmaster cried, "Welcome to the circus!"
2) "There are many formulas used in solving this equation," the teacher announced.
3) "Is there only one doughnut left?" asked Sue.
4) "Touchdown!" yelled the announcer.
5) Did Mrs. Scott say, "Matthew cannot go"?

Review Activities

Choose only the skills your student needs to review.

1. *Suffixes*
   Add the suffix to each of the following words. Be sure to double the last consonant if it is necessary.

   Ex: sit + er = sitter

   a. clap + ing
   b. trot + ed
   c. train + er
   d. sad + est
   e. lean + ing

2. *Prefixes and Suffixes*
   Using your list of prefixes and suffixes, add the prefix or suffix that is indicated by the definition in parentheses. In the space following the prefixes, indicate whether the root is bound or free.

   Ex: __in__ stead (*not* or *into*) <u>free</u>

   a. _____caution (*before*) _____
   b. _____cove (*to, towards*) _____
   c. _____definite (*not*) _____
   d. paint ____ (*one who, that which*) _____
   e. rest _____ (*full of*) _____

1.
a. clapping
b. trotted
c. trainer
d. saddest
e. leaning

2.
a. precaution, free
b. alcove, free
c. indefinite, free
d. painter, free
e. restful, free

3. *Adjectives*
Underline the correct adjective in the following sentences.

Ex: Mary can finish her math problems (<u>quicker</u>, quickest)
    than Samantha.

a. Of the two athletes, Mary is (*faster*, *fastest*).
b. In our family Matthew is the (*taller*, *tallest*).
c. Why is this dress (*more expensive*, *expensiver*) than the other one?
d. This butterfly is the (*most beautiful*, *beautifullest*) of them all.
e. This storm is (*badder*, *worse*) than the one we had earlier.

4. *Personification*
Write two sentences describing a tree using personification.

5. *Punctuation (Quotation marks, commas, period, exclamation mark)*
Add the correct punctuation mark in the following sentences.

a. How long does it take a caterpillar to become a butterfly Jim asked
b. His teacher replied Once the caterpillar forms a pupa it takes about two weeks for the transformation to be complete
c. That's amazing declared Martha
d. Dan commented I once saw a butterfly emerge from its pupa. It looked rather wet and crumpled at first
e. Blood pumping from the abdomen into the veins causes the wings to unfold, and when they are dry, the butterfly is able to fly away remarked his teacher

3.
a. faster
b. tallest
c. more expensive
d. most beautiful
e. worse

4. Answers will vary.

5. a. "How long does it take a caterpillar to become a butterfly?" Jim asked.

b. His teacher replied, "Once the caterpillar forms a pupa it takes about two weeks for the transformation to be complete."

c. "That's amazing!" declared Martha.

d. Dan commented, "I once saw a butterfly emerge from its pupa. It looked rather wet and crumpled at first."

e. "Blood pumping from the abdomen into the veins causes the wings to unfold, and when they are dry, the butterfly is able to fly away," remarked his teacher.

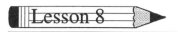
✎ **Teacher's Note:** As your student completes each lesson, choose skills from the Review Activities that he needs. The Review Activities follow each lesson.

Jesus closed the book and gave it back to the attendant. The waiting congregation seemed to surge forward and to hold its breath. Again that voice made the blood leap in Daniel's veins.

"I say to you, the time is fulfilled, and the kingdom of God is at hand. Repent, and believe."

Now! Daniel leaned forward. Tell us that the moment has come! Tell us what to do! Longing swelled unbearably in his throat.

But Jesus went on speaking quietly. A rippling murmur passed across the crowd. Others too waited for the word that was not spoken. What had the man meant? He had said liberty for the oppressed. Why didn't he call them to arms against the oppressor? Repent, he said now. Repent. As though that could rid them of the Romans. Disappointed and puzzled, Daniel leaned back. The fire that had leaped up in him died down. The man's voice had been like a trumpet call. Yet where did the call lead?

The Bronze Bow by Elizabeth George Speare. Used by permission Houghton Mifflin.

1.

a. Allow for discussion

1. a. Read the literature passage. Good biblical fiction, while adding details, will remain true to what the Bible teaches. Can you find an account in Scripture that could be the setting for this passage? Where would you begin looking?

b. Allow for discussion

b. How did Daniel feel as he listened to Jesus? Why was he disappointed? Explain to your teacher what it means to repent.

c. Write the literature passage from dictation. Be sure to use quotation marks to punctuate the direct quotation. Notice how the writer has identified the speaker as Jesus in the text a few sentences prior to the actual quotation instead of directly prior or directly after. This method allows the text to flow more smoothly and still leaves no question as to who is speaking.

d. Look at the word *repent* in the literature passage. The prefix **re-** means *back* or *again*. Is the root of this word bound or free? Add this prefix to your list. Be sure to write the definition and word examples.

e. Make a list of spelling words from any words you misspelled in the dictation or use the following suggested list.

quietly	believe	died
veins	oppressed	oppressor

> ## Spelling Tip
> It is easy to confuse the **ie** with the **ei** letter combination. **ie** is used in most words; **ei** is used after the letter **c** and in words that make the long /ā/ sound. The following rhyme will help you to remember which to use: **ie** or **ei**. I before **e** except after **c**, and in words that say /ā/ as *neighbor* and *weigh*.

f. Write **ie** or **ei** in the following words.

1) sl___gh   6) fr___nd
2) rec____ve   7) ch____f
3) sh____ld   8) y____ld
4) fr___ght   9) v ___n
5) bel___ve   10) conc___ve

1.
d. free
    re-; back or again
    Possible examples:
    review, repeat

✎ **Teacher's Note:** Read the words aloud to the student so he can fill in the letters.

f. 1) sleigh
    2) receive
    3) shield
    4) freight
    5) believe
    6) friend
    7) chief
    8) yield
    9) vein
    10) conceive

g. oppress

2.

a. **The man's voice had been <u>like</u> a trumpet call. The man's voice and a trumpet call are being compared.**

g. Two of the words from the suggested spelling list have the same root or base word. What is the root? Knowing the root of a word will help you remember how to spell it.

2. a. Remember that a simile compares two unlike things using the words *like* or *as*. Find the simile in this paragraph and underline it. What two things are being compared?

b. A **sentence** expresses a complete thought and has two parts. The part which tells who or what the sentence is about is called the **complete subject**. The other part of the sentence which tells what the subject is or does and is called the **complete predicate**. Most sentences can be divided between the complete subject and the complete predicate.

   Ex: The family / enjoys the amusement park.
        Mary Anne / is my friend.

c. Very often the subject comes at the beginning of the sentence, but not always. The subject always has a noun as its focal point. The predicate always has a verb as its focal point telling what the subject is or what action the subject is doing. It is usually easier to locate the predicate of the sentence first. Read the following sentence.

   The runner raced across the finish line.

   Now ask yourself the following questions to help locate the subject and predicate of the sentence.

   1) What action is taking place?
   2) Who or what is doing the action?

   The answer to the first question is the predicate of the sentence, and the answer to the second is the subject.

c.

1) raced across the finish line
2) the runner

d. It is a little harder to find the subject in a sentence which asks a question. Try putting the question in statement form.

Ex: What had the man meant?
  Make it into a statement: The man had meant *what*.
  By doing this you put the subject in front of the verb, making it easier to find.

e. Look at the first three sentences in the last paragraph of the literature passage. Draw a line dividing the complete subject from the complete predicate as in **2b**. Be sure to first locate the predicate and then find the subject.

f. Every sentence has to have a subject and predicate to be complete. A sentence that does not contain both parts or does not express a complete thought is called a **fragment**. A writer should always be careful to only use complete sentences in his writing.

Ex: Going to the store. (fragment - subject missing)
  Mary is going to the store. (complete sentence)

  My brother and his friend. (fragment - predicate missing)
  My brother and his friend went with us. (complete sentence)

  While we were at the beach. (fragment - incomplete thought)
  While we were at the beach we found a starfish. (complete sentence)

g. Read the following sentences. If the sentence is a complete sentence, write **C** in front of the sentence. If it is a fragment, write **F** in front of it, and rewrite the sentence to add whatever is necessary to make it a complete sentence.

_____1) Going to the mall.
_____2) The butterfly flew from flower to flower.
_____3) The sixth grade class at church.
_____4) As we were climbing up the mountain.
_____5) When he realized his error.

2.

e. But Jesus/ went on speaking quietly.
A rippling murmur/ passed across the crowd.
Others too/ waited for the word that was not spoken.

✎ **Teacher's Note: Writers often stray from this rule, but your student should use complete sentences**

2.

g. 1) F- Possible answer: I am going to the mall.
2) C
3) F- Possible answer: The sixth grade class at church sang a hymn.
4) F- Possible answer: We saw a bald eagle as we were climbing up the mountain.
5) F- Possible answer: It was too late when we realized his error.

3. a. There are four types of sentences, each expressing a different purpose.

Sentence Types

1) A **declarative sentence** makes a statement and ends with a period.
   Ex: Chickens are a type of bird found on most farms.

2) An **interrogative sentence** asks a question and ends with a question mark.
   Ex: Who is coming skating with us?

3) An **imperative sentence** gives a command or makes a request. They often contain the understood subject *you*. An imperative sentence ends with a period or exclamation mark.
   Ex: Come over here now!
       Please put these books back on the shelf.

4) **An exclamatory** sentence expresses strong emotion or surprise and ends with an exclamation point.
   Ex: What a noise those dogs make!
       You scared me!

---

b. Notice that in imperative sentences the subject is often said to be understood. This means that although the subject is not stated, the sentence is understood to have the subject *you*. Read the following sentence.

   Close the door.

   Who is directed to close the door? The understood subject *you* is the one being directed to close the door.

c. There are four imperative sentences in the literature passage. Locate these sentences and circle them. *Who* is the understood subject.

3.
c. Repent and believe.
   Tell us that the moment has come!
   Tell us what to do!
   Repent.
   ***You* is understood to be the subject.**

d. Look at the literature passage and find an example of a declarative sentence and an interrogative sentence. Check with your teacher to make sure you are correct.

e. Practice writing your spelling words, sounding them out by syllables. Remember to apply your spelling rule to help you in writing **ie** in the correct order.

4. a. In **3a** you learned there are four types of sentences: declarative, interrogative, imperative, and exclamatory. Read each of the following sentences and decide if they are declarative (**D**), interrogative (**I**), imperative (**Imp**), or exclamatory (**E**). Fill in the blanks and add the correct punctuation at the end of each sentence.

   Ex: _I_ Where are you going?

   ____ 1) Be sure to wash the dishes
   ____ 2) How beautiful the stars are
   ____ 3) There is a great variety of life in a rainforest
   ____ 4) Where will you be going this evening
   ____ 5) The races will begin at this evening at dusk
   ____ 6) Who will be cooking dinner tonight
   ____ 7) Go to your room right now
   ____ 8) What a surprise to see you
   ____ 9) What is the agenda for tonight's meeting
   ____ 10) Northern lights are a beautiful sight to see

b. Read the literature passage again. Write a short paragraph explaining to Daniel what you think Jesus meant as He spoke.

c. Take an oral or written spelling pretest. Review any words you have trouble with.

5. a. Choose one of the following activities.

   1) Write the literature passage from dictation paying special attention to spelling and punctuation.

   2) Choose skills from the *Review Activities* on the next page.

---

d. **Declarative - Jesus closed the book and gave it back to the attendant. (There are many other examples of declarative sentences in the literature passage) Interrogative - What had the man meant? Why didn't he call them to arms against the oppressor? Yet where did the call lead?**

4.
a. 1) Imp. - (.)
**   2) E - (!)**
**   3) D - (.)**
**   4) I - (?)**
**   5) D - (.)**
**   6) I - (?)**
**   7) Imp. - (!)**
**   8) E - (!)**
**   9) I - (?)**
**   10) D - (.)**

b. Answers will vary.

Review Activities

Choose only the skills your student needs to review.

1. *Prefixes*
Add the prefix **re-** to the following words. How does the prefix change the meaning of the root word?

   a. _____turn
   b. _____form
   c. _____examine

2. *Similes*
Complete the following examples of similes.

   a. as fancy as _____
   b. fluffy like _____

3. *Complete Subject and Complete Predicate*
Draw a vertical line between the complete subject and the complete predicate.

   Ex: Birds / are the only animals that have feathers.

   a. The ostrich is the largest bird in the world.
   b. Down feathers keep birds warm in cold weather.
   c. Penguins use their wings as flippers to help them swim faster.
   d. Birds build many different types of nests.
   e. Baby birds are always hungry.

4. *Fragments*
Read the following sentences. If it is a complete sentence, write **C** in the space provided. If it is a fragment, write **F**.

   a. _____When I travel on the bus.
   b. _____This road has some dangerous curves.
   c. _____Going to the beach this afternoon.
   d. _____Since you will not be able to come with us.
   e. _____The beautiful green forest.

1.
a. return
b. reform
c. reexamine

2. Possible answers
a. a peacock
b. clouds

3.
a. The ostrich/ is the largest bird in the world.
b. Down feathers/ keep birds warm in cold weather.
c. Penguins/ use their wings as flippers to help them swim faster.
d. Birds/ build many different types of nests.
e. Baby birds/ are always hungry.

4.
a. F
b. C
c. F
d. F
e. F

5. *Types of Sentences*

Identify each of the following types of sentences. On the line
next to each sentence write **D** for declarative, **I** for interrogative,
Imp for imperative, or **E** for exclamatory, and fill in the correct
punctuation at the end of sentence.

a. _____ Watch out for that bee

b. _____ Why do bees fly from flower to flower

c. _____ Bees collect nectar from the flowers

d. _____ What hard workers they are

5.

a. Imp

b. I

c. D

d. E

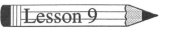

Icicles were forming on Sham's feelers, yet his body was wet with sweat. He backed up. He lowered his head, and as the whip struck him, he made a snatching pull. The load moved, and as if by some supernatural power Sham kept on going up the incline. When almost at the top, however, his forefeet began slipping. He clawed with them. The whip snarled and cracked. It cut deep into his hide. Groaning, he tried again, and again. His veins swelled to bursting.

King of the Wind by Marguerite Henry.
Used by permission, Macmillan Publishing Co.

1.

b. fore-; before in time
Possible examples:
forerunner, forefeet

1. a. Read the literature passage. Copy the passage from dictation and compare your copy to the model. Correct any errors.

   b. Look at the fifth sentence of the literature passage and find the prefix **fore-**. This prefix means *before in time*. Does knowing the meaning of this prefix help you to understand the meaning of the word *forefeet*? Add this prefix to your prefix list along with its definition and some word examples.

   c. Look over the first sentence of the literature passage. Why is an apostrophe used in Sham's feelers? Review the rules for use of apostrophes in Lesson 6 if you are not sure.

   d. Choose two to six words for your spelling words or use the following suggested list:

snatching	snarled	cracked
groaning	tried	slipped

e. *Snatching* **is used as an**
adjective to describe *pull.*

   e. Note that each of the spelling words has the suffix **-ed** or **-ing**. Usually words with these suffixes are verbs; however, one of these words is used as an adjective. Read each of the words in the context of the sentence in the literature passage. Can you identify the word that is used as an adjective?

f. In Lessons 4 and 7, you learned *Spelling Tips* for adding suffixes to words. Two of the tips are as follows:

Drop the silent e from a word before adding a suffix that begins with a vowel.

When a one-syllable word ends with a short vowel followed by a consonant, then the last consonant is doubled before adding a suffix beginning with a vowel.

Find the word in the suggested spelling list that follows one of these *Spelling Tips* and tell your teacher which rule it follows.

g. Find the word *tried* in the suggested spelling list. The **y** in the root word *try* has been changed to an **i** before the suffix **-ed** was added.

> ### Spelling Tip
> When a word ending in **y** is preceded by a consonant, the **y** is changed to **i** before adding a suffix, except for a suffix beginning with **i** such as **-ing**. If a word ends with **y** preceded by a vowel, then just add the suffix.

Copy these words. Say the words aloud as you write them. Remember there is no change made in the root word when adding the suffix **-ing**.

Root Word	-ed	-ing
play	played	playing
hurry	hurried	hurrying
empty	emptied	emptying
carry	carried	carrying

1.

f. **slipped** - When a one-syllable word ends with a short vowel followed by a consonant, the last consonant is doubled before adding a suffix beginning with a vowel.

✎ **Teacher's Note:** Some exceptions to this rule are *paid, said, gaily,* and *gaiety.*

1.

h. 1) married, marrying
2) cried, crying
3) prayed; praying
4) chopped, chopping
5) sneezed, sneezing
6) strayed; straying
7) traded, trading
8) dripped, dripping
9) applied, applying
10) copied, copying

h. Add the suffixes **-ed** and **-ing** to the following words. Be sure to follow the rules for adding suffixes.

Root Word	**-ed**	**-ing**
Ex: fry	fried	frying
stay	stayed	staying
1) marry		
2) cry		
3) pray		
4) chop		
5) sneeze		
6) stray		
7) trade		
8) drip		
9) apply		
10) copy		

2. a. A sentence expresses a complete thought and has two parts, the complete subject and the complete predicate.

   Ex: Three boys / were playing basketball.
   (complete subject) (complete predicate)

   b. The **simple subject** of a sentence is the noun or pronoun that is the focal point of the complete subject without any modifiers.

   Ex: Three boys / were playing basketball.
   (*boys* is the simple subject)

   c. The **simple predicate** of a sentence is the verb or verb phrase that tells the action of the subject without any modifiers. A verb phrase is the main verb and one or more helping verbs.

   Ex: Five girls / played tennis.
   (*played* is the simple predicate or verb)

   Three boys / were playing basketball.
   (*were playing* is the simple predicate or verb phrase)

d. Look at the last sentence of the literature passage. Divide the complete subject and complete predicate with a vertical line. Underline the simple subject and circle the simple predicate.

e. Often sentences contain more than one simple subject. A **compound subject** consists of two or more subjects.

   Ex: Sara and Anna had a wonderful time at the park.

   This sentence has a compound subject since both *Sara* and *Anna* are part of the complete subject.

   Sentences with more than one verb (or simple predicate) have a **compound verb**.

   Ex: Joe went to the store and bought some milk.

   Since both the verbs, *went* and *bought*, are telling what action was taken by the subject, *Joe*, the sentence has a compound verb.

f. Find a sentence in the literature passage that contains a compound verb. Double underline the compound verb.

g. Write one sentence with a compound subject and one with a compound verb.

3. a. A **conjunction** is a connecting word used to connect words, groups of words, or sentences.

Common Conjunctions
and but or nor so yet

2.

d. His veins / swelled to bursting.

f. The whip snarled and cracked.

89

3.

c. Icicles were forming on Sham's feelers, (yet) his body was wet with sweat.

He lowered his head, (and) as the whip struck him, he made a snatching pull.

The load moved, (and) as if by some supernatural power Sham kept on going up the incline.

d. See commas in 2c.

✎ Teacher's Note: The word *however* in the literature passage also connects a compound sentence, but it is a conjunctive adverb, not a coordinating conjunction. This will be taught in a higher level book.

b. When two complete sentences are joined together by a conjunction, it forms a **compound sentence**.

Ex: The two girls went on a picnic together, but they had to return before dark.

The conjunction *but* connects the two complete sentences:
The two girls went on a picnic together.
They had to return before dark.

c. Read over the literature passage. Find three compound sentences connected by conjunctions, and circle those conjunctions.

d. In compound sentences, a **comma** is always used before the coordinating conjunction. Find the commas that appear before the coordinating conjunctions in the three compound sentences.

e. Read the compound sentences from the literature passage as two separate sentences leaving out the conjunction. Now read them as the author wrote them. Which way do you like better?

f. Read the literature passage again. Tell your teacher in your own words what is happening. What information is not given? What words give you a clear picture of the scene? Write a paragraph to add to the passage, explaining what may have happened next to Sham. Use words that enable the reader to envision a clear picture of the events. Try to use compound sentences.

g. Practice writing your spelling words. Keep in mind the rules for adding suffixes as you practice your words.

4. a. The author of the literature passage makes good use of adjectives, adverbs, and descriptive verbs to create a word picture that helps you to not only see, but feel and hear what was happening. For example, instead of just saying "The whip struck him.", the author describes it as "The whip snarled and cracked." Reread the literature passage and examine the author's use of descriptive language.

b. Today you are going to write a paragraph describing a
   strenuous activity. You could describe a sport you enjoy, or
   describe an active animal such as a cat stalking prey.

c. Begin by brainstorming about your ideas. Choose your
   subject, such as the cat. Draw a circle and place your subject
   in the middle. Make lines extending outward from the
   circle. On these lines you will write your ideas. You are
   drawing a circle word picture. Record anything that comes
   to mind. You will use some of the ideas but not all of them.
   Write down any descriptive words you could use in your
   paragraph.

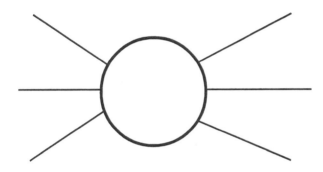

d. Beginning with a good topic sentence, take your ideas and
   form a good paragraph describing your subject. Using
   some of your ideas, write sentences supporting your topic
   sentence.

e. Take an oral or written spelling pretest.

5. Choose one of the following activities.

1) Write the literature passage from dictation.

2) Continue to work on your descriptive paragraph from **4a-d**.
   Draw a picture illustrating the paragraph.

3) Choose skills from the *Review Activities* on the next page.

Review Activities

Choose only the skills your student needs to review.

1. *Prefixes*
   Examine the words listed below that contain the prefix **fore-**. Guess the meaning of each word and then use your dictionary to check the definition. Does knowing the meaning of the prefix **fore-** help you in determining a word's meaning?

   a. foredoom
   b. forefather
   c. forecast

2. *Suffixes*
   Add the suffixes in parentheses to the following root words.

   a. plenty + (ful) =
   b. buy + (er) =
   c. hurry + (ing) =
   d. apply + (ed) =
   e. busy + (est) =

3. *Simple Subject and Verb*
   Underline the simple subject once and the verb twice in the following sentences.

   a. The tall plant waved in the breeze.
   b. The football player ran down the field for a touchdown.
   c. Mary can knit very quickly.
   d. The garden show will begin in ten minutes.
   e. The white flowers smell very sweet.

1.
a. foredoom: to condemn in advance
b. forefather: an ancestor, one who came earlier in a family line
c. forecast: to predict in advance

2.
a. plentiful
b. buyer
c. hurrying
d. applied
e. busiest

3.
a. The tall <u>plant</u> <u>waved</u> in the breeze.
b. The football <u>player</u> <u>ran</u> down the field for a touchdown.
c. <u>Mary</u> <u>can knit</u> very quickly.
d. The garden <u>show</u> <u>will begin</u> in ten minutes.
e. The white <u>flowers</u> <u>smell</u> very sweet.

4. *Conjunctions, Compound Subjects, Compound Predicates, and Compound Sentences*

Underline the conjunctions in the following sentences. On the line before each sentence, write if it contains a compound subject (**CS**), a compound verb (**CV**), or if it is a compound sentence (**CSent**). Also, add punctuation if the sentence is a compound sentence.

a. _____The daisies and marigolds made a lovely combination.

b. _____The *Nina*, *Pinta*, and *Santa Mari*a sailed to America.

c. _____We will walk to the park and catch the bus.

d. _____I will check with my mother but I do not think I will be able to go to the movie.

e. _____The children played games, ate lunch, and listened to a story.

f. _____We will go shopping at the mall or we can go to the shopping center.

4.
a. **and**, CS
b. **and**, CS
c. **and**, CV
d. I will check with my mother, but I do not think I will be able to go to the movie. CSent
e. and, CV
f. We will go shopping at the mall, or we can go to the shopping center. CSent

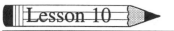

"At last the hole was cut, and I could push myself in. There was my father right below me, there on the wheel. The wheel was leaning against the side of the boat. With his last strength my father had climbed to the hub to be as close to me as possible while I sawed, to be within reach. I leaned in; I grabbed him under the arms; I lifted him out. I was small, but I was strong. Right then I could have lifted the church and the tower. Too, my father was just a light skeleton."

The Wheel on the School by Meindert DeJong.
Used by permission, Harper and Row.

1.
a. This is a direct quotation.

1. a. Look over the literature passage taking special notice of the punctuation. What do the quotation marks at the beginning and end of the passage tell you? Write the literature passage from dictation. Compare your copy to the model and correct any errors.

   b. Make a spelling list of any misspelled words from your dictation or use the following suggested list.

skeleton	strength	myself
possible	within	against

   Write the spelling words, dividing them into syllables. Remember, each syllable has to contain a vowel.

c. gh is silent

   c. It is important to be familiar with letters that are silent when they appear in certain letter combinations. Some words spell the long /i/ sound with **igh** as in *light*. What letters are silent?

> **Spelling Tip**
> Some words spell the long /i/
> sound with **igh** as in **light**.

d. Copy the words and underline the **gh**. Say the words aloud as you write them. Do you ever hear a /g/ sound?

1) freight   6) bright
2) light   7) sight
3) right   8) weight
4) might   9) might
5) height   10) twilight

e. Sometimes words can be tricky. In the first sentence, the word *hole* is used. How would the meaning change if the author had used the word *whole* instead? The words *hole* and *whole* are homonyms. **Homonyms** are words that sound the same, have different meanings, and are usually spelled differently.

   Whole means entire, and *hole* means an opening. When writing, be careful to use the correct word.

✏ **Teacher's Note:** Some grammar books refer to these words as homophones.

f. Listed below are five words from the literature passage that have corresponding homonyms. List the homonyms for each word. Be careful, some words have more than one homonym.

   Ex: eight - ate
   1) right   4) too
   2) there   5) in
   3) be   6) I

f. 1) write
    2) their, they're
    3) bee
    4) to, two
    5) inn
    6) eye

g. Choose one set of homonyms and write a sentence using all the homonyms for that word in the sentence.

   Ex: The *eight* of us *ate* supper at the deli.

2. a. The person telling a story is called the **narrator**. The **point of view** is the angle from which the story is told. The point of view will depend upon who is telling the story, whether it is told from the point of view of one of the characters in the story or from the point of view of someone outside the story.

b. The **first person** point of view is when the story is told from the point of view of one of the story characters. One indication that a story is being told from the first person point of view is the use of the pronoun *I* in the telling of the story. Although the character is usually a person, the character telling the story could be an animal or even an object.

  Ex: *I* was breathless with anticipation as the box was opened.

c. The **third person** point of view is used when the story is told from the point of view of someone outside the story. The use of the pronouns he, she, and they often indicate the use of third person.

  Ex: *She* was breathless with anticipation as the box was opened.

d. Examine the literature passage. From what point of view is this story being told? Does the context of the passage let you know who the narrator is? Which words give you clues in identifying the narrator?

e. Examine some other stories and determine the point of view from which they are written.

f. Rewrite the literature passage into the third person point of view. Look over the two versions of the literature passage. Which version do you find more enjoyable to read? Why?

2.
d. first person;
   Yes, the son;
   my father, myself, I

✐ **Teacher's Note:** Often it is more enjoyable to read a story written from first person point of view because you feel more connected with the character in the story.

f. Answers will vary.

3. a. Locate the three separate sentences joined together by semicolons (;) in the literature passage. The use of semicolons indicates that each part of the sentence is independent and could stand alone. An **independent clause** contains a complete thought which can stand alone as a sentence. **Semicolons** are used to join together independent clauses when they are not connected by a conjunction.

   Ex: The wind blew through the trees; the leaves rustled.

   Phrases that do not contain both subject and predicate are not independent. They are often listed together in a series with a conjunction joining the last phrase or item of the series. When three or more phrases or items are used together in a series, commas are used to separate the phrases or items, with a final comma used before the conjunction.

   Teacher's Note: Some grammar books teach this skill by omitting the last comma before the conjunction.

   Ex: I will be driving to the store, shopping for some groceries, and coming home.
   I love the peaches, plums, and nectarines that are ripe this time of year.

   Find the three independent clauses in the literature passage that are joined by semicolons. Rewrite them into one good sentence containing phrases in a series. Some words will have to be omitted, but the meaning of the sentence should not change. Be sure to use commas to separate the phrases.

   b. Having only one paragraph from an entire book restricts your information. However, there are certain things revealed in the literature passage. It can be determined there is a struggle taking place. Can you guess what is happening?

   c. Reread the literature passage. Can you tell how the person telling the story feels? The emotion created by the author is called the **mood** of the story. A good author uses descriptions that draw the reader into the action happening in the story and allows the reader to share in the mood created. How would you describe the mood created in this paragraph? Discuss with your teacher how the author succeeded in creating this mood.

3.
a. I leaned in, grabbed him under the arms, and lifted him out.

b. Allow your student to make any guess. The following is what actually took place: A son is rescuing his father who is trapped inside an overturned boat.

c. Possible answers: anxious, worried, hurried

The author succeeded in creating this mood by his dramatic description of each step of the rescue.

d. How would you feel if you were trying to rescue your father or a friend? Write a paragraph describing a tense situation. Use descriptions that create the mood you want and help the reader to feel what you feel.

e. Review your spelling words and prepare for a practice test.

4. a. Every story has a plot. The **plot** is the sequence of events and actions that take place in the story. Every good plot contains the five main elements listed below:

Plot Line

1) **Opening**: This is the part of the story that introduces the characters, explains the background of the story, the setting, and the present situation.

2) **Rising Action**: This is a series of problems and struggles which are building toward a climax.

3) **Climax**: The climax is the turning point or action peak of the story. Usually this is the point at which the action and anticipation is at the fullest.

4) **Falling Action**: The point in the story at which the action of the turning point or high point is worked out and a solution is at hand.

5) **Conclusion**: The part of the story in which the solution comes to a conclusion and the problem is solved. This usually provides the story with its ending.

A graphic representation of the elements of the plot of a story is called a **plot line**. A plot line can help you envision the sequence of the elements and how they are put together to form the plot of a story.

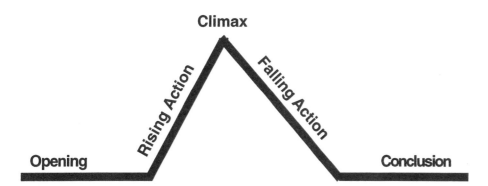

b. Which element of the plot is present in the literature passage? Which sentence of the passage best describes the turning point or action peak?

c. Although the literature passage only supplies us with a small amount of information concerning the situation, it does allow us to speculate what problems might have occurred prior to the rescue. These problems would be considered part of the rising action of the story. Imagine what problems would lead up to the situation described in the literature passage. Write a paragraph or two describing events and problems that may have led up to the climax in the literature passage.

Read the paragraphs you have written with the literature passage. Does your version of the rising action supply a series of events that lead up to the climax?

d. Take an oral or written spelling pretest.

5. a. Choose one of the following activities.

1) Write the literature passage from dictation.

2) Write a short story that contains the five elements of a plot. Map out your ideas on a plot line to make sure you have all the ingredients necessary for a effective plot.

3) Choose skills from the *Review Activities* on the next page.

4.
b. Rising Action and Climax.

I lifted him out.

Review Activities

Choose only the skills your student needs to review.

1. *Homonyms*
Choose the correct word in the parentheses to complete the sentence.

   a. (There, Their) will be a children's concert this evening.
   b. We will be going (to, too) the pottery class soon.
   c. I will (right, write) to my friend in Ireland.
   d. The (be, bee) kept buzzing around her head.
   e. The (in, inn) was already full when Mary and Joseph came.

2. *Narrator, Point of View, and Mood*
Read the following paragraph. Who is the narrator? From what point of view is the story told? What mood has been created?

    I surveyed all the land below me with a careful and calculated eye looking for the slightest possible movement. The rustle of a leaf, a shift of a blade of grass was all that was necessary to lead me to my prey. Suddenly, it happened! I detected movement! Quick as a flash I swooped from my treetop vantage point and clutched a small mouse in my talons.

3. *Commas*
Add commas as necessary.

   a. On our summer vacation we will visit the seashore climb a mountain and ride a horse.
   b. I looked inside reached down and picked up the rabbit.
   c. For the party I need to buy balloons cake decorations and gifts.
   d. The bee buzzed flipped and dove around the flowers.
   e. My grandparents have visited England France and Spain.
   f. Bring your lunch a thermos and a blanket.

4. *Plot*
What are the five main elements to a good plot?

1.
a. There
b. to
c. write
d. bee
e. inn

2.
Narrator: Hawk
Point of View: First Person
Mood: tense, anticipating

3.
a. On our summer vacation we will visit the seashore, climb a mountain, and ride a horse.
b. I looked inside, reached down, and picked up the rabbit.
c. For the party I need to buy balloons, cake decorations, and gifts.
d. The bumblebee buzzed, flipped, and dove around the flowers.
e. My grandparents have visited England, France, and Spain.
f. Bring your lunch, a thermos, and a blanket.

4. opening, rising action, climax, falling action, conclusion

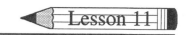

Everybody laughed, but the teacher's eyes weren't pleased. "True, true," he said. "That's right, Eelka. We can't think much when we don't know much. But we can wonder! From now until tomorrow morning when you come to school again, will you do that? Will you wonder why and wonder why? Will you wonder why storks don't come to Shora to build their nests on the roofs, the way they do in all the villages around? For sometimes when we wonder, we can make things begin to happen."

The Wheel on the School by Meindert DeJong.
Used by permission, Harper and Row.

1. a. Read the literature passage paying special attention to the punctuation marks. Write the passage from dictation. Proofread and correct your work.

   b. The literature passage contains four contractions. Locate the contractions and circle them. List each of the contractions, and write the two words that make up each contraction next to it.

   c. Find the word in the literature passage that is using an apostrophe (') to show possession and underline it. What is it showing possession of?

   d. Make a spelling list from any misspelled words from your dictation or use the following suggested list:

tomorrow	villages	happen
wonder	around	morning

   e. Look through the literature passage and find nouns that are plural (more than one). A noun is made plural by adding **s** or **es** to the word. The nouns in the literature passage have been made plural by adding just **s**.

✎ **Teacher's Note:**
As your student completes each lesson, choose skills from the Review Activities that he needs. The Review Activities follow each lesson.

1.
b. weren't - were not
   that's - that is
   can't - cannot
   don't - do not

c. <u>teacher's</u> eyes - the eyes of the teacher

Spelling Tip

Most nouns form their plural form by just adding **s**. However, to form the plural of nouns ending in **sh**, **ch**, **x**, **s**, and **z**, add **es**.

In words that end in **y** preceded by a consonant, change the **y** to **i** and add **es**. If the word ends in **y** preceded by a vowel, then just add **s**.

1.

f. s, es: no meaning;
forms plural nouns;
Possible examples:
pigs, beaches

g. 1) cherries
2) dishes
3) boys
4) foxes
5) rocks
6) dresses
7) churches
8) daisies
9) insects
10) buzzes

2.

a. The children try to find a way to get the storks to come back to Shora.

b. The mood of the teacher is serious, and he wants the students to be serious, too. The teacher is challenging the students to make a discovery and perhaps solve the problem.

Ex: beach - beaches   wish - wishes   box - boxes
       glass - glasses   waltz - waltzes
Ex: puppy - puppies   ray - rays

f. Add **s** and **es** to your list of suffixes. Under parts of speech write forms plural nouns. These suffixes have no meanings. Be sure to fill in some word examples.

g. Write each of the following nouns in its plural form.

1) cherry   6) dress
2) dish   7) church
3) boy   8) daisy
4) fox   9) insect
5) rock   10) buzz

2. a. As you learned in Lesson 10, every plot has at least one conflict or problem to be resolved. From reading the literature passage, can you identify the main conflict in *The Wheel on the School*?

b. Can you determine the mood of the teacher in the literature passage? What do you think the teacher was challenging the students to do?

c. Find the direct quotation in the literature passage.

The quotation is divided with the words *he said*. When the quotation is divided after a complete sentence, both parts of the quotation are completely enclosed by quotation marks.

Ex: "I love a rainy spring day," said Mary. "My mother can't wait until the flowers begin blooming."

If the quotation is divided within a sentence, then the second part of the quotation does not begin with a capital letter. This is called a **split quotation**.

Ex: "I need to finish my chores," answered Mark, "and then I will be able to join you."

d. Add capitalization and punctuation, including quotation marks, commas, question marks, exclamation points, and periods to the following direct quotations. (For information on punctuating direct quotations, refer to Lesson 7.)

1) I will finish my shopping said Jerri and meet you at the game
2) drive to the house slowly said Mary we don't want to arrive too early
3) when will the leaves begin to change color asked Jimmy
4) Marilyn smiled it is a wonderful feeling to know I have such good friend
5) stop playing and start working yelled Natalie with frustration we need to have the float finished by noon
6) spring is in the air. I see birds beginning to build their nests. a warm breeze is blowing from the south said Anne with a smile.

e. Read the literature passage carefully once again. What do you think possibly happened just before this scene? Use your imagination to write a paragraph describing what could have happened.

2.

c. "True, true," he said. "That's right, Eelka. We can't...begin to happen."

e. 1) "I will finish my shopping," said Jerri, "and meet you at the game."
2) "Drive to the house slowly," said Mary. "We don't want to arrive too early."
3) "When will the leaves begin to change color?" asked Jimmy.
4) Marilyn smiled, "It is a wonderful feeling to know I have such a good friend."
5) "Stop playing and start working!" yelled Natalie with frustration. "We need to have the float finished by noon."
6) "Spring is in the air. I see birds beginning to build their nests. A warm breeze is blowing from the south," said Anne with a smile.

3.

a. Declarative - Everybody laughed, but the teacher's eyes weren't pleased. "True, true," he said. That's right, Eelka. We can't think much when we don't know much. For sometimes when we wonder, we can make things begin to happen.

Interrogative - From now until tomorrow morning when you come to school again, will you do that? Will you wonder why and wonder why? Will you wonder why storks don't come to Shora to build their nests on the roofs, the way they do in all the villages around?

Exclamatory: But we can wonder!

b. From now until tomorrow morning when you come to school again, will you do that?
Wonder from now until tomorrow morning when you come to school again.

Will you wonder why and wonder why?
Wonder why and wonder why.

Will you wonder why storks don't come to Shora to build their nests on the roofs, the way they do in all the villages around?
Wonder why storks don't come to Shora to build their nests on the roofs, the way they do in all the villages around.

3. a. Sentences can ask a question (interrogative), make a statement (declarative), express strong feeling (exclamatory), or give a command (imperative). Find an example of an interrogative, declarative, and exclamatory sentence in the literature passage. Remember, the type of punctuation a sentence has can help you to identify it.

  b. Find the three interrogative sentences in the literature passage again. Change these interrogative sentences into imperative sentences. Remember, the subject in an imperative sentence is often understood. Be sure to change the end punctuation.

     Ex: Will you please close the door? (interrogative)
          Please close the door. (imperative)

  c. Look at the third sentence of the literature passage. In this sentence, Eelka is addressed by name. This is called a **direct address**. When a name is used in a direct address, set it off with **commas**. A pair of commas is used if the name appears within the sentence, but only one comma is necessary if the name appears at the beginning or end of the sentence.

     Ex: Go to the kitchen, Nancy, and find my large platter.
          Jack, please help me lift this box.
          You do not have to come with me, Rick.

d. Punctuate the following sentences that use a direct address. Also, be sure to add the correct end punctuation.

1) Martha go see who is at the door
2) I really liked your part in the play William
3) The secret to success Lydia is to prepare for opportunity
4) Carol are you sure the meeting is today
5) Come here this minute Patrick

e. Review your spelling words and prepare for tomorrow's practice test.

4. a. Many important discoveries have been made or mysteries solved because someone was curious. Someone wondered, "What if? Why? How?" Think about how our lives have been enriched because someone wondered.

b. Eelka's teacher encouraged his students to think. One way to improve your thinking skills is to develop word analogies. A **word analogy** expresses a relationship between words. An analogy statement has two parts. In the first part of the statement two words are placed together that are in some way related, then in the second part of the analogy two different words are placed together that have a similar relationship.

Ex: eyes:sight :: ears:hearing

This word analogy would read: *Eyes are to sight as ears are to hearing.*

3.
d. 1) **Martha, go see who is at the door.**
   2) **I really liked your part in the play, William.**
   3) **The secret to success, Lydia, is to prepare for opportunity.**
   4) **Carol, are you sure the meeting is today?**
   5) **Come here this minute, Patrick.**

4.
b. object to use

In the previous example the relationship is that as eyes provide the sense of sight; ears provide the sense of hearing. There are many different ways words can be related. Some of the relationships used in word analogies are:

antonyms   good:bad :: happy:sad
synonyms   yell:shout :: soaring:flying
part/whole   fingers:hand :: toes:foot
characteristic   leaves:green :: snow:white
object/use   scissors:cut :: pencil:write
object/place   car:garage :: furniture:house
representative/object   teacher:student :: boss:employee
family   mother:daughter :: father:son
grammar   noun:adjective :: verb:adverb

What type of relationship is used in our example analogy (eyes:sight :: ears:hearing)?

c. Fill in the second part of the word analogies listed below. First decide what the relationship of the first two words is and then apply that relationship to the second part of the word analogy to fill in the blank.

c. 1) pasture
   2) mammal
   3) sour
   4) climbing
   5) tree

1) fish:water :: cow:_____
2) ant:insect :: dog:_____
3) candy:sweet :: pickle: _____
4) beach:swimming :: mountain:_____
5) petals:flower :: leaves: _____

d. Take an oral or written spelling pretest.

5. a. Choose one of the following activities.

1) Write the literature passage from dictation. "Listen" for the punctuation as your teacher reads the paragraph.

2) Look at the paragraph below. Correct all errors in capitalization, punctuation, and other writing mechanics. When you are finished, compare to model and correct.

5.
a. 2) **See literature passage.**

everybody laughed but the teachers eyes werent pleased. true true he said. thats right Eelka. we cant think much when we dont know much. but we can wonder. from now until tomorrow morning when you come to school again, will you do that. will you wonder why and wonder why. will you wonder why storks dont come to shora to build their nests on the roofs the way they do in all the villages around. for sometimes when we wonder, we can make things begin to happen.

3) What are some things that cause you to wonder? Write one thing and spend some time wondering about it. You can do this by thinking about it, talking about it, and/or looking up information about it.

4) Choose skills from the *Review Activities* on the next page.

Review Activities

Choose only the skills your student needs to review.

1. *Plurals*
   Write the plural form of the following words.

   a. brush
   b. guess
   c. lily
   d. turkey
   e. ax

2. *Direct Quotations*
   Add quotation marks and punctuation to the following sentences.

   a. We will begin the canoe trip at this point announced Luke and then paddle downstream to the campgrounds
   b. Who is going to the concert asked Adam I will be leaving in an hour
   c. I do not know the answer to the problem said Anna Can you help me
   d. The soccer equipment is expensive at this store remarked Will
   e. Nicki shouted Catch the ball

3. *Direct Address*
   Add punctuation to the following sentences.

   a. Judy will you please open the door for me.
   b. I located the bird nest Kate in the old oak tree.
   c. Explain the bike safety rules to the club Lewis.

4. *Word Analogy*
   Fill in the word that correctly finishes the word analogy.

   a. black:white :: tall:_____
   b. run:sprint :: walk: _____
   c. uncle:nephew :: aunt:_____
   d. rabbit:hutch :: bird: _____
   e. ruler:measure :: spoon: _____

---

1. a. brushes
   b. guesses
   c. lilies
   d. turkeys
   e. axes

2. a. "We will begin the canoe trip at this point," announced Luke, "and then paddle downstream to the campgrounds."
   b. "Who is going to the concert?" asked Adam. "I will be leaving in an hour."
   c. "I do not know the answer to the problem," said Anna. "Can you help me?"
   d. "The soccer equipment is expensive at this store," remarked Will.
   e. Nicki shouted, "Catch the ball!"

3. a. Judy, will you please open the door for me?
   b. I located the bird nest, Kate, in the old oak tree.
   c. Explain the bike safety rules to the club, Lewis.

4. Possible answers:
   a. short
   b. stroll
   c. niece
   d. nest
   e. stir

Assessment 2
(Lessons 7 - 11)

1. Give an example of an interrogative sentence. What punctuation would you use?

2. Rewrite the following imperative sentence with the subject (*Sarah*) understood but not stated.

   Sarah, put the dog out.

3. Write a word with the prefix **re-**.

4. Write a sentence with a compound subject.

5. Write a sentence with a compound verb.

6. Circle the conjunction in each of the following sentences.

   a. He ran down the beach and shouted for joy.
   b. We would like to come but cannot at this time.
   c. Sam or Sue could do the job.

7. Combine the following two sentences to form one sentence with a compound verb.

   Bob opened the door. Bob stepped aside for his mother.

8. Copy the following sentences, adding the correct punctuation.

   Could you come over today Mary asked We could study together

---

1. **Answers will vary. A question mark is placed at the end of an interrogative sentence.**

2. **Put the dog out.**

3. **Possible answers: repaint, return, redo, etc.**

4. **Answers will vary.**

5. **Answers will vary.**

6. **a. and**
   b. but
   c. or

7. **Bob opened the door and stepped aside for his mother.**

8. **"Could you come over today?" Mary asked. "We could study together."**

9. Conflict - The Wind wanted to show the Sun that he was greater.

Climax - The climax of the story is when the Sun's rays caused the main to remove his cloak.

9. Read "The Wind and the Sun." What is the conflict and climax of the story?

The Wind and the Sun

One day a man strolled contentedly down a village road. The Sun warmed the man gently with its rays as he looked up and smiled. At this, the Wind came and taunted, "You think you are so mighty and great, but I will show you that I am stronger than you."

"Very well," said the Sun.

"Whoever has the ability to take the cloak off the man strolling on the road shall be claimed the victor," said the Wind assuredly.

"Very well," said the Sun again. " You may go first."

The Wind bellowed out the fiercest gust of wind that he could, but the man held on to his cloak. The Wind blew more ferociously than before. He blew and blew, but the man clutched his cloak tighter.

Now it was the Sun's turn. As the Wind moved over to the side, the Sun gleamed his bright face in the sky. The man loosened his grip. Sun beamed, radiating his warmth to the man below. Looking upward, the man squinted, removed his cloak, and continued on his way.

HOW TO CONDUCT

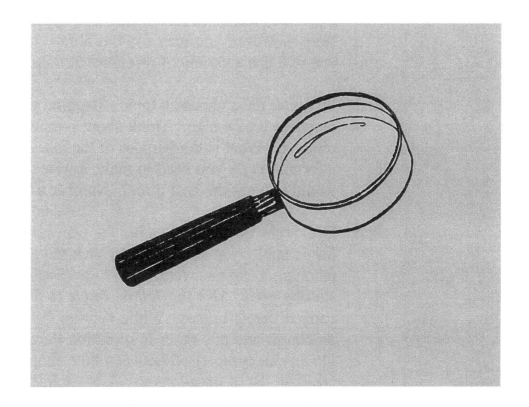

Personal Research

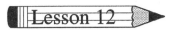

✏ Teacher's Note: The Persona. Research unit continues in Lesson 13.

1. a. In last week's lesson we discussed how our lives had been enriched by someone's curiosity. Many times curiosity naturally leads to research. Think of something that interests you. It could be something you desire to purchase: a pet, a bike, computer, or sports equipment. Perhaps you would even like to know which fast food chain offers the highest quality burger. For the next few days you will explore an enjoyable form of research written in the form of a story. Many times the purpose of research is extensive study of a topic with lots of library work. In your personal research story, however, you may use the library if you choose, but you will use a variety of resources as well.

   b. First you must choose a topic. Imagine you are going to purchase a new bike. Think about possible questions to research. What is the purpose of the research? What information do you need to make a wise purchase? Where would you get the best price? Number and list your ideas.

2. a. Decide the best way to gather the necessary information. If, for example, you choose to research the topic of bikes, planning a trip to several local bike shops would be a great starting point. Use the *Yellow Pages* to find bike shops that carry different brands. While visiting the shops, gather brochures and any other information they make available. Do a price comparison between bike shops. Prepare a standard list of questions to ask at each shop. Look at the following questions. Take notes and keep track of the information you gather.

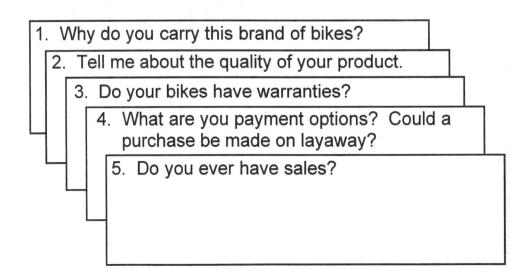

1. Why do you carry this brand of bikes?
2. Tell me about the quality of your product.
3. Do your bikes have warranties?
4. What are you payment options? Could a purchase be made on layaway?
5. Do you ever have sales?

3 - 5. Plan to interview several friends who own different brands
of bikes. Make a list of questions for them. Use the rest of
the week to thoroughly gather the following information.

1. Why did you choose this brand over another?

2. Have you enjoyed your bike?

3. Would you purchase this brand again?

4. Have you had any problems with your bike?

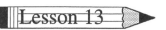

1. a. Use a consumer report to read about different bikes. Check your library for a junior version of a standard consumer report.

   b. Compare the prices you found in the bike shops to the prices in discount stores.

2-3.

   a. Check to see if you are satisfied with the information you have gathered. If you are prepared to write your research story, follow the steps listed below in organizing your information.

Student Checklist

☐ 1) Make sure all your information is related to the topic you are writing about.

☐ 2) Make a list of the various ideas about your subject that you wish to write about.

☐ 3) Group your ideas into several main ideas and number these grouping as to the order in which you want them to appear in your paper.

☐ 4) Write an introductory paragraph for your research paper. This paragraph should explain the purpose of your research and give a brief summary of what your paper will be about.

☐ 5) Write your supporting paragraphs. Make sure that all the information presented supports the main topic presented in your introductory paragraph.

☐ 6) End your paper with a concluding paragraph that again summarizes your topic and ends with a closing sentence.

---

b. Spend two days compiling your research story. Since this is a research "story," it may be written informally and may include your own opinions and comments. Putting your story in a folder and adding sketches or pictures from brochures would add to the presentation of your research.

4. a. Examine your research story. Was your research helpful in making a decision about your purchase? Would it be helpful to someone else making a similar choice?

   b. Check your paper for any errors in spelling, grammar, capitalization, and punctuation.

5.   Look over your research story once more. Make a final, neat copy for your teacher.

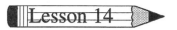

"Jest 'Fore Christmas"
by Eugene Field

*Father calls me William, sister calls me
   Will,*
*Mother calls me Willie, but the fellers call
   me Bill!*
Mighty glad I ain't a girl — ruther be a boy,
*Without them sashes, curls, an' things
   that's worn by Fauntleroy!*
*Love to chawnk green apples an' go
   swimmin' in the lake —*
*Hate to take the castor-ile they give for
   belly-ache!*
*'Most all the time, the whole year round,
   there ain't no flies on me,*
*But just 'fore Christmas I'm as good as I
   kin be!*

*Got a yeller dog named Sport, sic him on
   the cat;*
*First thing she knows she doesn't know
   where she is at!*
*Got a clipper sled, an' when us kids goes
   out to slide,*
*'Long comes the grocery cart, an' we all
   hook a ride!*
*But sometimes when the grocery man is
   worrited an' cross,*
*He reaches at us with his whip, an' larrups
   up his hoss,*
*An' then I laff an' holler, "Oh, ye never
   teched me!"*
*But jest 'fore Christmas I'm as good as I
   kin be!*

*Gran'ma says she hopes that when I git to
   be a man,*
*I'll be a missionarer like her oldest brother,
   Dan,*
*As was et up by the cannibuls that lives in
   Ceylon's Isle,*

*Where every prospeck pleases, an' only man
    is vile!*
*But Gran'ma she has never been to see a
    Wild West show,*
*Nor read the Life of Daniel Boone, or else I
    guess she'd know*
*That Buff'lo Bill an' cowboys is good
    enough for me!*
Excep' *jest 'fore Christmas, when I'm good
    as I kin be!*

*And then old Sport he hangs around, so
    solemn-like an' still,*
*His eyes they keep a-sayin': "What's the
    matter, little Bill?"*
*The old cat sneaks down off her perch an'
    wonders what's become*
*Of them two enemies of hern that used to
    make things hum!*
*But I am so perlite an' 'tend so earnestly to
    biz,*
*That Mother says to Father: "How
    improved our Willie is!"*
*But Father, havin' been a boy hisself,
    suspicions me*
*When, jest 'fore Christmas, I'm as good as I
    kin be!*

*For Christmas, with its lots an' lots of
    candies, cakes, an' toys,*
*Was made, they say, for proper kids, an' not
    for naughty boys;*
*So wash yer face an' bresh yer hair, an'
    mind yer p's and q's,*
*An' don't bust out yer pantaloons, and
    don't wear out yer shoes;*
*Say "Yessum" to the ladies, an' "Yessur" to
    the men,*
*An' when they's company, don't pass yer
    plate for pie again;*
*But, thinkin' of the things yer'd like to see
    upon that tree,*
Jest 'fore Christmas be as good as yer kin be!

1.

a. fellers, mighty glad, ain't, ruther, an', chawnk, swimmin', just, 'fore, kin

c. But jest 'fore Christmas I'm as good as I kin be!

Repetition gives the poem continuity and rhythm

d. 1) before
2) can
3) and
4) laugh
5) polite
6) prospect
7) himself
8) just
9) thinking
10) worried
11) castor-oil

2.

b. Father calls me William, sister calls me Will, Mother calls me Willie, but the other boys call me Bill!
I'm very glad I'm not a girl, I would rather be a boy, (continue)

1. a. Listen as your teacher reads the bolded section of the poem. Does the pronunciation of the words used in the poem sound different than the way you speak? Sometimes an author will use pronunciation peculiar to a certain region, called **dialect,** to express himself. This is an effective way to make his character seem true to life. What are some examples of regional dialect in the first stanza of this poem? Try reading the first two stanzas of the poem aloud.

   b. Look over the poem. Note that the first word of every line of the poem is capitalized. Often in poetry the first word of every line is capitalized even when the word does not begin a sentence.

   c. Find the phrase in the poem that is repeated in each stanza. The technique of repeating a phrase or word in a poem for emphasis or for rhythm is called **repetition**. What effect does the use of repetition have in this poem?

   d. Look over your list of dialect words and pronounce them the way they are spelled. Sometimes words are purposely misspelled to allow for dialect pronunciation.

   Listed below are some of the words in the literature passage which are misspelled for this purpose. Find the words in the literature passage, and use context clues to decide what the correct word for the dialect word would be. Opposite each of the words write the proper spelling.

   Ex: ruther - rather
   1) 'fore   7) hisself
   2) kin   8) jest
   3) an'   9) thinkin'
   4) laff   10) worrited
   5) perlite   11) castor-ile
   6) prospeck

2. a. Read the entire poem today.

   b. Rewrite the first two stanzas in standard English. Read each version aloud. Which do you like better? Can you see how effective the use of dialect can be?

c. Look over the poem again. Circle any words that are capitalized other than at the beginning of a line poetry and the pronoun *I*. In Lesson 6 you learned that words were capitalized for three main reasons:

1) to indicate the beginning of a sentence
2) to help the reader quickly identify proper names and titles
3) to show respect when referring to God and the Bible

Which of the reasons listed is the reason for the capitalization of the words you circled? Note that Christmas, the name of a holiday, is considered a proper name. The entire name of holidays are always capitalized.

Ex: Fourth of July   Mother's Day
       Thanksgiving Day   Good Friday

d. Find the capitalized words that also indicate a family relationship. When a family relationship word is used in place of a name or in front of a person's name, the word is capitalized. However, when the word is not used to replace a name or is used with a personal pronoun such as *my*, *our*, or *her*, then the word is not capitalized.

Ex: Grandpa Joe came for a visit.
     Grandpa came for a visit.
     My grandpa came for a visit.

e. Correct any errors in capitalization in the following sentences as needed.

1) My Mother said I could go when I am finished.
2) Where is your Father going?
3) Aunt mary and uncle ralph will be visiting this week.
4) When will Grandma be arriving?
5) It will be wonderful to have all the Aunts and Uncles visit for christmas.

c. William (2)
Willie (2)
Bill (2)
Fauntleroy (2)
Christmas (2)
Sport (2)
Oh (1)
Dan (2)
Ceylon's Isle (2)
Gran'ma (2)
Wild West (2)
Life of Daniel Boone (2)
Buff'lo Bill (2)
What's (1)
Mother (2)
How (1)
Father (2)
Yessum (2)
Yessur (2)

d. Father, Mother, Gran'ma

✐ **Teacher's Note: The word *sister* should also be capitalized but the author chose not to do so.**

e. 1) My *mother* said I could go when I am finished.
2) Where is your *father* going?
3) Aunt Mary and *Uncle Ralph* will be visiting this week.
4) No change.
5) It will be wonderful to have all the *aunts* and *uncles* visit for *Christmas*.

3.
a. Yes

b. Where the Boats Go -
   abab
   Autumn Fires - abcb

3. a. Poetry that rhymes usually follows a certain pattern called a **rhyme scheme**. In order to identify the rhyme scheme, assign a letter to each line that rhymes. For example, the rhyme scheme for the first stanza of "Jest 'Fore Christmas" is **aabbccdd**, because the last word in the first two lines rhyme (**aa**), the last word in the next two lines is a new rhyme (**bb**), and so on. Does the second stanza follow the same rhyme scheme?

   b. Read the following poetry selections by Robert Louis Stevenson. Assign a letter to each line that rhymes and identify the rhyme schemes of the stanzas of the poems.

   (from) Where The Boats Go

   Dark brown is the river,
   Golden is the sand.
   It flows along forever,
   With trees on either hand.

   (from) Autumn Fires

   Sing a song of seasons!
   Something bright in all!
   Flowers in the summer,
   Fires in the fall!

   c. The poems you have been reading have only end rhyme. Other poems contain rhyme words within a line of poetry to create **internal rhyme.**

   Ex: Jack *Sprat* could eat no *fat.*

   Note that the words *Sprat* and *fat* rhyme within the same line of the poem creating an internal rhyme.

d. Read the selections below, find the internal rhymes, and underline them. Remember, in order for a poem to have internal rhyme the words that rhyme must be within one line of the poem.

Whisky Frisky

author unknown

Whisky Frisky,
Hippity-hop
Up he goes
To the treetop!

Whirly, twirly,
Round and round,
Down he scampers
To the ground.

Intery, Mintery, Cutery Corn

Mother Goose Rhyme

Intery, mintery, cutery corn,
Apple seed and apple thorn
Wire, brier, limber-lock,
Three geese in a flock;
One flew east, and one flew west,
And one flew over the cockoo's nest.

e. Write the end rhyme schemes for *"Whisky Frisky"* and *"Intery, Mintery, Cutery Corn."* Do you like the effect created when the poet combines end rhyme and internal rhyme?

3.

d. whisky, frisky;
   whirly, twirly;
   round, ground

   intery, mintery, cutery;
   wire, brier

e. *"Whisky Frisky"* - abcb
   "Intery, Mintery, Cutery
   ***Corn"* - aabbcc**

4. a. Another device used in poetry is the repetition of beginning consonant sounds within a poem. This is called **alliteration**.

   Ex: **D**iddle, **d**iddle, **d**umpling, my son John,

   The consonant **d** is repeated in this example of alliteration. When alliteration is used often throughout the poem, it has a tongue-twisting effect. Read the following example:

   Peter Piper

   Peter Piper picked a peck of pickled peppers;
   A peck of pickled peppers Peter Piper picked.
   If Peter Piper picked a peck of pickled peppers,
   Where's the peck of pickled peppers Peter Piper picked?

   b. "Jest 'Fore Christmas" is about a rather naughty boy. Can you imagine him with a very good little sister? Using the poem below as a model, write another poem from the sister's point of view.

   Father calls me Millicent, brother calls me Mills,
   Mother calls me Milly, and dresses me in frills!
   Mighty glad I'm not a boy, glad to be a girl,
   Wouldn't touch a frog or toad for anything in the world!
   Love to dress up pretty and have tea parties in the lane,
   Hate to be a bother, or cause anyone the slightest pain.

   c. Using the example poem in **4b**, complete the last two lines. Remember to follow the rhyme scheme and to use Mr. Field's poem as your model. After you have completed your poem read the original version and the poem from the sister's point of view. Which version do you like better?

d. The literature passage poem is fun to memorize and recite. Try to memorize just the first stanza of the poem. Follow these tips when reciting poetry or any oral presentation.

Tips on Poetry Recitation

1) Read the poem aloud several times. Try to understand the meaning and the mood of the poem.

2) Use your voice where emphasis is needed and pause accordingly.

3) Speak clearly and loudly.

4) Look at your audience as if you are speaking directly to them.

5) Stand straight; do not slouch.

---

5. a. Choose one of the following activities.

   1) Continue rewriting the other stanzas of the poem from the sister's point of view.

   2) Examine a book of poetry. Try to find examples of poems with internal rhyme and alliteration. Write the rhyme scheme for some of the poems with end rhyme.

   3) Decide what rhyme scheme you like best and write an original poem that uses that rhyme scheme.

   4) Choose skills from the *Review Activities* on the next page.

Review Activities

Choose only the skills your student needs to review.

1. *Poetry*
Read the following poem. What is the rhyme scheme? Identify the following elements: **alliteration**, **internal rhyme**, **end rhyme**, and **repetition**.

> *Roaring, rippling river races toward the sea.*
> *Swirling, twirling waters laugh with joyful glee.*
> *Listen to the waters, listen to them sing.*
>
> *Whipping, whirling waves crashing on the shore.*
> *Reeling, keeling ocean groans and moans its lore.*
> *Listen to the waters, listen to them sing.*

2. *Capitalization of Holidays*
Capitalize the names of the following holidays.

   a. independence day
   b. fourth of july
   c. memorial day
   d. thanksgiving day

3. *Dialect*
Identify the words and expressions in the following paragraph that indicate a regional dialect.

   She ain't a purty horse, like sum are, but she shure is a strong one. Then again, them brown eyes of hers have a way of lookin' at ya that let ya know she's a smart one too.

1.
rhyme scheme - aab

alliteration - <u>r</u>oaring, <u>r</u>ippling <u>r</u>iver <u>r</u>aces; <u>wh</u>ipping, <u>wh</u>irling <u>w</u>aves

internal rhyme - swirling, twirling; reeling, keeling; groans, moans

end rhyme - sea, glee; shore, lore

repetition - Listen to the waters, listen to them sing

2. a. Independence Day
   b. Fourth of July
   c. Memorial Day
   d. Thanksgiving Day

3. ain't, purty, sum, shure, them, lookin', ya

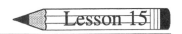

The pigeons now flew up to crevices in the rocks, the fowls perched themselves on our tent pole, and the ducks and geese waddled off, cackling and quacking, to the marshy margin of the river. We, too, were ready for repose, and having loaded our guns and offered up our prayers to God, thanking Him for His many mercies to us, we commended ourselves to His protecting care, and as the last ray of light departed, closed our tent and lay down to rest.

The Swiss Family Robinson by Johann Wyss.

1. a. Read the literature passage. Write the passage from dictation. Proofread your copy. Make any necessary corrections.

   b. In the last sentence of the literature passage the family thanks God "for his many mercies." For what mercies do you think this family was thankful? Are there mercies in your life for which you are thankful?

   c. Find the word in the last sentence of the literature passage that contains the prefix **re-**. Check with your prefix list and find the meaning of **re-**. Often knowing the meaning of a prefix can help you define an unfamiliar word. The root of *repose* is *pose*. *Pose* means *to be in a certain position*. The prefix **re-** means *back* or *again*. When you put the prefix and root together, you have back position as a possible choice to help you define the word *repose*. *Repose* means *to lay at rest*, therefore, back position gives a good hint as to the definition of the word.

   d. Find the prefixes **pro-** and **de-** in the last sentence of the literature passage. The prefix **de-** means *from* or *down* and the prefix **pro-** means *forward* or *in favor of*. Add these prefixes to your prefix list along with their definitions and word examples.

Teacher's Note: As your student completes each lesson, choose skills from the Review Activities that he needs. The Review Activities follow each lesson.

1.
b. Allow for discussion

c. re-: back or again

d. de-: from or down
   Possible examples:
   deplore, design

   pro-: forward or in favor of
   Possible examples:
   prorate, protrude

e. Use any words you misspelled in your dictation for your spelling words or use the following suggested list.

ourselves	crevices	themselves
margin	repose	offered

f. The words ourselves and themselves contain the plural of the words self, spelled **s-e-l-v-e-s**. The **f** is changed to **v** before the **es** is added because the **/f/** sound in self changes to a **/v/** sound in selves.

To determine if the **f** or **fe** should be changed to **v** in order to form a plural, say the plural of the noun. If you hear a **/v/** sound, then make the change; if you do not hear a **/v/** sound, then just add **s**.

Ex: reef - reefs

Spelling Tip
When forming the plural of a word ending in **f** or **fe**, change the **f** or **fe** to **v** and add **es**. If the **/f/** sound remains, just add **s**.

g. Write the plural form of the following nouns.

1) wife	5) self
2) leaf	6) roof
3) life	7) chief
4) calf	8) wolf

2. a. Look over the literature passage and list ten pronouns. Remember, pronouns are words that take place of nouns. Refer to the Personal Pronoun Chart in Lesson 4 if you need help.

1.
g. 1) wives
**   2) leaves**
**   3) lives**
**   4) calves**
**   5) selves**
**   6) roofs**
**   7) chiefs**
**   8) wolves**

2.
a. our, We, our, our, Him, His, us, we, His, our

✎ **Teacher's Note: The pronouns *themselves* and *ourselves* are reflexive or compound pronouns and will be covered in a higher level book. If your student chose these words as pronouns, it is correct.**

b. Personal pronouns may also be classified into persons; either first, second, or third persons.

Personal Pronouns			
First Person (The one speaking)	I we	my, mine our, ours	me us
Second Person (The one being spoken to)	you	you, yours	
Third Person (The one being spoken about)	he she it they	his her, hers its their, theirs	him her them

A **first person pronoun** is the one speaking.
Ex: I took the bus to town.
    I is used as a first person pronoun.

A **second person pronoun** is the one being spoken to.
Ex: You come with me immediately!
    You is used as a second person pronoun.

A **third person pronoun** is the one being spoken about.
Ex: Frequently, Bill visits his grandmother.
    His is used as a third person pronoun. Bill is not the person speaking or being spoken to, but he is being spoken about.

c. Once again look at your list of personal pronouns from the literature passage. Indicate if they are first, second, or third person pronouns by writing 1, 2, or 3 by them.

2.
c. our-1
   We-1
   our-1
   our-1
   Him-3
   His-3
   us-1
   we-1
   His-3
   our-1

d. first person

3.

a. pigeons, crevices, rocks, fowls, ducks, geese, guns, prayers, mercies

geese

b. mercies

d. You learned in Lesson 10 that a story is told from a first person point of view (when one of the characters of the story narrates the story from his point of view) or third person point of view (when someone from outside the story is narrating). Read over the literature passage and decide from what point of view this story is being told. The pronouns used can help you to identify the correct point of view.

3. a. Look at the literature passage and underline all the plural nouns. Note that most plurals are formed by adding **s** or **es**. However, some nouns form plurals by changing the spelling of the word. These are called **irregular nouns**.

   Ex: man - men

   Locate the word in your list of plural nouns that follows this rule.

   b. Circle the plural that requires the **y** ending to be changed before the **s** is added.

   c. Look over the following summary of the spelling rules for forming plurals you have covered so far.

Spelling Tips for Plurals

1) To form the plural of most words just add **s**.
2) To form the plural of nouns ending in **ch**, **s**, **sh**, **x**, or **z** add **es**.
3) To form the plural of a noun ending in **y** preceded by a consonant, change the **y** to **i** and add **es**.
4) To form the plural of most words ending in **f** or **fe**, change the **f** to **v** and add **es**. If the plural word keeps the /**f**/ sound, just add **s**.
5) Some words change their spelling to form the plural form.

---

d. Using these *Spelling Tips*, write the correct plural form for the following nouns.

1) shelf   6) woman
2) monkey   7) loaf
3) church   8) mass
4) box   9) baby
5) sock   10) company

e. Review your spelling words for a practice test tomorrow.

4. a. A capital letter is always used when referring to God or the Bible, even if it is a pronoun. Find the three pronouns in the literature passage that are used in reference to God and underline them.

b. Many words are tricky and good writers must exercise extra care not to misuse them. Find the word *lay* used in the last sentence of the literature passage. Locate this example and circle it. The word *lay* is often confused with the word *lie*. If you know the meaning of each word, it will help you to use the correct word when writing.

lay - to put or place something down
      lay, laying, laid, (have) laid
      Please *lay* the paper on my desk.

lie - to rest or recline
      lie, lying, lay, (have) lain
      It is time for you to *lie* down and go to sleep.

Although both words are verbs, only the word *lay* has an object. Look at this sentence again.

Please *lay* the paper on my desk.

The object is paper. The word *lay* usually has an object, but the word *lie* never has an object.

---

d. 1) shelves
    2) monkeys
    3) churches
    4) boxes
    5) socks
    6) women
    7) loaves
    8) masses
    9) babies
    10) companies

4.
a. Him, His, His

c. Some other troublesome words are *to, too, two*. These words are homonyms, words with the same sound but different meanings. Again, being familiar with the meaning of each word will help you choose the correct word.

to - to move toward or in the direction of
We will be going *to* the park this afternoon.

too - also
He is on the team, *too*.

two - a number
I need to buy *two* apples.

d. Choose the correct word.

1) My cat likes to (*lay, lie*) in front of the fireplace.
2) Make sure you (*lay, lie*) your clothes out for the next day.
3) Do you want to see the movie (*to, too*).
4) What friend do you want (*too, to*) visit?
5) (*Lay, Lie*) down and rest before the trip home.
6) Do the (*two, too*) of you want to come along for the ride?
7) (*Lay, Lie*) your books on the table.
8) Your game has been (*laying, lying*) on the floor all day.
9) The tiger was (*laying, lying*) in wait for its prey.
10) I have an appointment for (*two, to*) o'clock, (*too, to*).

e. Take an oral or written spelling pretest.

5. a. Choose one of the following activities.

1) Write the literature passage from dictation.

2) Imagine what it would be like to be shipwrecked with your family on an isolated, uninhabited island. Write a few paragraphs telling how you would feel and how you would prepare for living there.

3) Choose skills from the *Review Activities* on the next page.

4.
d. 1) lie
  2) lay
  3) too
  4) to
  5) Lie
  6) two
  7) Lay
  8) lying
  9) lying
  10) two, too

Review Activities

Choose only the skills your student needs to review.

1. *Prefixes*
   Add the prefixes **re-**, **de-**, or **pro-** to each of the following roots. If you are unsure of the meaning of the new word, look it up in the dictionary.

   a. _____juvenate (prefix meaning *back* or *again*)
   b. _____jector (prefix meaning *forward* or *in favor of*)
   c. _____preciate (prefix meaning *from* or *down*)

2. *Personal Pronouns and Point of View*
   Rewrite the following paragraph by substituting personal pronouns for the underlined words. Write 1 (*first person*), 2 (*second person*), or 3 (*third person*) above each pronoun to indicate which person the pronoun is. Also, tell from what point of view this story is being told.

   Marcy loved visiting <u>Marcy's</u> cousin, Jeanette at <u>Jeanette's</u> farm. <u>Marcy and Jeanette</u> would wake up early in the morning because Jeanette needed to feed all <u>Jeanette's</u> animals. <u>Jeanette</u> had chickens, goats, pigs, and cows. However, Marcy's favorite animals were the horses. Jeannette had two horses named Thunder and Whisper. As soon as the chores were done, <u>Marcy and Jeanette</u> would ride for hours through the woods and pastures. <u>Marcy and Jeanette</u> had such fun together!

3. *Plurals*
   Circle the correct plural form in each of the following sentences.

   a. Many people dressed as (*elfs*, *elves*) at the party.
   b. We drove through many (*valleys*, *valleies*) on our trip.
   c. The meadow was full of (*daisys*, *daisies*).
   d. All the (*dishs*, *dishes*) must be washed before you can leave.
   e. We must finish putting the garden (*tools*, *tooles*) away before it starts raining.

1.
a. rejuvenate - to be made young again
b. projector - a device that shows light images on a screen
c. depreciate - to come down in value

2. Marcy loved visiting <u>her</u>[3] cousin, Jeanette, at <u>her</u>[3] farm. <u>They</u>[3] would wake up early in the morning because Jeanette needed to feed all <u>her</u>[3] animals. <u>She</u>[3] had chickens, goats, pigs, and cows. However, Marcy's favorite animals were the horses. Jeanette had two horses named Thunder and Whisper. As soon as the chores were done, <u>they</u>[3] would ride for hours through the woods and pastures. <u>They</u>[3] had such fun together!

Point of view - third person

3.
a. elves
b. valleys
c. daisies
d. dishes
e. tools

4. Answers will vary.

5.
a. to
b. too
c. two

6. God, Him, He, God

4. *Lie and Lay*
   Use each word correctly in a sentence.

5. *To, Too, and Two*
   Underline the correct word.

   a. We will travel (*to*, *too*) Switzerland on the train.
   b. Will Henry be coming along (*to*, *too*)?
   c. The trip will cost (*too*, *two*) hundred dollars.

6. *Capitalization*
   Capitalize all references to God in the following sentence.

   We worship a holy god, and therefore it is important that we
   worship him with a spirit of reverence and remember that he
   is a loving, but just god.

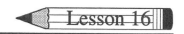

> *Suddenly a mottled green fish, a yard long, with a dark back and white underneath, came to the top. It lifted an enormous head right out of the water, and opened a great white mouth, and shook itself. A little perch flew high in the air. Roger's rod straightened. For a moment the great fish lay close to the top of the water, looking wickedly at the crew of the* <u>Swallow</u> *as they looked at it. Then, with a twist of its tail that made a great twirling splash in the water, it was gone.*

Swallows and Amazons by Arthur Ransome.
Used by permission, David R. Godine Publishers Inc.

✎ **Teacher's Note:** As your student completes each lesson, choose skills from the Review Activities that he needs. The Review Activities follow each lesson.

✎ **Teacher's Note:** Titles of ships will be covered in Lesson 27.

1. a. Listen as your teacher reads the literature passage. Write the passage from dictation. Circle every word you are not sure is spelled correctly. Compare your copy with the passage.

   Do you know why *Swallow* is underlined? The name of a ship is capitalized and underlined. (Use italics if computer-generated.) If you did not underline the ship's name in your dictation, do so now.

   b. Make a spelling list from the words you misspelled or use the following suggested list.

mottled	underneath	enormous
straightened	twist	swirling

   c. Try to imagine the scene described in the literature passage. Describe to your teacher how you think the crew felt when the big one got away. If you'd like, draw a picture of what you think the fish looked like.

   d. Find the word *underneath* in the literature passage. This word contains the prefix **under-** which means *beneath.* Although **under** is also a word which can stand alone, in this word it is acting as a prefix. Add the prefix **under-** to your list of prefixes and include the definition and some word examples.

1.
d. under-: beneath
   Possible examples:
   underneath, underline

1.

e. it - the green fish
   they - the crew of the
   Swallow

f. the fish having
   possession of its tail

g. 1) It's
   2) its
   3) its
   4) it's
   5) its

e. Locate all forms of the pronoun *it* in the literature passage and draw a box around them. Remember, an antecedent is the noun that the pronoun stands for. What is the antecedent of *it* in the literature passage? What is the antecedent for the pronoun *they* in the literature passage?

f. Note that the pronoun *its* used in the last sentence of the literature passage is a possessive pronoun. What is the pronoun showing possession of in this sentence?

It is important not to confuse the possessive pronoun its with the contraction it's. If you are using the pronoun in a sentence, it should be showing possession and should not have an apostrophe. If you are using the contraction, the word should have an apostrophe. You can check to make sure you are using the correct form by substituting the words, it is, in the sentence. If the words, it is, make sense in the sentence, then the contraction form is correct.

g. Complete the sentences correctly with *its* or *it's*.

   1) _____ going to be a beautiful morning.
   2) I need to get the horse _____ bridle.
   3) The peacock spread _____ tail in a breathtaking display.
   4) When the alarm rings, _____ six o'clock.
   5) The cat will let you pet _____ kittens.

2. a. Look at the literature passage. Find and underline the
       adjectives (words that describe nouns) and circle the nouns
       they describe.

   Ex: <u>mottled, green</u> (fish)

   b. Read the paragraph aloud, leaving out the adjectives you
       underlined. Read it again with the adjectives. What
       difference do adjectives make? Which way does the
       paragraph sound better?

       Adjectives help you to picture the scene. Without adjectives
       it would be hard for you to envision what the author wants
       you to see. The paragraph would be dull and boring to read
       without adjectives.

   c. Find the two words in the literature passage that end in the
       suffix **-ly**. These two words are adverbs, words that describe
       verbs. Most words ending in **-ly** are adverbs. Some
       exceptions are *friendly* and *lovely*; they are adjectives. Look
       at the sentences where these words are located. Identify the
       verbs they are describing.

3. a. Locate the word *perch* in the literature passage. Although it
       identifies a kind of fish, it is not capitalized. It is only when
       a particular variety of fish is identified that the name is
       capitalized, such as Yellow Perch.

   Ex: pine tree (not capitalized)
        Norfolk Pine (specific name - capitalized)

2.
a. <u>dark</u> (back)
     <u>white</u> (underneath)
     <u>enormous</u> (head)
     <u>great white</u> (mouth)
     <u>little</u> (perch)
     <u>great</u> (fish)
     <u>great twirling</u> (splash)

2.
c. suddenly - came
     wickedly - looking

135

b. Read the following capitalization rules.

Capitalization Rules

1) Capitalize the name of a club, organization, association, team, or political party.
   Ex: Boy Scouts, Red Cross, Striker Soccer Team, Republican Party

2) Capitalize the names of languages, religions, races, and nationalities.
   Ex: French, Catholic, Indian, African

3) Specific school courses are capitalized, but a field of study is not.
   Ex: History 101 (specific course)
   history (field of study)

4) The brand name of a product is capitalized, but the common noun that appears after the brand name is not capitalized.
   Ex: Whirlpool oven

5) Capitalize the first and all important words in the titles and chapters of books, poems, plays, magazines, television programs, art works, movies, newspapers, musical compositions, articles, and stories.
   Ex: *The Last of the Mohicans* (book)
   My Fair Lady (movie)
   New York Times (newspaper)

6) Capitalize the names of historical events and time periods.
   Ex: French Revolution (event)
   Middle Ages (time period)

---

7) Names of people, buildings, pets, boats, planes, trains, planets, bridges, monuments, and documents are capitalized.

   Ex: Statue of Liberty (monument)
        Jupiter (planet)
        Titanic (boat)

8) Capitalize the names of days of the week, months, holidays, and special events, but do not capitalize the names of seasons (spring, summer, fall, winter) unless they are part of the name of an event.

   Ex: Thursday (day of the week)
        September (month)
        Valentine's Day (holiday)
        Spring Livestock Show (event)
        spring rain storm (season)

9) Capitalize geographical places:

   Ex: bodies of water - Lake Superior, Mississippi
             River, Atlantic Ocean
        cities - Birmingham
        countries - Switzerland
        counties - Pinellas County
        continents - Asia
        islands - Hawaiian Islands
        mountains - Mount St. Helen
        parks - Yellowstone National Park
        provinces - Alberta
        sections of the country - the West (do not
             capitalize when referring to direction only
             - west of town)
        states - Florida
        streets, avenues, etc. - Grand Boulevard,
             Twenty- first Street (**Note:** The second
             part of the number is not capitalized.)

3.

c. Roger - name of a person
Swallow - name of a boat

3.
d. 1) A
   2) A
   3) B
   4) B
   5) B
   6) B
   7) A
   8) A
   9) B
   10) A

4.

a. *Articles are underlined
once, nouns twice.*
a mottled green *fish*
a yard
a dark *back*
the top
an enormous *head*
the water
a great white *mouth*
a little *perch*
the air
a moment
the great *fish*
the top
the water
the crew
the Swallow
a twist
a great twirling *splash*

c. Review the literature passage and find proper nouns that are capitalized. Why are they capitalized?

d. Refer to the capitalization rules to help you choose the correct phrases.

	A	B
Ex: __B__	the asian culture	the Asian culture
1) ____	a geometry assignment	a Geometry assignment
2) ____	Fifty-second Street	fifty-second street
3) ____	saturn's orbit	Saturn's orbit
4) ____	lake area 4-H club	Lake Area 4-H Club
5) ____	ocala national forest	Ocala National Forest
6) ____	boy scouts	Boy Scouts
7) ____	Statue of Liberty	Statue of liberty
8) ____	Sony stereo	Sony Stereo
9) ____	the sound of music	The Sound of Music
10) ____	Lake Superior	lake superior

e. Review your spelling words for a practice test tomorrow.

4. a. Adjectives are words that describe nouns. Look at the following sentence:

An elephant picked up the peanut with a spoon.

Look at the words that come before *elephant, peanut,* and *spoon. An, a,* and *the* are special adjectives called **articles**. Articles can be signals to tell you that a noun will follow. Usually, the nouns directly follow the articles. Sometimes other adjectives separate the article from the noun, but a noun always follows an article.

Ex: the round orange

The word *round* seperates the article from the noun but the noun, *orange* still follows the article, *the*. Find all the articles in the literature passage, and locate the nouns they describe.

b. **Synonyms** are words that have the same or similar meanings. A **thesaurus** is a book of synonyms. Use your thesaurus to find synonyms for the adjectives you underlined in **2a**. Check to make sure your synonym makes sense in the content of the literature passage. For example, the word *great* appears three times as an adjective in the literature passage, but each time its meaning is a little different.

c. Rewrite the literature passage using the synonyms you found. Which way do you like better?

d. Take an oral or written spelling pretest.

5. a. Choose one of the following activities.

   1) Write the literature passage from dictation again. Did you spell all the words correctly?

   2) Read the literature passage again. Imagine you are Roger, and you have just battled with a great fish. Its tail makes a splash, and it's gone. How do you feel? Write down your thoughts on paper. Using these ideas, record a journal entry for Roger. A journal entry is written in the first person. This means you are the one speaking or telling the story. Use descriptive words to express how you feel. Edit your work. Check for errors in spelling, punctuation, and writing mechanics.

4.
b. Possible Answers
   dark - dusky (back)

   white - pale (underneath)

   enormous - immense (head)

   great white - large blanched (mouth)

   little - small (perch)

   great - magnificent (fish)

   great twirling - vast twisting (splash)

5.

c. a) Christopher Columbus crossed the Atlantic Ocean to discover America.
b) Her high school schedule included geometry, biology, and Word Processing 102.
c) Their trip to New York City included visits to the Statue of Liberty and the Empire State Building.
d) She is considered bilingual because she can speak both English and Spanish fluently.
e) He wasn't sure whether to purchase the Oldsmobile station wagon or the Ford van.
f) There will be no classes on President's Day and Memorial Day.
g) The Boy Scouts of America will sponsor a food drive at the Glenville Baptist Church.
h) The directions tell us to turn left at the next street and follow Bayview Avenue to the auditorium.
i) I will be working on Tuesday, Thursday, and Saturday of this week.
j) We have short winters and long summers in the South.

3) Read each sentence below. Look for capitalization errors and correct them.

Ex: Many indians were moved to Reservations as people moved west.

Correct - Many Indians were moved to reservations as people moved West.

a) Christopher columbus crossed the atlantic ocean to discover america.

b) Her High School schedule included geometry, biology, and word processing 102.

c) Their trip to New York city included visits to the statue of liberty and the empire state building.

d) She is considered bilingual because she can speak both english and spanish fluently.

e) He wasn't sure whether to purchase the Oldsmobile Station Wagon or the Ford Van.

f) There will be no classes on president's day and memorial day.

g) The Boy scouts of America will sponsor a food drive at the Glenville baptist church.

h) The directions tell us to turn left at the next Street and follow Bayview avenue to the auditorium.

i) I will be working on tuesday, thursday, and saturday of this Week.

j) We have short Winters and long Summers in the south.

Review Activities

Choose only the skills your student needs to review.

1. *Prefixes*

Add the prefix **under-** to the following root words. How does the addition of the prefix change the meaning of each word? If you are unsure of the meaning of the new word, look it up in the dictionary.

a. _____line
b. _____growth
c. _____age

2. *Its and It's*

Complete the following paragraph by choosing the correct word.

The sun is at the center of our solar system. (*Its*, *It's*) gravitational force holds the planets in their orbits. (*Its*, *It's*) known that the sun is made of the gases hydrogen and helium, and that (*its*, *it's*) surface temperature is about sixty times hotter than boiling water. The sun provides our planet with warmth and light, and (*its*, *it's*) impossible for life to exist without it.

3. *Articles and Adjectives*

Underline any articles you find in the following sentences and draw an arrow to the noun that follows it. Circle any adjectives.

a. A beautiful border of flowers ran along the garden path.
b. The array of flowers made the garden a pleasant place to visit.
c. The visitors enjoyed the colorful butterflies that were attracted by the honeysuckle.
d. The tiny honeybees buzzed amongst the fragrant blossoms.
e. An afternoon spent in the lovely garden left you with a peaceful feeling.

1.
a. underline - to draw a line beneath
b. undergrowth - small shrubs that grow beneath trees
c. underage - below the age required by law

2.   The sun is at the center of our solar system. Its gravitational force holds the planets in their orbits. It's known that the sun is made of the gases hydrogen and helium, and that its surface temperature is about sixty times hotter than boiling water. The sun provides our planet with warmth and light, and it's impossible for life to exist without it.

3.
a. A (beautiful) border of flowers ran along the (garden) path.

b. The array of flowers made the garden a (pleasant) place to visit.

c. The visitors enjoyed the (colorful) butterflies that were attracted by the honeysuckle.

d. The (tiny) honeybees buzzed amongst the (fragrant) blossoms.

e. An afternoon spent in the (lovely) garden left you with a (peaceful) feeling.

4.

a. She (walked) quickly down the sidewalk.

b. The ground (quaked) violently beneath their feet.

c. We seldom (travel) this road.

d. She (rushed) into the room.

e. We (will find) the answer tomorrow.

5. The *Gainesville Sun* featured an article on the Micanopy Historical Committee's plan to renovate many buildings of historical value in Micanopy. The First Methodist Church located on Twenty-second Street will be the first project the committee will undertake. Also many houses built during the Civil War are slated to be renovated. The renovations should begin this spring.

6.

a. The (mare) whinnied at its young foal.

b. The youth (group) enjoyed their trip to mountains.

c. (Jean and Sue) went swimming, and then they played volleyball on the beach.

d. (Mike) usually played first base, but sometimes he played shortstop.

7. Possible answers

a. pretty, gorgeous

b. enormous

c. stiff, strict

d. fragile

4. *Adverbs*
Underline the adverbs in the following sentence. Circle the verb or verb phrase they modify.

a. She walked quickly down the sidewalk.
b. The ground quaked violently beneath their feet.
c. We seldom travel this road.
d. She rushed into the room.
e. We will find the answer tomorrow.

5. *Capitalization*
Correct any errors in capitalization by placing a slash through any incorrect letters and placing the correct letter above it.

The Gainesville sun featured an article on the micanopy historical committee's plan to renovate many buildings of historical value in Micanopy. The first methodist church located on twenty-second street will be the first project the committee will undertake. Also many houses built during the civil war are slated to be renovated. The renovations should begin this Spring.

6. *Personal Pronouns and Antecedents*
Underline each personal pronoun in the following sentences. Circle the noun that is its antecedent.

a. The mare whinnied at its young foal.
b. The youth group enjoyed their trip to mountains.
c. Jean and Sue went swimming, and then they played volleyball on the beach.
d. Mike usually played first base, but sometimes he played shortstop.

7. *Synonyms*
Using a thesaurus, write a synonym for each of these adjectives.

a. beautiful
b. tremendous
c. rigid
d. brittle

The

Research Essay

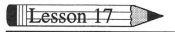
✐ Teacher's Note: As your student completes each lesson, choose skills from the Review Activities that he needs. The Review Activities follow each lesson.

✐ Teacher's Note: For the next three lessons your student will learn how to use the library for research.

Library Learning

1. Public libraries will be very helpful as you learn to write and research. The librarian has been trained to assist you. If you can't find what you are looking for, ask for help. Most libraries are divided into sections or departments.

   a. **Reference Department** - This is where you will find periodicals, pamphlets/fliers, newspapers, magazines, city/county directories, literary criticisms, consumer reports, and encyclopedias.

   b. **Adult Department** - Here you will find adult literature, fiction/nonfiction, videos, books on audio tapes, large print books, science fiction, CD's, cassettes.

   c. **Youth Department** - This is where you will find many of your resources. This department is almost like a library in itself containing much of what you find in the reference and adult departments. The books, however, are written for youth. You will find readers of all levels, nonfiction, books on audio tapes, cassettes, encyclopedias, biographies, and a youth reference section.

   d. **Card Catalog** - Here you will find titles, authors, and their reference (call) numbers. In many libraries the card catalog is now obsolete and everything can be found on the library computer.

   Plan a trip to your local library. Ask your librarian to help you become familiar with each department. Ask her to instruct you in using the card catalog or computer.

2. a. There are many books in each department. It would be an overwhelming task to search for a title without the help of the Dewey Decimal System. This system of numbers serves as a way to classify nonfiction books into ten major categories.

Dewey Decimal System

000-099 General Works - encyclopedias, computer information

100-199 Philosophy - conduct, manners

200-299 Religion - Bibles, Bible stories, books about religion, religions of different countries

300-399 Social Science - Folk lore, fairy tales

400-499 Language - dictionaries, sign language, foreign language dictionaries, language helps

500-599 Science - experiments, animals, biology, chemistry, etc.

600-699 Technology - (how things work) health, body, medicine, etc.

700-799 Arts - fine arts, artists, crafts, sports, music, photography

800-899 Literature - (nonfiction) poetry, writing, books, plays

900-999 History/Geography - countries, states, Indians, U.S./World History

---

2.

b. 1) 500-599 *Earth Science for Every Kid*, Janice Van Cleave

2) 100-199 *The Teenage Book of Manners...PLEASE*, Fred Hartley

3) 200-299 *Intimate Moments with the Savior*, Ken Gire

4) 400-499 *The Thorndike Barnhart Children's Dictionary*, HarperCollins

5) 800-899 *A Child's Treasury of Verse*, Eleanor Doan

6) 900-999 *The Reader's Digest Children's World Atlas*

7) 300-399 *Happy Hours in Storyland*

8) 800-899 *World War II Day* by Day, Donald Sommerville 900-999

b. Using the Dewey Decimal System, write the correct number category where you would find the following books.

1) *Earth Science for Every Kid*, Janice Van Cleave
2) *The Teenage Book of Manners...PLEASE*, Fred Hartley
3) *Intimate Moments with the Savior*, Ken Gire
4) *The Thorndike Barnhart Children's Dictionary*, HarperCollins
5) *A Child's Treasury of Verse*, Eleanor Doan
6) *The Reader's Digest Children's World Atlas*
7) *Happy Hours in Storyland*
8) *World War II Day by Day*, Donald Sommerville 900-999

c. During a trip to your library use the Dewey Decimal System to find an example from each category.

3. a. Fiction books (novels, mysteries, etc.) can usually be found in a special section of the library. They are arranged in alphabetical order by the author's last name. If the author has more than one title on the shelf, they are placed in alphabetical order by title.

Ex: *Summer of the Monkeys*; Rawls, Wilson
        Where the Red Fern Grows; Rawls, Wilson

If the title begins with a small word like *A* or *The*, disregard it, and alphabetize according to the next word. For example, to look up the book title, *The Courage of Sarah Noble*, look under **C** for *Courage*.

b. Arrange the following fiction titles in the order you would find them on the library shelf by placing the order number in the space provided.

_____ *Call It Courage*; Sperry, Armstrong
_____ *The Tale of Jeremy Vole*; Lawhead, Stephen
_____ *Mr. Popper's Penguins*; Atwater, Richard and Florence
_____ *The Big Wave*; Buck, Pearl S.
_____ *The Tale of Anabelle Hedgehog*; Lawhead, Stephen
_____ *Island of the Blue Dolphins*; O'Dell, Scott
_____ *Rabbit Hill*; Lawson, Robert
_____ *The Sign of the Beaver*; Speare, Elizabeth George
_____ *The Road to Damietta*; O'Dell, Scott
_____ *Farmer Boy*, Wilder; Laura Ingalls

c. Usually a library has a special section given to biographies and autobiographies. Do you know the difference between the two? If not, use a dictionary to look up the terms. You will find the books in this nonfiction section arranged in alphabetical order by the last name of the subject. If more than one biography has been written about a person, then the biographies are put in order by the author's last name.

Ex: *Benjamin Franklin*; d'Aulaire, Ingrid and Edgar Parin
Meet Benjamin Franklin; Scarf, Maggi
Benjamin Franklin; Stevenson, Augusta

A **biography** is the story of a person's life written by someone other than that person.

An **autobiography** is a person's life story that that person has written.

d. Arrange the following biographies in the order you would find them on the library shelf by placing the order number in the space provided.

_____ *Susanna Wesley*; Ludwig, Charles
_____ *Daniel Webster*; Allen, Robert
_____ *George Frideric Handel*; Ludwig, Charles
_____ *Robert E. Lee*; Roddy, Lee
_____ *Christopher Columbus*; Rhodes, Bennie

3.

b. _9_ *Call It Courage*; Sperry, Armstrong
_4_ *The Tale of Jeremy Vole*; Lawhead, Stephen
_1_ *Mr. Popper's Penguins*; Atwater, Richard and Florence
_2_ *The Big Wave;* Buck, Pearl S.
_3_ *The Tale of Anabelle Hedgehog*; Lawhead, Stephen
_6_ *Island of the Blue Dolphins*; O'Dell, Scott
_5_ *Rabbit Hill;* Lawson, Robert
_8_ *The Sign of the Beaver*; Speare, Elizabeth George
_7_ *The Road to Damietta*; O'Dell, Scott
_10_ *Farmer Boy;* Wilder, Laura Ingalls

3.

d. _5_ *Susanna Wesley* by Charles Ludwig
_4_ *Daniel Webster* by Robert Allen
_2_ *George Frideric Handel* by Charles Ludwig
_3_ *Robert E. Lee* by Lee Roddy
_1_ *Christopher Columbus* by Bennie Rhodes

4.

a. Vol. 2 - American
Revolution
Vol. 1 - Amazon River

b.

1) 1922
2) The Newbery Award is
awarded to the
American author
contributing the finest
book for children for
that year.
3) Children's Services
Division of the
American Library
Association (ALA)
4) It was named after
John Newbery, an
18th century English
bookseller.
5) 1949 - *King of the Wind*
by Marguerite Henry
1961 - *Island of the
Blue Dolphins* by Scott
O'Dell
6) Answers will vary.

5.

a. Answers will vary.

4. a. At the library, ask the Reference Librarian where you can
find the children's research books. Review the reference
books to determine which books you would use for the
following topics:

1) The American Revolution
2) The Amazon River

This method allows you to find your subject easily. In an
encyclopedia set arranged as listed in the example, which
volume would you find information about the American
Revolution?

Which volume would you find information about the
Amazon River?

b. Each year a special acknowledgement called the Newbery
Award is made to certain books. Ask your librarian where
you can find information on Newbery Award winners.

1) In what year was the first Newbery Award given?
2) How does a book win this award?
3) Who issues the award?
4) Why was it named "Newbery" Award?
5) What was the title and author of the 1949 award winner?
The 1961 award winner? Last year's winner?
6) List some or all of the Newbery Award winners you
would like to read.

5. a. Use your library's computer, or card catalog if available, to
make a list of all the books your favorite author has written.
How many have you read? Would you like to read other
books by this author?

b. Use the reference area of your library to find out more information about your author. One good reference source is "Something About the Author." Look for this or a similar reference book to research your author.

c. Does the information you found about the author help you determine whether or not the author is a Christian?

d. Choose skills from the *Review Activities* on the next page.

Review Activities

Choose only the skills your student needs to review.

1. *Departments of the Library*
   Refer to your list of library departments to answer the following questions.

   a. In what department would you find a magazine article on nutrition?
   b. In what department would you find young children's books?
   c. In what department would you go to locate a video on Spain?
   d. What department would help you in locating a book?

2. *Dewey Decimal System*
   Use the Dewey Decimal System to classify each of the following books. Write the correct number category next to each selection.

   a. *First Guide to the Universe*
   b. *Amazing Machines and How They Work*
   c. *Art Through the Ages*
   d. *Religions of Many Lands*
   e. *World Book Encyclopedia*

3. *Fiction*
   Arrange the following fiction books in the correct order they would appear on the library shelf of fiction by placing the number of their appearance on the space provided.

   a. _____ *Silver for General Washington*; Meadowcroft, Enid
   b. _____ *The Legend of Fire*; Roddy, Lee
   c. _____ *The Bronze Bow*, Speare; Elizabeth George
   d. _____ *Amos Fortune, Free Man*; Yates, Elizabeth
   e. _____ *Gift From the Midado*; Fleming, Elizabeth

1.
a. Reference
b. Youth
c. Adult
d. Card Catalog

2.
a. 500-599
b. 600-699
c. 700-799
d. 200-299
e. 000-099

3.
a. 2
b. 3
c. 4
d. 5
e. 1

4. *Biographies*

Arrange the following biographies in the correct order they would appear on the library shelf by placing the number of their appearance on the space provided. If the book is an autobiography, circle the number.

a. _____ *Michael Faraday, Father of Electronics*; Ludwig, Charles

b. _____ *Isaac Newton: Mastermind of Modern Science*; Knight, David

c. _____ *Inventor, Scientist & Teacher: Isaac Newton*; Tiner, John

d. _____ *Ben Carson*; Carson, Ben

e. _____ *Martin Luther: Hero of Faith*; Nohl, Frederick

f. _____ *The World of William Penn*, Foster; Genevieve

5. *Encyclopedia*

Indicate in which volume you would find the following information.

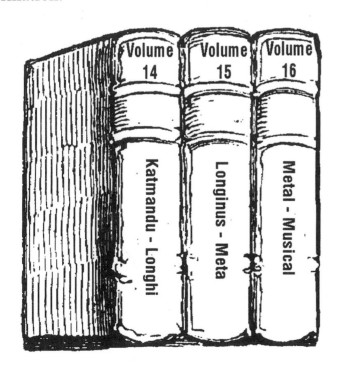

a. Vol. _____ - minerals

b. Vol. _____ - monarchy

c. Vol. _____ - Kitty Hawk

d. Vol. _____ - mathematics

e. Vol. _____ - library

6.

  1) 1938

  2) The Caldecott Medal is awarded to the American artist/ illustrator contributing the finest picture book for children and exhibiting the most unique and distinctive style.

  3) The American Library Association (ALA)

  4) 1940 - *Abraham Lincoln* by Ingri and Edgar Parin d'Aulaire 1963 - *The Snowy Day* - Ezra Jack Keats

  5) Robert McCloskey; Marcia Brown

  6) Robert Lawson

  7) Randolph Caldecott, an English illustrator

  9) Answers will vary.

6. *Research*

You did some research on the Newbery Award. Another special acknowledgment is the Caldecott Award. Use an encyclopedia or other resource to answer the following questions.

1) In what year was the first Caldecott award given?
2) How does a book qualify to win the award?
3) What organization issues the award?
4) What was the title and author of the 1940 award winner? The 1963 award winner? Last year's winner?
5) Has any one person ever won the Caldecott medal more than once?
6) Has any one person ever won both the Newbery and Caldecott Awards?
7) For whom was the Caldecott medal named?
8) List some of the Caldecott winners you have read.

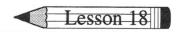

✐ Teacher's Note: As your student completes each lesson, choose skills from the Review Activities that he needs. The Review Activities follow each lesson.

✐ Teacher's Note: The Research Essay unit continues in Lesson 19.

At last either Betsie or I would open the Bible. Because only the Hollanders could understand the Dutch text we would translate aloud in German. And then we would hear the life-giving words passed back along the aisles in French, Polish, Russian, Czech, back into Dutch. They were little previews of heaven, these evenings beneath the light bulb. I would think of Haarlem, each substantial church set behind its wrought-iron fence and its barrier of doctrine. And I would know again that in darkness God's truth shines most clear.

The Hiding Place by Corrie Ten Boom.
Used by permission, Chosen Books, 25 Turner Dr., Chappaqua, NY 10514.

1. a. Copy the literature passage. Compare your copy with the passage and correct any errors.

   b. Why are the words French, Polish, Russian, Czech, and Dutch capitalized?

   c. Find the word *substantial* in the literature passage. This word contains the prefix **sub-** which means *under*. Add this prefix to your prefix list along with its definition and some word examples.

   d. Make a spelling list from any misspelled words from your dictation or use the following list.

aisles	wrought	barrier
substantial	translate	doctrine

   e. The word *wrought* is spelled with a silent **w** and **r** to make the /r/ sound.

1.
b. Names of countries and ethnic groups are always capitalized.

> ### Spelling Tip
> Some words spell the **/r/** sound with **wr** as in write.

153

Copy the following words and underline **wr**. Say the words aloud as you write them.

write	wren
wreath	wreck
wrestle	wrinkle
wrong	wrap

2. a. Read the last two sentences of the literature passage. Discuss with your teacher what you think the author means.

2.
b. first-person

   b. The author of this novel is Corrie Ten Boom. *The Hiding Place* is the story of her experiences during World War II. Examine the literature passage and determine from what point of view the story is written.

   c. Although most of the information presented in *The Hiding Place* is based on firsthand experience, the author does present many facts about World War II that she obtained through research.

   During the next two weeks, you will research the topic of your choice and write an essay about the subject. When various books, magazines, and other reference materials are used as sources of information for an essay that documents a subject, the resulting paper is referred to as a **research essay.**

3. a. This lesson will use World War II as a sample topic of research in order to guide you through the process of preparing a research essay.

   b. Research requires proper planning. It is important that you follow the steps in the order presented without omitting any steps of research. Keep track of your research planning by using the student checklist in Lesson 19. Each time you complete a step on the checklist, mark the box and move to the next step.

c. Begin your research by first deciding the topic you want to research. Think of a subject you might like to know more about. Then take a trip to your library. Use books, magazines, or an encyclopedia to help you choose an interesting topic. (Your librarian can help you with any questions you may have.) Your research paper will be only five or six paragraphs so you must narrow down your topic to a specific topic you would like to explore.

> Ex: **General area of interest**: Battles of World War II
> **General topic**: Battle at Pearl Harbor
> **Limited topic**: The Destruction of the American Fleet at Pearl Harbor

d. Write a statement of purpose for your essay. This statement is called the **thesis statement** and should express the **main idea** of the essay in a sentence or two. Think of your thesis statement as your focus point. You want your research paper to center around what is said in your thesis statement.

> Ex: The destruction of the American fleet at Pearl Harbor had more of an effect on the United States than any other event of World War II.

e. Look back at the Dewey Decimal System in Lesson 17. Write the number or name of the category you would find each of the following books.

1) Books on World War II
2) An encyclopedia
3) A biography of a famous person involved in World War II

3.
e. 1) 900-999
   2) 000-099
   3) Biographies

f. What section would you find books on the subject of your choice?

g. Spend time today at the library gathering and deciding which books or reference you will use to research your topic. You may include pictures (drawn or otherwise) with your paper. In making your choices include at least one encyclopedia or reference book, one magazine or newspaper (if possible), and one book.

4. a. Once you have narrowed your broad topic to a more specific topic, begin reading the information you have gathered. Use the index (or subtopics in an encyclopedia) to aid you in your search of specific information. You don't have to read the entire magazine article or book unless you want to. Focus just on the parts that deal with your specific topic.

   b. Keep your ideas focused. Make a list of questions on 3 x 5 index cards. For example, with the topic, The Destruction of the American Fleet at Pearl Harbor, you might write the following questions. One question per card.

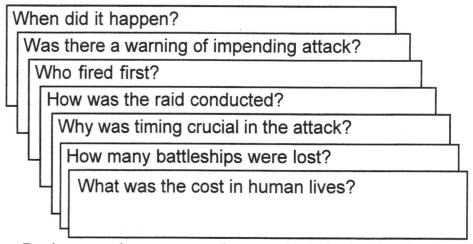

When did it happen?

Was there a warning of impending attack?

Who fired first?

How was the raid conducted?

Why was timing crucial in the attack?

How many battleships were lost?

What was the cost in human lives?

   c. Begin answering your questions on the index cards. Be sure to use your own words. Do not copy information. This is against the law; it is called **plagiarism**. When you use a reference, write where you got your information on the back of the card. You will need this when you make a list of references that goes on the last page of your research paper.

   d. Review your spelling words. Remember to be careful of words with silent letters.

   e. Continue gathering information and recording it on your note cards.

   f. Take an oral or written spelling pretest.

5. a. Choose one of the following activities.

      1) Take the literature passage from dictation again.

      2) You may continue to gather information on your note cards.

1. a. Now you must put your notes in order. Focus first on your main idea and then follow with details. Look over your note cards and ask yourself these questions.

   ☐ Do all my note cards apply to my subject?

   ☐ Do I need to discard some that do not apply?

   ☐ Do I have enough information on my topic?

   b. Decide what the main points of your essay will be and list them. Group the remaining ideas under these main points forming a **topical outline**. A topical outline uses words or phrases to express ideas; it does not use sentences. The most important points of your outline should be numbered with Roman numerals and the subheadings should be listed by capital letters. Any remaining supporting details should be listed numerically under the subheading they support. Be sure to place a period after each of the numbers and letters used in the outline formation and indent each level. One of the rules used in forming an outline is that you never have just one subheading or just one detail listed under a subheading. You always have at least two subheadings or at least two details. Often this rule is expressed: "You never have an *A* without a *B* and you never have a *1* without a *2*." Look over the following sample topical outline and then create your own outline for the topic you have chosen.

The Destruction of the American Fleet at Pearl Harbor

I. The Japanese Attack on Pearl Harbor

   A. Situation Prior to Attack

      1. U. S. Naval base located on Oahu Island, Hawaii
      2. The bulk of the US fleet was at its base
      3. Japanese diplomats in talks with U.S.
      4. American fleet not on a wartime alert

   B. The Attack

      1. Japanese planes attacked at 7:55 A.M.
      2. First destroyed planes
      3. Second attacked fleet in harbor

II. U.S. losses at Pearl Harbor

   A. Damage to U.S. Fleet

      1. Battleships: 4 sunk; 4 damaged
      2. Cruisers: 3 damaged
      3. Destroyers: 3 sunk

   B. Lives loss or wounded

      1. Number of Americans killed: 3,581
      2. Number of Americans wounded: 1,168

III. Results of Battle

   A. Gave Japanese fleet temporary command of western Pacific

   B. United States enters World War II

2. a. With your teacher's help, review your outline and notes. Pay special attention to any suggestions your teacher makes. Work on an opening paragraph developed from your thesis statement. The **opening paragraph** should contain your thesis statement.

    Ex: World War II was raging, but the United States was still attempting to isolate itself from involvement. All this would change early the morning of December 7, 1941. The destruction of the American fleet at Pearl Harbor had more of an effect on the United States than any other event of World War II.

  b. Use your outline to continue writing the body of your research paper. This is only your first draft. You may make changes without worrying about being neat.

3. a. You must close your research paper. Develop a good **closing paragraph** concluding your research.

    Ex: The attack at Pearl Harbor gave Japan temporary command of the Western Pacific. Japan thought it could defeat America before our military forces had time to fight back; instead their attack drew the United States into the war. America had just begun the road to victory.

  b. Complete the **first draft** of your research paper.

  c. If you choose to include sketches or pictures, neatly mount them onto paper.

  d. Ask your teacher to look over your first draft.

4. a. Discuss your essay with your teacher, and pay special attention to any suggestions that your teacher makes. Review your research essay using a red pencil to make corrections as you check your grammar and spelling. If there are any words you have used too often, use your thesaurus to find synonyms to replace them.

b. In checking over your essay it would be helpful to ask yourself the following questions:

☐ Did I follow my outline?

☐ Did I follow the main idea of my research essay?

☐ Are the opening paragraph and closing paragraph interesting?

☐ Did my thoughts flow well through the paper?

☐ Does it make sense?

c. Using the information on the back of your index cards, make a list of references to go on the last page of your research paper. This list is called a **bibliography**. List only the references you used in your research essay. A bibliography entry should include the author's name (last name first), the title of the book (underlined) or article (in quotation marks), and publication information (state and name of company). Follow the format used in the following example. The words in italics are not to be copied; they are for reference.

Bibliography

Holmes, Richard. The World Atlas of Warfare. New York: Viking Penguin, Inc. (*Book*)

"Pearl Harbor Disaster". Collier's Encyclopedia. 1967. (*Reference book*)

Jones, Harold. "The Attack of Pearl Harbor." History Chronicles (6, July, 1997): pp 14-18. (*Magazine*)

5. Make a neat final copy to give to your teacher. Look over
    your paper once more. When you are pleased with your
    work, put your paper in order: outline the research essay,
    pictures/sketches, and bibliography. A nice way to end your
    work would be to place it in a folder with the title of your
    research essay on the front.

Student Checklist

☐ Choose a subject.

☐ Narrow topic.

☐ Select research materials.

☐ Prepare note cards/take notes
   recording any references used.

☐ Conduct interview (optional).

☐ Write a statement of purpose.

☐ Write an outline.

☐ Write first draft.

☐ Revise first draft

☐ Add sketches or pictures
   (optional).

☐ Write reference list
   (bibliography).

☐ Write final copy.

☐ Place in order and put in a
   folder.

Assessment 3
(Lessons 12 - 19)

1. abaabcc

1. Read the following poem. What is its rhyme scheme?

When Mother Reads Aloud

When Mother reads aloud, the past
Seems real as every day;
I hear the tramp of armies vast,
I see the spears and lances cast,
I join the trilling fray;
Brave knights and ladies fair and proud
I meet when Mother reads aloud.

When Mother reads aloud, far lands
Seem very near and true;
I cross the desert's gleaming sands,
Or hunt the jungle's prowling bands,
Or sail the ocean blue.
Far heights, whose peaks the cold mists shroud,
I scale, when Mother reads aloud.

When Mother reads aloud, I long
For noble deeds to do—
To help the right, redress the wrong;
It seems so easy to be strong,
So simple to be true.
Oh, thick and fast the visions crowd
My eyes, when Mother reads aloud.

2. Answers will vary.

2. Use the verb *lie* correctly in a sentence.

3. Answers will vary.

3. Use the verb *lay* correctly in a sentence.

4. copying information without giving the author credit

4. What is plagiarism?

5. his, He, He, his, him, he, his, He, his, he, His

5. Find the pronouns in the literature passage in Lesson 9.

6. Write the following singular nouns as plural nouns.

   a. book
   b. goose
   c. baby

7. Circle the adjectives in the following sentence.

   The ragged, dirty shirt hung on the line.

8. Using your thesaurus, rewrite the above sentence replacing the adjectives with synonyms.

9. Find two articles in the literature passage in Lesson 2.

10. Arrange the following authors' names in alphabetical order.

   Arthur Ransome, Laura Ingalls Wilder, Elizabeth George Speare, Meindert Dejong

11. Arrange the following information in outline form.

   Cars, Motorcycles, Places People Live, Condominiums, Apartments, Trucks, Vehicles, Houses

---

6.
a. books
b. geese
c. babies

7. ragged, dirty

8. Possible answer:
The shabby, filthy shirt hung on the line.

9. the, a

10. DeJong, Ransome, Speare, Wilder

11.
A. Places People Live
  I. Houses
  2. Apartments
  3. Condominiums
B. Vehicles
  I. Cars
  2. Trucks
  3. Motorcycles

BOOK STUDY

on

Big Red

Big Red by Jim Kjelgaard
**Published by Bantam
Skylark**

Readability level: 7th grade

Introducing
Big Red

Jim Kjelgaard spent his childhood years in a country setting much like what is described in *Big Red*. He enjoyed exploring the vast wilderness that surrounded him.

Summary

It was love at first sight. "Spellbound, Danny returned the dog's gaze ... never before had he seen any dog that revealed at first glance all the qualities a dog should have." Danny's love was a sleek and silky Irish setter named Cheapen Sylvester's Boy, but Danny simply called him Red. Danny's first thought on seeing Red was how much he wanted to own him. He found out that Mr. Haggin, the wealthy man who owned thousands of acres in the Wintapi, had paid seven thousand dollars for the dog. That was more money than Danny and his father, Ross, had made in their entire lives hunting, trapping, and doing odd jobs.

Mr. Haggin was a man who made his fortune sizing up men. He knew Danny had what it takes to become a good dog handler and also knew that like himself, Danny could love and understand a great dog. That is how Danny ended up as caretaker for Red. He wanted to start Red's education by training him to hunt partridge, knowing Red had the makings of an exceptional partridge dog, if he could only be cured of his interest in other varmints. This was taken care of by a close encounter with a skunk.

Red and Danny spend an eventful winter together, where both grow in knowledge and strength. Not only does Red help to save Ross' life, but he and Danny have an exciting encounter with a wolverine and end up in the biggest contest of their lives battling the cunning and dangerous bear, Old Majesty. One of Danny's dreams begins to come true as Red acquires a mate and begins a family which Danny hopes to see as the first in a long line of champions. Finally, the best dream of all comes true as Danny becomes the owner of Red.

Jim Kjelgaard wrote an exciting story of courage and sense of duty in both man and beast. His childhood was spent in much the same way as Danny's and he brings his love of the wilderness to each of his books.

Vocabulary

Find each of the following words in the chapters indicated and use context clues to decide the meaning of each word. Then, look up each word in the dictionary and write a definition.

1. ravenous - (Chapter 1)

2. profoundly - (Chapter 2)

3. careening - (Chapter 6)

4. indispensable - (Chapter 9)

5. hypodermic - (Chapter 11)

Choose the correct word from the words listed above to complete the following sentences.

6. A carpenter's tools are _____ for his work.

7. Mother is _____ against the use of pesticides.

8. The patient grimaced as the doctor placed the _____ needle in his arm.

9. The race car went _____ into the stands.

10. The young boy had a _____ appetite.

1. ravenous - very hungry
2. profoundly - with deep feeling
3. careening - moving swiftly
4. indispensable - necessary
5. hypodermic - introduced under the skin

6. indispensable
7. profoundly
8. hypodermic
9. careening
10. ravenous

Discussion Questions

1. Mr. Haggin entrusts Danny with his valuable dog. What does he see in Danny's character that makes him do this?

2. What are some examples of his character traits found in Chapter 1?

3. Examine your own character. How do you think people see you? What strengths can you identify? What weaknesses?

4. Mr. Haggin explains why people exhibit their dogs. The reason he gives is "he ... will know that he has built on what competent men have declared to be the very best. He will know also that he, too, can go one step nearer the perfection that men must and will have in all things." Is there such a thing as perfection? Why would men seek for perfection?

5. There are two major conflicts between Danny and Ross in the story. Are they resolved? If so, how?

---

1. Danny has proved himself to be hard working, thoughtful, dependable, loyal, and truthful.

2. Possible answers:
   1) He tracks a bull for Mr. Haggin and completes the job.
   2) He goes beyond what was asked of him by acting to prevent the bull from spoiling.
   3) He bravely hunts Old Majesty, which he has done since he was 12 years old.
   4) Mr. Haggin comments that he will call Danny next time anything goes astray.
   5) Mr. Haggin appreciated Danny's perceiving the value of Big Red and protecting him from possible injury.

3. Answers will vary.

4. Allow for discussion.

5. The first conflict had to do with Red's education. Ross' solution to the problem of Red running after every varmint he encountered was to give him a licking. Danny felt that Red was too sensitive and he would lose Red's trust if he struck him. The conflict was resolved when Red chased a skunk and was sprayed. This made him stop chasing varmints.

   The second conflict arose over Red's being trained as a partridge dog. Ross thought this was a waste of a good dog and made him look down on Red. This was resolved when Red saved Ross' life by finding him in the snow, causing Ross to love and appreciate Red.

6. Do you think Danny lied to his father about how Red found Ross in the snow?

7. What made Danny change his mind about taking Big Red to hunt Old Majesty?

8. "He was young, but old enough to know that life was seldom easy. And it seemed to him that in the future there would be a great many bears to meet. How he met them depended in great measure on what he did now with Old Majesty." Could Danny have been thinking of something other than real bears that he would have to meet in the future? What kind of bears do you think he meant?

   Can you apply this to your life? In what ways?

9. Danny made the choice to take Mr. Haggin's valuable dog into the forest to meet Old Majesty. What was Mr. Haggin's reaction? Do you think he made the right decision?

10. Foreshadowing in literature is a suggestion of what is to come later in the story by giving hints or clues. What is the major event that is foreshadowed in this book?

---

6. Allow for discussion.

7. After Old Majesty had killed their animals and attacked Ross, Danny felt that Old Majesty was asserting his supremacy over all the Wintapi. No animal or man would ever be safe there again unless this challenge was met. Danny also realized that how he met this challenge would determine how he would meet other challenges that were sure to come to him in life.

8. Allow for discussion.

9. Mr. Haggin agreed with Danny's decision. He felt that a man's life was worth more than an animal's, even such a valuable animal as Red.
Allow for discussion.

10. In the beginning of the book, Danny and Big Red have a confrontation with Old Majesty which is not resolved because Danny is afraid of hurting Big Red. This conflict is resolved at the end of the book.

Activities

The following activities are intended to help you understand the friendship that Danny and Red formed as well as what Danny's life was like. Choose two or three activities to complete your study.

1. If you have a dog, sign up for dog training classes. These are usually held at community centers or you can call your local veterinarian. Even if you do not have a dog, you can attend these classes and observe the relationship between a dog and his owner.

2. Go to the library or look in the encyclopedia for pictures of different dog breeds. How are dogs grouped? What characteristics determine the different groups?

3. Research the American Kennel Club. What is it? When and why was it formed? What purpose does it serve?

4. Attend a dog show. Talk to the owners and find out what characteristics judges look for in each breed of dog represented.

5. Since money was scarce, Danny and Ross were used to doing things for themselves. For instance, they knew basic first aid and could treat small injuries and illnesses. Think about things around your house that you could do yourself that would save your family money.

6. Ross and Danny made their living hunting and trapping animals. Do you know anyone who hunts? Most hunting today is for the purpose of sport. There are arguments against this as well as arguments in favor. What do you think? Write a paper defending your position.

7. Read other books about Irish setters written by Mr. Kjelgaard, *Irish Red* and *Outlaw Red*, as well as his other books about the wilderness.

I C.A.N. Assessment

for

Big Red - Book Study C

After the *Book Study* is completed, check off each I C.A.N. objective with your teacher.

____ C I can **complete** my work.

____ I can be **creative**.

____ A I can be **accurate**.

____ I can do my work with a good **attitude**.

____ N I can do my work **neatly**.

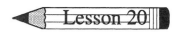

*The time I spent upon the island is still
so horrible a thought to me, that I must pass
it lightly over. In all the books I have read
of people cast away, they had either their
pockets full of tools, or a chest of things
would be thrown upon the beach along with
them, as if on purpose. My case was very
different. I had nothing in my pockets but
money and Alan's silver button; and being
inland bred, I was as much short of
knowledge as of means.*

Kidnapped by Robert Louis Stevenson.

1. a. Read the literature passage aloud paying close attention to
punctuation. Notice the semicolon which joins the two parts
of the last sentence. When you read the literature passage,
be sure to pause at the semicolon as for a comma. Write the
literature passage from dictation, then make any corrections.

b. The main character in the literature passage is also the
narrator. What did the narrator in the literature passage think
of stories of other castaways? What emotion or mood does
the author create concerning the character's island
experience? Did he have any practical experience in
survival or even roughing it?

c. Explain what you think the first sentence of the literature
passage means.

d. Make a spelling list from the words you misspelled in your
dictation or use the following suggested list:

horrible	either	different
inland	button	knowledge

e. The word *knowledge* is spelled with a silent **k** and **n** to
make the **/n/** sound. **Gn** also makes a **/n/** sound. Words may
begin with **kn** or **gn**, but **kn** will usually not end a word.

✐ **Teacher's Note:** As your
student completes each
lesson, choose skills from
the Review Activities that he
needs. The Review
Activities follow each
lesson.

1.
b. **The narrator thought
stories of other
castaways were
unrealistic because they
were always supplied
with the tools or other
means to survive.**

**The mood is one of
frustration and concern.**

**No. The narrator
indicates he is *inland
bred* and has little
knowledge of survival
skills.**

c. **The memories are so
unpleasant that he does
not like to dwell on them.**

2.
a. first person

b. Alan's; the use of 's

> ### Spelling Tip
> Some words spell the /n/ sound with **kn** or **gn**; but **kn** will usually not end a word.

Copy the following words and underline **kn** and **gn**. Say the words aloud as you write them.

knee	gnaw
knight	gnat
knife	gnarl
knit	reign
knock	sign
knob	align
knuckle	design

2. a. Look at the literature passage again, paying special attention to the pronouns. In which person (first, second, or third) are the pronouns used?

   b. Underline the noun that shows possession in the literature passage. How do you know it shows possession?

   c. Another method of showing possession is the use of possessive pronouns. **Possessive pronouns** are words that take the place of nouns that show possession. The possessive pronouns most commonly used are:

Commonly Used Possessive Pronouns					
my	his	her	its	your	our
their	mine	hers	yours	ours	theirs

Hint
Possessive pronouns do not use an apostrophe to show possession.

d. Find and list the three possessive pronouns in the literature passage. Beside each one, write what each pronoun is showing possession of.

e. Usually possessive pronouns are used as adjectives in the structure of a sentence. All the possessive pronouns in bold print listed above are used as adjectives.

f. Write the correct possessive pronoun in the space provided in the following sentences.

   Ex: *Mary* went to __her__ Spanish lesson.

   1) *Matthew and Lane* went to _____ favorite fishing spot.
   2) The *car* slowed down to stay in _____ correct lane.
   3) *I* want you to see _____ new shoes.
   4) *Lydia* likes to finish _____ homework before going to softball practice.
   5) *Mike* will achieve _____ goals because he believes in working hard.

g. Being cast away on a deserted island with just money and a silver button would put you in a very difficult situation. Think of some things you would need if you were stranded on a deserted island. Think about the reasons why you would need those particular things. Spend some time talking about it with your teacher to help you clarify your thoughts. Put your thoughts on paper and save it for tomorrow's work.

2.
d. their pockets
   my case
   my pockets

f. 1) their
   2) its
   3) my
   4) her
   5) his

3. a. **Essays** are used to explain an idea, describe how something is done, argue a point of view, or interpret something you read. In Lessons 18 and 19 you wrote a research essay. Today you will begin work on a different type of essay. It will be an essay in which you express your ideas and views about a survival situation. Use what you wrote yesterday to guide you in formulating a thesis statement. Place your thesis statement at the top of your outline. This will help you remember to keep your thoughts focused on your main idea.

   Ex: Although many items would be useful in a survival situation, I think the three items that would be crucial to my survival would be a knife, matches, and a Bible.

   b. The next step in writing an essay is to complete a topical outline in order to better organize your thoughts. First list the three most important items you would need to survive on the island. Each of these main ideas will be numbered with a roman numeral.

   c. Under each main idea list at least two reasons why this item would be important to your survival. Note these **supporting details** with a capital letter.

   I. Knife

       A. Make weapons for hunting
       B. Cut up food to prepare for eating
       C. Make a shelter

   II. Matches

       A. Cook food
       B. Keep warm

   III. Bible

       A. Keep from being lonely
       B. Receive comfort from God

d. Any further supporting details should be listed in numerical order under the subheading shown with a capital letter. (See the outline in Lesson 19.) Save your outline for tomorrow.

e. Review your spelling words.

4. a. Use your outline from yesterday to write the first draft of a short essay. Look over your outline. The first thing you need to do is develop a good opening paragraph. Just as you greet a friend, "Hello!" on the telephone, you must introduce your reader to your idea of the essay. Use your thesis statement as a basis to build your opening paragraph. As you begin your writing, write on every other line. This will make revising your work easier.

b. Now take each main idea and supporting details to form three good paragraphs.

c. You now must close your paragraph. Just as you say, "Goodbye," to a friend as you finish your telephone conversation, you now must conclude your thoughts on paper.

d. Today you have completed a rough draft of your essay. You are building a house, and the bricks are your words! It doesn't need to be perfect. You are working to get your thoughts down in an organized form.

e. Take an oral or written spelling pretest.

5. a. All writers work to get their words just right. Today you will rearrange and add to your rough draft from yesterday. This is the process of editing, revising, and rewriting. This is an important step in writing your essay. Carefully look at each paragraph and decide what you want to change, rearrange, or reword. Perhaps you need to add more details or information.

b. Use your thesaurus to improve the quality of your words. Doing this will make your writing more interesting and increase your vocabulary.

c. Check your rough draft for spelling and punctuation. Read your composition aloud. When you are satisfied with the way it sounds, have your teacher check it for grammar, spelling, and content. Write a neat final copy.

d. Choose one of the following activities.

  1) Write the literature passage from dictation or just take a final spelling test.

  2) Choose skills from the *Review Activities* on the next page.

Review Activities

Choose only the skills your student needs to review.

1. *Possessive Pronouns*
   Underline the possessive pronouns in the following sentences.

   a. Their home near the creek is large and roomy.
   b. My teacher said I wrote an excellent essay.
   c. He grows a variety of different vegetables in his garden.
   d. Our family enjoys spending time together.

2. *Outline*
   Arrange the following information in outline form. The title of your outline is: *Eating a Healthy Diet.*

Vegetables	Foods You Should Eat
Candy	Cake
Fruit	Foods You Should Avoid
Carbohydrates	Whole-grain bread
Carrots	Fried foods
Broccoli	Apples
Fried chicken	High-sugar foods
French fries	Peaches
Cereal	

1.
  a. Their
  b. My
  c. his
  d. Our

2.
Eating a Healthy Diet

I. Foods You Should Eat
  A. Vegetables
    1. Broccoli
    2. Carrots
  B. Fruit
    1. Apples
    2. Peaches
  C. Carbohydrates
    1. Cereal
    2. Whole-grain bread
II. Foods You Should Avoid
  A. Fried foods
    1. French fries
    2. Fried chicken
  B. High-sugar foods
    1. Candy
    2. Cake

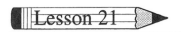

September 30. *I was now come to the unhappy anniversary of my landing. I cast up the notches on my post, and found I had been on shore three hundred and sixty-five days. I kept this day as a solemn fast, setting it apart to religious exercise, prostrating myself on the ground with the most serious humiliation, confessing my sins to God, acknowledging His righteous judgments upon me, and praying to Him to have mercy on me through Jesus Christ.*

Robinson Crusoe by Daniel DeFoe.

✐ **Teacher's Note:** As your student completes each lesson, choose skills from the Review Activities that he needs. The Review Activities follow each lesson.

1. a. Copy the literature passage or write it from dictation. Notice the date which begins the paragraph. This is Robinson Crusoe's journal entry for September 30. A **journal** is a record of a person's thoughts and observations. Most entries begin with the date the entry is made.

✐ **Teacher's Note:** *Judgments* may also be spelled *judgements*.

b. When you complete your dictation, be sure to check your work for any spelling or punctuation errors. Make your spelling list from any misspelled words or use the following suggested list:

judgments	acknowledging
prostrating	humiliation
righteous	religious

c. -ion, -sion, -tion - act of, state of, or result of
Possible examples: tension, graduation

-ous, -ious, -eous - full of or having
Possible examples: religious, gorgeous

c. All of the words in the suggested spelling list have a suffix. Two of the suffixes are **-ion** and **-ous**. The suffix **-ion** means the *act of, state of,* or *result of.* This suffix can also be spelled **-sion** or **-tion**. The suffix **-ous** means *full of* or *having.* This suffix can also be spelled **-ious** or **-eous**. Add each of these suffixes to your list, along with the definition and some word examples.

d. Suffixes make it possible to change a word from a noun to an adjective, from a verb to a noun, and from an adjective to an adverb. Use your list of suffixes to complete the following.

Ex: Change the noun, *mathematics,* to an adjective meaning *having an ability in mathematics:* mathematical

1) Change the noun *beauty* to an adjective meaning *full of beauty.*
2) Change the verb *inject* to a noun that means *the act of being injected.*
3) Change the verb *teach* to a noun that means *one who teaches.*
4) Change the adjective *quick* to an adverb that means *in the manner of being quick.*

1.
d. 1) **beautiful**
   2) **injection**
   3) **teacher**
   4) **quickly**

e. Some words like *judgments* and *acknowledging* are spelled with **dg** to make the **/j/** sound. The letters **dg** is used only after a single short vowel when making the **/j/** sound.

> ### Spelling Tip
> Words are often spelled with **dg** or **dge** following a single short vowel to make the **/j/** sound.

f. Copy these words and underline **dg**. Say the words aloud as you write them.

bridge   fudge
midget   edge
badger   hedge
lodge

g. How would you describe Robinson Crusoe? Was he happy or unhappy? Can you determine his relationship to God from the literature passage?

g. **Answers will vary.**

2.

a. I, myself, my, me

2.

c. 1) sit
   2) Set
   3) sits
   4) sit
   5) set

2. a. Many people write in journals or diaries to record their thoughts or events in their lives. Journals are written in the first person because events are being recorded from the perspective of one of the characters in the story. Look over the literature passage. What pronouns are used that indicate the passage is written in first person?

   b. Find the word *setting* in the literature passage. The verb *set* means *to place something*. It is often confused with the word *sit* which means *to rest or be seated*. When using the verb *set*, an object should be named that is being placed; the verb *sit* has no object.

      Ex: Please *sit* in this seat.
         Jim *set* his game on the table. (*game* is the object being placed)

   c. Complete the following sentences with the correct form of *sit* or *set*.

      1) Will you _____ with me during the concert?
      2) _____ your purse down and stay for a visit.
      3) My dad always _____ in that chair.
      4) Joanna likes to _____ on the beach.
      5) Would you _____ the package on the chair?

   d. Pretend you are a historical person who lived long ago. (George Washington at Valley Forge, a Pilgrim on the Mayflower, etc.) Take time today to gather some information on your character and an event which takes place. Jot down notes to use tomorrow.

3. a. Taking the notes you gathered yesterday, create a journal entry for your historical character. Be sure to add enough detail to make it interesting and to understand how the narrator is feeling. Be sure to date your entry.

   b. Review your spelling words.

4. a. In the third sentence of the literature passage notice the phrase *prostrating myself on the ground.* The word *on* shows the relationship between the pronoun (myself) and the verb (prostrating). This word is called a preposition. **Prepositions** show the relationship between a noun or pronoun and the other words in a sentence.

A preposition begins a **prepositional phrase**. For example, *on the ground* is the prepositional phrase. *On* is the preposition.

b. Look over the list of some of the most commonly used prepositions.

List of Commonly Used Prepositions				
aboard	at	during	off	under
about	before	except	on	until
above	behind	for	onto	up
across	below	from	outside	upon
after	beneath	in	over	with
against	beside	inside	past	within
along	between	into	since	without
among	beyond	like	through	
around	by	near	to	
as	down	of	toward	

There are fourteen prepositional phrases in the literature passage. Using the list of prepositions, underline the prepositional phrases and circle the prepositions.

c. Complete the following sentences with a preposition.

1) We will walk _____ Mary's house _____ the sewing class.
2) Joan's house is _____ the road and _____ the corner.
3) It is important to be quiet _____ the concert.

d. Take an oral or written spelling pretest.

4.
b. (to) the unhappy anniversary
(of) my landing
(up) the notches
(on) my post
(on) shore
(as) a solemn fast
(to) a religious exercise
(on) the ground
(with) the most serious humiliation
(to) God
(upon) me
(to) him
(on) me
(through) Jesus Christ

c. Possible answers:
1) to, with
2) down, around
3) during

5. a. Choose one of the following activities.

   1) Write the literature passage from dictation.

   2) Add another entry to the journal you began in **3a**.

   3) Think about how you would feel if you had been marooned on a island by yourself for a year. Write a journal entry telling how you would feel and what you would do on the one year anniversary of your arrival.

   4) Choose skills from the *Review Activities* on the next page.

Review Activities

Choose only the skills your student needs to review.

1. *Suffixes*
   Add the correct suffix to the following words. Following each sentence write what part of speech (noun, verb, adverb or adjective) each new word is.

   Ex: The singer sang a joy<u>ful</u> (*full of*) song. ____adjective____

   a. She lacked the motivat____ (*state of*) to finish the job. _____

   b. The stereo amplifi____ (*that which*) was turned up too loud. _____

   c. She is very graci____ (*full of* or *having*) person to allow us to stay in her home. _____

   d. The audience applauded loud____ (*like* or *manner of*) at the conclusion of the performance. _____

2. *Sit and Set*
   Choose the correct form of *sit* or *set* in the following sentences.

   a. She will (*sit, set*) the plant down on the table.
   b. We will (*sit, set*) here for lunch.
   c. Please (*sit, set*) the box down carefully.
   d. Jim likes to (*sit, set*) by the window.
   e. Did you (*sit, set*) my wallet here?

3. *Prepositions*
   Underline the prepositions in the following sentences.

   a. The girls walked under the bridge and across the street to the church.
   b. The car traveled through the tunnel before reaching its destination.
   c. Before you leave, turn off the light beside the door.
   d. Beyond this valley is the roadway to the campsite.
   e. Until the project is finished we will be inside the house.

4. *Journal Entry*
   Write a journal entry for a day in your own life. Be sure to date the entry and use descriptive words to tell about your day.

✏ **Teacher's Note:** As your student completes each lesson, choose skills from the Review Activities that he needs. The Review Activities follow each lesson.

"You don't seem to see," continued Toad, "that this fine horse of mine is a cut above you altogether. He's a blood horse, he is, partly; not the part you see, of course— another part. And he's been a Prize Hackney, too, in his time— that was the time before you knew him, but you can still tell it on him at a glance, if you understand anything about horses. No, it's not to be thought of for a moment. All the same, how much might you be disposed to offer me for this beautiful young horse of mine?"

The Wind in the Willows by Kenneth Grahame.

1. a. Look at the first sentence of the literature passage. Notice that this literature passage contains a split quotation. The quotation is interrupted with *continued Toad*. The comma is placed after the first part of the quotation, and after *continued Toad*. The quotation mark will always go outside the comma, period, exclamation mark, or question mark.

   b. Copy the literature passage from dictation. Proofread and check your work. Make a spelling list from any misspelled words or use the following suggested list.

altogether	understand	glance
disposed	thought	hackney

   c. The word *thought* is spelled with **ough** to make the short /o/ sound. Most of these words are followed by the letter **t** when making this sound.

   > ### Spelling Tip
   > Some words like **thought** are spelled with **ough** to make the short /o/ sound.

Copy these words and underline **ough**. Say the words aloud as you write them.

bought   fought   sought   brought   wrought

d. Look up the word *hackney* in the dictionary and find out its meaning and etymology. Is it a word that we would hear used today? Why or why not?

e. Make a list of all the contractions you find in the literature passage. Opposite each contraction write the two words that make up the contraction.

Ex: they're - they are

f. Read the literature passage aloud. Does it sound funny? Do you think Toad really wants to sell his horse? Describe what kind of personality you think Toad would have.

2. a. Look at the fourth sentence of the literature passage. A comma is used to set off introductory words when they begin a sentence. These words are called interjections. An **interjection** is a word or phrase expressing strong or sudden feeling.

Common Interjections
no   yes   well
wow   oh my

An interjection may be separated by a comma or an exclamation mark. Be sure to capitalize the next word if using an exclamation mark.

Ex: Yes, I will help you.
     Wow! Did you see that?

1.
d. a horse used for carriage driving or riding etymology - Middle English

It is not used much today as horses are not used as a means of transportation and are rarely used to pull a carriage.

e. don't - do not
He's - he is
it's - it is

f. The passage is meant to be humorous. Yes, he wants to sell the horse, but you get the impression that Toad's representation of the horse is not quite truthful. From the literature passage we can guess that Toad is the type of character who exaggerates and is not quite truthful, but also that he is rather silly and not real clever.

2.
b. of course, all the same

b. Expressions used in a sentence for emphasis, to set off contrasting ideas, or to indicate an attitude by the speaker are called **parenthetical expressions**. These expressions are independent to the meaning of the sentence, and are set off by commas to separate it from the rest of the sentence. The sentence is independent if it is complete without the expression. Find two parenthetical expressions in the literature passage. Some of the most commonly used parenthetical expressions are listed below.

Common Parenthetical Expressions	
after all	incidentally
all the same	in fact
as a matter of fact	in my opinion
by the way	naturally
consequently	nevertheless
for example	of course
however	on the other hand
I believe (hope, suppose)	therefore

c. 1) Yes, I completed my homework before leaving for the game.
2) Natalie, on the other hand, does not need to practice the piano for a long time to learn a piece.
3) George, of course, will be happy to go with you.
4) No, I was not aware of the change made in your classes.
5) Incidentally, the time of the delivery has been changed to 9:00 A.M.

c. Add commas where needed in the following sentences to set off interjections or parenthetical expressions.

1) Yes I completed my homework before leaving for the game.
2) Natalie on the other hand does not need to practice the piano for a long time to learn a piece.
3) George of course will be happy to go with you.
4) No I was not aware of the change made in your classes.
5) Incidentally the time of the delivery has been changed to 9:00 A.M.

3. a. The literature passage is an example of humorous writing called **irony**. Irony always suggests something different from what is actually said.

    Ex: My doctor said I needed an activity to help calm my nerves so I decided to go skydiving.

    As we read the literature passage it is obvious that Toad's horse is not all he claims. What are some clues the author gives us in the passage to help us see this?

  b. Try writing a paragraph using the technique of irony. Look at Toad's example. Think of something amusing and make it have the opposite meaning.

  c. Review your spelling word for a practice test tomorrow.

4. a. Read the literature passage aloud, pausing for commas and dashes. Add expression and read the passage again as if you were Toad trying to convince someone to buy this horse. Can you envision the humor of this scene?

  b. Look at the classified advertisements section of your newspaper. Look over the advertisements for horses and other pets. Male horses are either called *stallions* or *geldings*. A female horse is called a *mare*. If you do not have a newspaper available, use the following example.

    FOR SALE: Chestnut Gelding, 12 years old, 14 hands, gentle for anyone to ride. Good-looking horse. $800. Call 1-437-555-8436 anytime.

    Notice that the height of a horse is described in *hands*. Each hand measurement is approximately 4 inches. If a horse is described as being 14 hands, then the horse is approximately 56 inches tall.

  c. When you have read a few ads, think of how Toad might describe his horse in a newspaper ad. Write an advertisement for Toad's horse as he might have written it.

  d. Take an oral or written spelling pretest.

3.
a. not the part you see ....

that was the time before you knew him .....

4.
c. Possible answer:
   FOR SALE: Prize Hackney Horse, young and beautiful, great blood lines, gentle disposition. A real steal at $5,000. Call Toad at (843)-555-8712.

5. a. Choose one of the following activities.

   1) Write the literature passage from dictation. Compare it with the model and correct any mistakes.

   2) Write another ad for an object you would like to sell. For example, you might write an ad to sell a bicycle, a skateboard, or a dog.

   3) Choose skills from the *Review Activities* on the next page.

Review Activities

Choose only the skills your student needs to review.

1. *Punctuation and Capitalization (Quotations and interjections)*
Rewrite the following paragraph correcting any mistakes in capitalization and adding any needed punctuation.

   yes there are many different breeds of horses continued the instructor some breeds are known for the size and strength of the horses while other breeds are known for their speed.

2. *Irony*
Which of the following sentences contain an example of irony?

   a. It was a beautiful day, so Marie decided to go to the beach.
   b. The one time Jack arrived at work on time the store was closed.

1. "Yes, there are many different breeds of horses," continued the instructor. "Some breeds are known for the size and strength of the horses while other breeds are known for their speed."

2. b

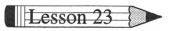

Teacher's Note: As your student completes each lesson, choose skills from the Review Activities that he needs. The Review Activities follow each lesson.

Before they had gone half a mile, the storm broke with all its strength. Lightning and thunder crashed and flashed together in a perfect fury! Stunned by the force of it, the children ran for shelter under the great oak tree that marked the halfway point between home and school. Its branches lashed and creaked, but it was something sturdy to cling to. Caddie and Warren and Hetty clung together under the tree, but Tom urged them on.

Caddie Woodlawn by Carol Ryrie Brink.
Used by permission, Macmillan Publishing Company.

1. a. Write the literature passage from dictation. Compare your copy to the passage and correct any errors. Make a list of any misspelled words or use the following list.

    strength   lightning   stunned
    sturdy   thunder   shelter

   b. Look at the spelling words *thunder* and *shelter*. The letter combination **er** is the most common way words make the **/er/** sound.

   Three other ways to spell the **/er/** sound is **ir**, **ur**, and **ear**.

   > **Spelling Tip:**
   > The **/er/** sound may be spelled er, ir, ur or ear.

   Copy these words and underline **er**, **ir**, **ur**, and **ear**. Say the words aloud as you write them.

term	sir	hurt	earth
serve	first	purse	early
fern	bird	burn	learn
certain	dirt	curl	pearl

1.

c. (with) all its strength
   (in) a perfect fury
   (by) the force
   (of) it
   (for) shelter
   (under) the great oak tree
   (between) home and school
   (under) the tree

c. Underline the prepositional phrases in the literature passage.
Circle the prepositions. Review the list of prepositions from
Lesson 21 if you need help.

d. Find and draw a box around the possessive pronoun *its* each
time it appears in the literature passage. What is the
antecedent of *its* in the first sentence of the literature
passage? What is the antecedent of *its* in the fourth
sentence?

e. Find two words in the literature passage with the prefix **be-**.
Review your list of prefixes and find its meaning.

f. Using your prefix list, add a prefix to each of the following
underlined root words to correctly complete each sentence.

   1) If an item is _____available, it means you will not be able
   to obtain it.
   2) The cat is _____active if it is sleeping.
   3) If you broke the vase, you will have to _____place it.
   4) I hope the weatherman's _____cast is correct for
   this weekend.
   5) We will _____port this product for sale in France.

1.
d. 1st - the storm;
   4th - the oak tree

e. be- on or away;
   Possible examples:
   before, between

f. 1) unavailable
   2) inactive
   3) replace
   4) forecast
   5) export

2. a. It is important not to confuse the possessive pronoun *its*
with the contraction *it's*. Write two sentences using the
words *its* and *it's* correctly.

b. Look at the first sentence in the literature passage.

Before they had gone half a mile, the storm broke with all its
strength.

This sentence contains a comma separating a phrase from the
remaining sentence.

Read the first part of this sentence: *Before they had gone
half a mile.* This phrase does not express a complete
thought and cannot stand alone as a sentence. This is called
a **dependent clause.**

Now read the second part of the sentence: *the storm broke with all its strength.* This phrase expresses a complete thought and can stand alone as a sentence. This is called an **independent clause**.

When a dependent clause begins a sentence, it is separated from the independent clause by a comma.

Ex: *Although the wind had blown hard*, there was no damage done to the house.

2.

c. 1st part - dependent clause;
2nd part - independent clause

c. Look at the third sentence in the literature passage. Is the first part of the sentence a dependent or independent clause? Is the second part of the sentence a dependent or independent clause?

d. Underline the dependent clauses in the following sentences. If the sentence begins with a dependent clause, be sure to place a comma between the dependent and independent clause.

d. 1) <u>Since I started jogging,</u> I have been steadily losing weight.
2) <u>If you wish to attend the meeting,</u> you must be ready at 9:00 A.M.
3) I will practice playing the piano <u>until I have mastered the skill.</u>
4) <u>When other people have needs,</u> we should try to help them.
5) Everyone rejoiced <u>when he arrived home safely.</u>

1) Since I started jogging I have been steadily losing weight.
2) If you wish to attend the meeting you must be ready at 9:00 A.M.
3) I will practice playing the piano until I have mastered the skill.
4) When other people have needs we should try to help them.
5) Everyone rejoiced when he arrived home safely.

e. Read the literature passage aloud with expression. Be sure to pause at the commas and emphasize the second sentence of the passage.

f. Answers will vary.

f. What do you think will happen next? Write the next sentence as if you were the author.

3. a. Read the literature passage again. Make a list of the things in the order which they happened in the story. When we write about events in the order in which they happened, we are placing the events in correct **sequence**.

   Ex: The storm broke.
          Lightning and thunder crashed and flashed.

   b. Use your list to tell the story to your teacher. Did you have enough information? Are the events listed in the correct sequence? Add to your list if you need to.

   c. Using your list, write a paragraph about the literature passage without looking at it. Be sure to write the events in correct sequence. Compare your work with the model. Did you include everything? Are the events in the correct order?

   d. Review your spelling words.

4. a. The use of expressive verbs in the writing process allows the writing to come alive for the reader. It can be the difference between the writing being drab and uninteresting, or being captivating and exciting. Read the following sentences. Decide which of the sentences makes use of expressive verbs.

   1) As I walked down the beach, I saw the waves come ashore.
   2) As I strolled down the beach, I watched the waves crash ashore.

   b. Note that the only difference in the two sentences above is the verbs that were used. Look over the literature passage. What verbs would you consider expressive?

   c. Read over the paragraph you wrote in **3c**. Are there any verbs you can change to more expressive verbs? Use a thesaurus to help you find expressive verbs to add to your writing. Edit until you have done your best. Make a neat copy of your paragraph.

   d. Take an oral or written spelling pretest.

3.
a. 1) The storm broke.
   2) Lightning and thunder crashed and flashed.
   3) Children ran for the tree.
   4) Branches lashed and creaked.
   5) They clung together under tree.
   6) Tom urged them on.

4.
a. the 2nd sentence

b. Possible answer: broke, crashed, flashed, stunned, lashed, creaked, clung, urged

5. a. Choose one of the following activities.

    1) Write the literature passage from dictation. Be sure to use correct punctuation and spelling.

    2) Using the sentence you added to the literature passage in **2f**, continue writing the story as if you were the author. Be sure to make use of expressive verbs.

    3) Choose skills from the *Review Activities* on the next page.

Review Activities

Choose only the skills your student needs to review.

1. *Prepositions; Its and It's; and Antecedents*
   Underline the prepositions. Draw a box around the contraction
   for *it is*. Circle the possessive pronoun for *it,* and draw an
   arrow to the antecedent.

   The Privet Hawk Moth hides on tree bark or under leaves
   during the day, but after the sun sets, it flies around the area
   looking for nectar. The moth uses its long proboscis to
   drink nectar from flowers; it's similar to a straw. After the
   sun rises, the moth grabs onto a tree and remains there until
   dusk comes again.

2. *Dependent Clauses*
   Write one sentence with a dependent clause at the beginning of
   the sentence, and another sentence with a dependent clause at
   the end of a sentence. Be sure to punctuate the sentences
   correctly.

3. *Correct Sequence*
   Read over the following sentences. Decide the correct
   sequential order and place the correct order number in front of
   the sentence. The first one is done for you.

   _____ The thaw causes the streams and rivers to swell.
   __1__ Spring brings amazing change to the land.
   _____ As winter ends, the hours of daylight grow longer
          and the temperature grows warmer.
   _____ Finally, new buds begin to appear on the trees.
   _____ The land has completed its change, and a new season
          has begun.
   _____ The increased temperatures cause the winter snows to
          melt.
   _____ As the thaw continues, wildflowers and green grasses
          begin to bloom.

1. **The Privet Hawk Moth
   hides <u>on</u> tree bark or
   <u>under</u> leaves <u>during</u> the
   day, but <u>after</u> the sun
   sets, it flies <u>around</u> the
   area looking for nectar.
   The moth uses (its) long
   proboscis <u>to</u> drink nectar
   <u>from</u> flowers; it's
   similar <u>to</u> a straw. <u>After</u>
   the sun rises, the moth
   grabs <u>onto</u> a tree and
   remains there <u>until</u> dusk
   comes again.**

2. **Answers will vary.**

3. **4
    1
    2
    6
    7
    3
    5**

4. Possible answers:

a. squat, perch

b. step, march, amble, stroll

c. sprint, bound, dart, scamper

d. tell, state, announce, declare

e. observe, inspect, examine, gaze

4. *Expressive Verbs*

Using a thesaurus, write expressive verbs that could be substituted for the following verbs.

a. sit

b. walk

c. run

d. say

e. see

The Gettysburg Address

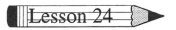

✐ **Teacher's Note:** Your student will continue with the Gettysburg Address in Lesson 25.

The Gettysburg Address

Fourscore and seven years ago our fathers brought forth on this continent a new nation, conceived in liberty, and dedicated to the proposition that all men are created equal. Now we are engaged in a great civil war, testing whether that nation, or any nation so conceived and so dedicated, can long endure. We are met on a great battlefield of that war. We have come to dedicate a portion of that field as a final resting place for those who here gave their lives that that nation might live. It is altogether fitting and proper that we should do this.

But, in a larger sense, we cannot dedicate -- we cannot consecrate -- we cannot hallow this ground. The brave men, living and dead, who struggled here, have consecrated it far above our poor power to add or detract. The world will little note nor long remember what we say here, but it can never forget what they did here. It is for us, the living, rather, to be dedicated here to the unfinished work which they who fought here have thus far so nobly advanced. It is rather for us to be here dedicated to the great task remaining before us, — that from these honored dead we take increased devotion to that cause for which they gave the last full measure of devotion; that we here highly resolve that these dead shall not have died in vain; that this nation, under God, shall have a new birth of freedom; and that government of the people, by the people, for the people, shall not perish from the earth.

Gettysburg Address by Abraham Lincoln.

1. a. Read the text of the *Gettysburg Address*. Carefully look over the bold text portion and write that part from dictation. Compare your dictation copy to the model to see if you made any mistakes. Correct any errors you find. Make a spelling list from any misspelled words or use the following suggested list.

conceived	portion	endure
proposition	continent	nation

   b. Most words spell **/shun/** as in nation with **-tion**. Other words spell it with **-sion**.

   > ### Spelling Tip
   > Most words spell the **/shun/** sound with **-tion**. Other words spell it with **-sion**.

   Copy these words and underline **-tion** and **-sion**. Say the words aloud as you write them.

emotion	division
lotion	lesion
caption	pension
sensation	vacation
tension	vision

   c. The speech in the literature passage contains a number of prefixes. Find the words that contain the prefixes **con-** and **en-**.

   Add these prefixes to your prefix list along with their definitions and word examples. The prefix **con-** means *together* or *with*, and the prefix **en-** means *in* or *into*.

1.

c. continent, conceived, consecrate
engaged, endure

con-: together or with
Possible examples:
confirm, continue

en-: in or into
Possible examples:
enrich, enact

d. 1) encompass
   2) construct
   3) constellation
   4) engage
   5) congregate

2.
a. 1) to form a concept or
idea
   2) to set apart for a
special purpose
   3) a purpose or plan that
is set forth
   4) four times twenty (80)
   5) become involved in
   6) to stand or bear

b. Possible answers:
   1) conceived - created
   2) dedicate - appropriate
   3) proposition - proposal
   4) fourscore - eighty
   5) engaged - undertook
   6) endure - tolerate

d. Add either the prefix **con-** or **en-** to complete the following words. Use the definitions provided to help you choose the correct prefix.

1) _____compass (to shut in all around)
2) _____struct (to build by fitting parts together)
3) _____stellation (a gathering of stars)
4) _____gage (to draw into, to involve)
5) _____gregate (to meet together)

2. a. Although the *Gettysburg Address* is a famous speech, there may be several words that you are unfamiliar with. Look up the following words in the dictionary and write a definition for each.

1) conceived   4) fourscore
2) dedicate   5) engaged
3) proposition   6) endure

b. Using the same words from **2a**, use your thesaurus to find synonyms for each word.

c. Look at the bolded part of the *Gettysburg Address* in the literature passage. Rewrite the passage using the synonyms you found in **2b**. Does this help you to better understand the speech?

3. a. Find the word *their* in the last sentence of the bolded part of the literature passage. The word *their* is a possessive pronoun, but it also has two homonyms. Remember, homonyms are words that sound the same but have a different meaning and usually a different spelling.

Ex: We will travel to *their* house.
      (*Their* is a possessive pronoun.)

      There will be a concert at the park. I will meet you over *there*.
      (*There* is usually an adverb.)

      They're good friends of ours.
      (*They're* is a contraction for they are.)

b. Complete the following sentences with *their*, *there* or *they're*.

1) _____ are many miles more to travel before we reach our destination.
2) _____ ideas really helped to make this project a success.
3) _____ very surprised they have been chosen to receive the award.
4) The ball flew over _____.
5) _____ dog loves to romp in our yard.

c. The *Gettysburg Address* is a powerful, moving speech. Using an encyclopedia, look under Abraham Lincoln or Gettysburg, and find out some information about the background of the speech. You may use the following questions as a guide.

1) When was the speech made?
2) Why was it given?
3) Why is it so powerful and remembered?
4) Where was it given?
5) How many copies did Lincoln make of the speech?
6) Did Lincoln add anything as he was speaking? (something not on the original draft)

d. Begin to study the *Gettysburg Address*. Plan to have it memorized by the end of next week's lesson. (Only the bolded text portion is necessary to memorize although you can memorize the whole speech if you wish.)

e. Review your spelling words.

4. a. Take your notes from **3c** and write two to three paragraphs sharing something that you found interesting about the *Gettysburg Address*.

b. Take an oral or written spelling pretest.

3.
b. 1) There
   2) Their
   3) They're
   4) there
   5) Their

c. 1) Nov. 19, 1863
   2) It was given as a dedication speech at a ceremony dedicating the battlefield of Gettysburg as a national cemetery for soldiers who were killed in that battle during the Civil War.
   3) The speech was remembered because it set forth the highest purposes of the Civil War and a statement of democracy.
   4) It was given at the battlefield of Gettysburg.
   5) five copies
   6) He added the words "under God" as he spoke.

5. a. Write the bolded text portion of the literature passage from dictation. This will also help you to memorize the speech. Check your copy for any mistakes in spelling or punctuation.

   b. Practice saying the bolded portion of the literature passage aloud paying special attention to the punctuation. Be sure to pause for the commas.

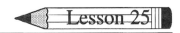

1. a. One method that will help you memorize the *Gettysburg Address* is to prepare index cards with key words or pictures to help you remember specific parts of the speech. For example, you might draw a picture of North America to give you a clue to the word *continent*. After you have finished preparing your cards, number them by placing a small number in the right hand corner. This will help you keep the cards in the correct order.

   b. Continue to study and memorize the speech using your index cards.

2. a. Read the entire *Gettysburg Address* slowly and carefully. Every good speech has several parts: the **introduction**, the **body**, and the **conclusion**. Identify these parts of the *Gettysburg Address* with your teacher.

   b. Continue memorizing the speech.

2.
a. Introduction - first sentence
Conclusion - last sentence
Body - the sentences in between

3. a. Prepare to make an oral presentation. Use your index cards to practice your speech. Record your speech with a tape recorder, then play it back and listen to yourself. Are there any parts you need to improve?

   b. Follow these guidelines when preparing an oral presentation.

Oral Presentation Checklist

___ 1) Read the speech aloud several times. Try to understand the meaning and the mood of the speech.

___ 2) Use your voice where emphasis is needed and pause accordingly.

___ 3) Speak clearly and loudly. Be sure not to rush through the speech.

___ 4) Look at your audience as if you are speaking directly to them.

___ 5) Stand straight; do not slouch.

___ 6) Practice in front of a mirror.

4. Give an oral presentation of the speech to your group or family. Ask them for any advice as to how you could improve your presentation.

5. You are now very familiar with the *Gettysburg Address*. Write a paragraph telling about the bolded part of the speech. This will show how well you understand what was said. A retelling of a speech (or any written material) in your own words is called a **paraphrase**.

   Ex: Eighty-seven years ago our forefathers formed a new government in this land, based on freedom etc.

Assessment 4
(Lessons 20 - 25)

1. Rewrite the first two sentences of the literature passage in Lesson 20 as if someone else were telling the story (third person).

2. Write a sentence using *to, two, too.*

3. How are pronouns used?

4. List at least three pronouns that show possession (ex: his). Do possessive pronouns ever need an apostrophe?

5. Rewrite the following phrases using possessive nouns:

   a. the book that belongs to John
   b. the bikes that belong to the boys
   c. the sister of Pat

6. Find at least three prepositions in the literature passage in Lesson 20.

7. Copy the following sentences and add the correct punctuation:

   In fact John said all we have to do is read the directions. I am sure we will be able to build the model by ourselves.

8. Write a word with the prefix **be-**.

9. Write a word with the suffix **-tion**.

1. He was now come to the unhappy anniversary of his landing. He cast up the notches on his post, and found he had been on shore three hundred and sixty-five days.

2. Possible answer:
   Give this *to* Bob.
   I have *two* cats.
   Bill will come with us, *too.*

3. Pronouns are used to replace nouns.

4. Possible answers: my, mine, your, yours, his, her, hers, its, our, ours, your, yours, their, theirs
   Possessive pronouns never use an apostrophe.

5.
   a. John's book
   b. boys' bikes
   c. Pat's sister

6. upon, with, to, in, of, along, on

7. "In fact," John said, "all we have to do is read the directions. I am sure we will be able to build the model ourselves."

8. Possible answers: become, beside, etc.

9. Possible answers: vacation, edition, etc.

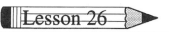

Teacher's Note: As your student completes each lesson, choose skills from the Review Activities that he needs. The Review Activities follow each lesson.

The dog-wanting disease never did leave me altogether. With the new work I was doing, helping Papa, it just kind of burned itself down and left a big sore on my heart. Every time I'd see a coon track down in our fields, or along the riverbanks, the old sore would get all festered up and start hurting again.

Just when I had given up all hope of ever owning a good hound, something wonderful happened. The good Lord figured I had hurt enough, and it was time to lend a helping hand.

It all started one day while I was hoeing corn down in our field close to the river. Across the river, a party of fishermen had been camped for several days. I heard the old Maxwell car as it snorted and chugged its way out of the bottoms. I knew they were leaving. Throwing down my hoe, I ran down to the river and waded across at a place called the Shannon Ford. I hurried to the camp ground.

Where the Red Fern Grows by Wilson Rawls.
Used by permission, Doubleday Books, Dell Publishing Group.

1.

a. The boy wanted a dog so badly that his heart ached not to have one.

1. a. Read the literature passage. This boy had a "dog-wanting disease" that left a big sore in his heart. Tell your teacher what you think this means.

   b. Write the bold part of the literature passage from dictation. Check your copy with the passage and make a list of any misspelled words or use the following suggested spelling list.

hoeing	waded
snorted	leaving
chugged	hurried

c. Each of the suggested spelling words has a suffix. Write the root word next to each word. What changes were made in each of the root words in order to add the suffix? Which spelling word is an exception to the rule concerning adding a suffix beginning with a vowel to a root word ending with a silent *e*?

d. Look at the literature passage. List all the words that are capitalized that are not the first word of a sentence or the pronoun *I*. Determine why each word is capitalized. If you are not sure, check with the capitalization rules in Lessons 6 and 16.

2. a. Find the contraction in the first paragraph of the literature passage. Write it as two words.

b. Find the word *its* in the third paragraph of the literature passage. Is it a possessive pronoun or a contraction? If it is a possessive pronoun, what is its antecedent?

c. Read the first sentence of the second paragraph of the literature passage. What do you think happened? Often the author gives us hints as to what is going to happen in the story. This is called **foreshadowing**. What hints do you find in the literature passage that help you to predict what will happen in this story?

d. Write the next paragraph of the story telling what you think happened.

3. a. Looking at the last paragraph of the literature passage, draw a box around all the prepositions. There are nine. If you are unsure of the prepositions, refer to your list of common prepositions oin Lesson 21.

1.
c. hoe (exception - just add *ing*),
snort (just add *ed*),
chug (double the last consonant before adding *ed*),
wade (drop the silent *e* before adding *ed*),
leave (drop the silent *e* before adding *ing*),
hurry (change the *y* to *i* before adding *ed*)

d. Papa - proper name
Lord - any name referring to God
Maxwell - brand name of a product
Shannon Ford - geographical place

2.
a. I'd - I would

b. its - possessive pronoun
antecedent - the old Maxwell car

c. The dog-wanting disease never did leave me altogether. Just when I had given up all hope of ever owning a good hound, something wonderful happened. The good Lord figured I had hurt enough, and it was time to lend a helping hand. Across the river, a party of fishermen had been camped for several days. I hurried to the camp ground.

d. Answers will vary

3.
a. in, to, Across, of, for, of, to, at, to

b. in-field,
   to-river,
   across-river,
   of-fishermen,
   for-days,
   of-bottoms,
   to-river,
   at-place,
   to-camp ground

c. 1) to - neighbor
   2) in - bookcase
   3) of - birds; by - river
   4) across - bridge; into - county
   5) outside - lines

b. For each preposition you boxed ask, "What?". Underline the noun that answers that question.

   Ex: in our field
   Ask yourself, "In what?" In field.

   Each word you underlined is called the **object of the preposition**. Some words that are used as prepositions can also be used as other parts of speech. Remember, for a word to be a preposition, it must have an object.

c. Circle the preposition and underline its object in the following sentences.

   Ex: We will spend the day swimming (at) the pool.

   1) Mary delivered fresh bread to her neighbor.
   2) I found the novel in the bookcase.
   3) We will look for different types of birds by the river.
   4) We must travel across the bridge and into the next county.
   5) The ball bounced outside the boundary lines.

d. Review your spelling words.

4. a. Have you ever wanted anything as badly as this boy? Did you receive what you wanted?

b. Write a friendly letter explaining your experience to a friend. Follow the format for a friendly letter found in Lesson 5. Be sure to include how you felt.

c. Take an oral or written spelling pretest.

5. a. Choose one of the following activities.

   1) Write the bolded part of the literature passage from dictation. Were you able to spell all the words correctly? Did knowing the root of a word help you with your spelling?

   2) Choose skills from the *Review Activities* on the next page.

Review Activities

Choose only the skills your student needs to review.

1. *Capitalization and Conjunctions*
Add capitalization and punctuation to the following paragraph.
Underline any conjunctions.

in europe during the middle ages falconry or hawking as it was sometimes called was a favorite sport. hawks falcons and eagles were trained to respond to their owners commands and hunt small prey. the bird was hooded and sat on his owners gloved arm. the hood was removed when small game was spotted and the bird would swoop down on its prey. the bird would catch the animal return to his owner with the prey and receive its reward of a piece of meat.

2. *Foreshadowing*
Write a paragraph that uses foreshadowing to give the reader a hint of what is going to happen next.

3. *Object of the Preposition*
Write two sentences that contain a preposition and its direct object.

4. *Friendly Letter*
Write a letter to someone who has done something nice for you recently telling that person how much you appreciate it.

1. **In Europe during the Middle Ages falconry, <u>or</u> hawking as it was sometimes called, was a favorite sport. Hawks, falcons, <u>and</u> eagles were trained to respond to their owner's commands <u>and</u> hunt small prey. The bird was hooded <u>and</u> sat on his owner's gloved arm. The hood was removed when small game was spotted, <u>and</u> the bird would swoop down on its prey. The bird would catch the animal, return to his owner with the prey, <u>and</u> receive its reward of a piece of meat.**

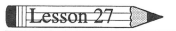
✐ **Teacher's Note:** As your student completes each lesson, choose skills from the Review Activities that he needs. The Review Activities follow each lesson.

It was always a pleasure to prowl where fishermen had camped. I usually could find things: a fish line, or a forgotten fish pole. On one occasion, I found a beautiful knife stuck in the bark of a sycamore tree, forgotten by a careless fisherman. But on that day, I found the greatest of treasures, a sportsman's magazine, discarded by the campers. It was a real treasure for a country boy. Because of that magazine, my entire life was changed.

Where the Red Fern Grows by Wilson Rawls.
Used by permission, Doubleday Books, Dell Publishing Group.

1. a. Write the literature passage from dictation. Compare your copy with the passage and make a list of any misspelled words or use the following suggested list.

sycamore	occasion	magazine
discarded	sportsman	fisherman

   Which of the suggested spelling words are compound nouns? What word is common to both compound nouns?

1.

a. sportsman, fisherman
   man

   b. Look at the title of the literature passage. Copy the title paying close attention to the capitalization. Capitalize the first word and every other important word of a title. If handwritten, underline the entire title; if computer generated, use italics.

   Ex: <u>Where the Red Fern Grows</u> - handwritten
   Where the Red Fern Grows - computer generated

c. careless
   care - root word
   The suffix changes the meaning from care to without care.

-less: without
Possible examples:
motionless, helpless

   c. This literature passage contains the suffix **-less**. Find the word in the passage that contains this suffix. What is the root of this word? The suffix **-less** means *without*. How does the suffix change the meaning of the root word? Add this suffix to your list along with its definition and word examples.

d. Find the prefix **dis-** in the literature passage. This prefix means *apart, away, reverse.* Add this to your prefix list along with its definition and word examples.

> ### Spelling Tip
> When adding a prefix to a word do not add or drop any letters. If the last letter of the prefix and the first letter of the root word are the same, the word will contain a double letter.

Add prefixes to the following root words.

1) dis + satisfied =
2) dis + appear =
3) un + necessary =
4) im + mature =
5) dis + similar =

e. Many times a prefix added to a word changes the meaning of the word to mean the opposite. Refer to your prefix list to make words of opposite meaning.

Ex: sufficient (not sufficient) - insufficient

1) necessary (not necessary) =
2) expensive (not expensive) =
3) correct (not correct) =
4) fair (not fair) =
5) ripe (not ripe) =

2. a. Look at the first sentence of the literature passage. The subject, *it,* is a singular subject, therefore the singular verb, *was,* is used. A verb must agree with the subject in number. If the subject is singular, then the verb must be singular. If the subject is plural, then the verb must be plural. The following information will help you in determining whether a verb is singular or plural.

1.

d. dis-: apart, away, reverse;
   Possible examples:
   discarded, disappear

d. 1) dissatisfied
   2) disappear
   3) unnecessary
   4) immature
   5) dissimilar

e. 1) unnecessary
   2) inexpensive
   3) incorrect
   4) unfair
   5) unripe

Singular Verbs

1) A verb ending in **s** is usually considered singular.
   Ex: He looks. Susan writes. The dog runs.
2) The verbs *am, is, was, does,* and *has* are singular.

Plural Verbs

1) Plural verbs usually do not end in *s*.
   Ex: They look. Susan and Jim write. The dogs run.
2) The verbs *are, were, do,* and *have* are plural.

b. The subject of a sentence determines whether a singular or plural verb is used. Look at the following guidelines for choosing a singular or plural verb.

A singular verb is used when:

1) The subject is singular.
   Ex: The cricket is chirping.

2) The subject is e*ach, nobody, anyone, everyone, either,* or *neither*. These are singular words.
   Ex: Everyone agrees with your choice.

3) The singular subjects are connected by the words *or* or *nor*.
   Ex: Linda or Mary is babysitting.

4) The subject is a collective noun (one that names a group).
   Ex: My family attends church together.

5) The subject expresses an amount of money.
   Ex: Two dollars is the amount I owe.

A plural verb is used when:

1) The subject is plural.
   Ex: The kittens are cute.

2) The subject is *you.*
   Ex: Are you coming with us?

3) The subjects are connected by *and.*
   Ex: Jim and Tom are working together.

4) Plural subjects are connected by *or* or *nor.*
   Ex: Horses or ponies are fun to ride.

---

c. Often word phrases separate the subject and verb in a
   sentence. Do not let these word phrases confuse you when
   determining subject/verb agreement.

   Ex: The *rabbits* <u>in the meadow</u> *eat* the clover.
        (The prepositional phrase *in the meadow* does not
        affect the subject/verb agreement of *rabbits eat.*)

2.

d. 1) sleeps
2) take
3) drinks
4) is
5) are
6) were
7) do
8) pray
9) loves
10) travel
11) was
12) is
13) have
14) are
15) agree

e. 1) The Princess and Curdie
2) The House of Sixty Fathers
3) Trail of Apple Blossoms
4) The Cabin Faced West

3.

a. it, I, my

d. Underline the verb that agrees with the subject in number in the following sentences.

1) Our dog often (*sleep*, *sleeps*) under the porch.
2) The students in the class (*take*, *takes*) their notebooks home.
3) The hummingbird (*drink*, *drinks*) from our feeders.
4) Three dollars (*is*, *are*) the price of admission.
5) Several runners (*is*, *are*) entered in this race.
6) The fish of the coral reef (*was*, *were*) very beautiful.
7) The leaves on this tree (*do*, *does*) not change color in the fall.
8) The members of the church (*pray*, *prays*) for our country.
9) The squirrel outside gathering acorns (*love*, *loves*) to jump through the trees.
10) People (*travel*, *travels*) on this roadway daily.
11) Each of the workers (*was*, *were*) capable of completing the job.
12) Either John or Hank (*is*, *are*) going to drive to the store.
13) (*Has*, *Have*) Martha and Deanna finished the assignment?
14) I hope you (*is*, *are*) coming with us to dinner.
15) Neither the boys nor the girls (*agree*, *agrees*) that the game was played fairly.

e. Capitalize and underline the following titles of books.

1) the princess and curdie
2) the house of sixty fathers
3) trail of apple blossoms
4) the cabin faced west

3. a. Pronouns are used to replace nouns. Find the three different pronouns in the literature passage.

b. The literature passage is written in the first person. This means that the author is writing from his point of view, using the pronoun *I*. Most stories, however, are written in the third person, using the pronouns *he, she,* and *they*. Rewrite the literature passage in the third person.

> Ex: It was always a pleasure to prowl where fishermen had camped. He usually could find . . .

c. You have learned to capitalize and underline titles of books. Here is a list of other titles that are also underlined.

magazines	works of art
newspapers	music albums
television programs	ships
movies	trains
plays	aircraft

d. Capitalize and underline titles in the following sentences.

> Ex: The Gainesville Sun is a source for daily news.
> The *Gainesville Sun* is a source for daily news.

1) where the red fern grows is an excellent book for young boys and girls to read. (book)
2) The space shuttle, columbia, is orbiting the earth at this time. (aircraft)
3) I am cooking a recipe I cut out of the family circle. (magazine)
4) The doulos will be docking here today. (ship)
5) Shakespeare's hamlet will be performed by the actors of the Community Theater. (play)

e. Review your spelling words.

4. a. An adverb describes a verb, adjective, or another adverb. They tell us how, when, where, or to what extent or degree. Find two adverbs in the literature passage.

3.

b. It was always a pleasure to prowl where fishermen had camped. He usually could find things: a fish line, or a forgotten fish pole. On one occasion, he found a beautiful knife stuck in the bark of a sycamore tree, forgotten by a careless fisherman. But on that day, he found the greatest of treasures, a sportsman's magazine, discarded by the campers. It was a real treasure for a country boy. Because of that magazine, his entire life was changed.

✐ **Teacher's Note: Titles may be underlined if handwritten; italicized if computer generated.**

d. 1) Where the Red Fern Grows OR *Where the Red Fern Grows*
2) Columbia OR *Columbia*
3) Family Circle OR *Family Circle*
4) Doulos OR *Doulos*
5) Hamlet OR *Hamlet*

4.
a. always, usually

b. Locate the punctuation mark used in the literature passage before the list of things the boy found. This mark is a **colon**. The colon (:) is used to introduce a list. Often the colon is preceded by summary words such as *things, as follows, the following,* or *these.*

Ex: Be sure to bring the following things: drawing paper, soft lead pencils, and erasers.

c. Colons are also used as follows:

1) Between the chapter and verse of a Bible reference
   Ex: Romans 10:9

2) After the salutation of a business letter
   Ex: Gentlemen:

3) Between the hour and minute when referring to time
   Ex: 2:45

d. Add colons and commas as needed in the following sentences. Remember that items in a series are separated by commas. (Refer to Lesson 10, **3a** if you need further review of this punctuation rule.)

1) These are the items we need for the trip coolers snacks sleeping bags and sheets.
2) The meeting will begin at exactly 8 00 P.M.
3) The children chosen for the team are as follows James Karen Robert Todd and Sandy.
4) My favorite Scripture verse is II Corinthians 5 17.

e. Pretend you are the young boy described in the literature passage. Write a business letter to *Field and Stream,* 2147 Bird Dog Avenue, Spokane, WA 63458, requesting information on purchasing a hunting dog. This letter will not be mailed; it is only for the purpose of acquainting you with the format of a business letter. Use the following model as an example for your letter. The parts of the business letter are labeled in italics for your information. Do not copy these words when you are writing your letter.

4.
d. 1) These are the items we need for the trip: coolers, snacks, sleeping bags, and sheets.
2) The meeting will begin at exactly 8:00 P.M.
3) The children chosen for the team are as follows: James, Karen, Robert, Todd, and Sandy.
4) My favorite Scripture verse is II Corinthians 5:17.

(*Heading*)
1234 Main Street
Seattle, WA 63782
September 8, 1997

(*Inside Address*)
Field and Stream
2147 Bird Dog Avenue
Spokane, WA 63458

(*Salutation or Greeting*)
Gentlemen:

(*Body*)
I read your article on purchasing hunting dogs in the August edition and would like to have the additional information you offer along with the list of breeders. Please send this information to me at the address listed below:

Mr. James Harris
1234 Main Street
Seattle, WA 63782

Thank you for your attention in this matter.

(*Closing*)
Sincerely,

(*Signature*)
James Harris

f. Take an oral or written spelling pretest.

5. a. Choose one of the following activities.

　　1) Write the literature passage from dictation and check your copy.

　　2) Write a paragraph describing your favorite magazine. Use adverbs to help describe why you find it so interesting. Remember to underline the title of the magazine and capitalize the first word and every important word in the title.

　　3) Choose skills from the *Review Activities* on the next page.

Review Activities

Choose only the skills your student needs to review.

1. *Suffix*
   Add a suffix from your list of suffixes to the following root words to fit the definition given. If you are not sure about a word, check your dictionary.

   a. heart_____ (*without heart or compassion*)
   b. thank_____ (*full of thanks*)
   c. quick_____ (*manner of quick*)
   d. connect_____ (*the state of being connected*)
   e. paint_____ (*one who paints*)

2. *Prefix*
   Add the prefixes to complete the following words.

   a. dis + solve =
   b. im + material =
   c. im + practical =
   d. un + written =
   e. un + navigable =

3. *Subject/Verb Agreement*
   Choose the correct verb to complete the following sentences:

   a. Everyone (*is, are*) going to the lecture tonight.
   b. The panther (*run, runs*) swiftly through the underbrush.
   c. (*Do, Does*) Rick and Mary know where to meet us?
   d. James or John (*has, have*) the skill to play the piano.
   e. The paintings on the wall (*contain, contains*) beautiful colors.

1. a. heartless
   b. thankful
   c. quickly
   d. connection
   e. painter

2. a. dissolve
   b. immaterial
   c. impractical
   d. unwritten
   e. unnavigable

3. a. is
   b. runs
   c. do
   d. has
   e. contain

4. a. 3 - He
b. 1 - I, my
c. 2 - You

4. *First, Second, and Third Person*
   Read each of the following sentences. Indicate whether the sentence is written in first (**1**), second (**2**), or third person (**3**). Underline the pronouns that help you in making your decision.

   a. _____He drove into the placid pool of water and broke through the surface of the water with a shout.
   b. _____I ran as I had never run before; my lungs were ready to burst.
   c. _____You must pay attention if you hope to succeed in mastering this skill.

5.
a. Miami Herald OR *Miami Herald*
b. Little Women OR *Little Women*
c. Mona Lisa OR *Mona Lisa*
d. Time OR *Time*
e. Christy OR *Christy*

5. *Titles*
   Capitalize and underline the titles in the following sentences.

   a. The miami herald printed a story about the many boating accidents in their area. (newspaper)
   b. little women is based on the life of author, Louisa May Alcott. (book)
   c. The mona lisa is on display at the Louvre in Paris. (painting)
   d. I read an article about the future of the economy in time. (magazine)
   e. The television program, christy, is based on the novel by Catherine Marshall. (television program)

6. a) 8:00 A.M.
b) Romans 10:9
c) the ground:
d) fall:

6. *Colon*
   Add colons to the following sentences.

   a) We will begin hiking the trail at 800 A.M.
   b) The pastor based his message on Romans 10 9.
   c) The following things were littering the ground cans, newspapers, and bottles.
   d) You will be taking these subjects this fall earth science, literature, and algebra.

7. *Business letter*
   Write a business letter to the company of your choice.

8. *Capitalization and Punctuation*
   Add punctuation and capitalization in the following paragraph.

what do you feel is our nation's greatest resource water is the greatest natural resource our country has we most often think of water in terms of drinking water and water for household needs there are many other ways that water is valuable some of these uses are as follows transportation irrigation and hydroelectric power the united states would not be the rich nation it is today without the ability to transport its goods down the mississippi river or use the waters of the colorado river to water farmland in the west much of the electrical power in the west is generated by hydroelectric power plants no other natural resource is as valuable to our nation as our water supply

8.   **What do you feel is our nation's greatest resource? Water is the greatest natural resource our country has. We most often think of water in terms of drinking water and water for household needs. There are many other ways that water is valuable. Some of these uses are as follows: transportation, irrigation, and hydroelectric power. The United Sates would not be the rich nation it is today without the ability to transport its goods down the Mississippi River or use the waters of the Colorado River to water farmland in the West. Much of the electrical power in the West is generated by hydroelectric power plants. No other natural resource is as valuable to our nation as our water supply.**

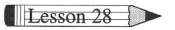

It was almost quite dark, the girls were getting tired, and as Bobbie said, it was past bedtime, when suddenly Phyllis cried, "What's that?"

And she pointed to the canal boat. Smoke was coming from the chimney of the cabin, had indeed been curling softly into the soft evening air all the time—but now other wreaths of smoke were rising, and these were from the cabin door.

"It's on fire—that's all," said Peter, calmly. "Serve him right."

*"Oh—how **can** you?" cried Phyllis. "Think of the poor dear dog."*

The Railway Children by E. Nesbit.

Teacher's Note: As your student completes each lesson, choose skills from the Review Activities that he needs. The Review Activities follow each lesson.

Teacher's Note: You may want to reassure your student that as the story continues, you find that the dog is unharmed.

1. a. Read the literature passage paying close attention to how quotation marks are used. Written conversation is called **dialogue**.

   b. The last part of the literature passage is a conversation. When writing dialogue, begin a new paragraph when there is a change in speaker.

   c. Write the literature passage from dictation. Proofread and correct your work. Make a spelling list from the words you misspelled or use the following suggested list.

bedtime	chimney	wreaths
suddenly	pointed	softly

   d. Some words, like *chimney* are spelled with the ending **ey**. Other words, like *candy* are spelled with just **y**. It is helpful to know the correct spelling of these words so you can spell the plural form correctly.

To form the plural of words ending with a consonant before the **y**, change the **y** to **i** and add **es**. To form the plural of words ending with a vowel before the **y**, just add **s**.

Ex: chimney - chimneys
    candy - candies

> ## Spelling Tip
> To form the plural of words ending in **y** preceded by a consonant, change the **y** to **i** and add **es**. Otherwise, just add **s**.

e. Copy these words and write its plural form.

chimney	monkey	donkey
candy	pony	sky

f. Which words from the suggested spelling list are used as adverbs in the literature passage? What suffix helps to identify these words as adverbs?

2. a. Locate the word *poor* in the literature passage. What does this word mean? The word *poor* has two meanings. If you are unsure, look the word up in the dictionary. The word *poor* also has two homonyms (words that sound the same but have different meanings and spellings). The homonyms are *pore* and *pour*. Look up the meanings in the dictionary for each of these words. You will find the word *pore* also has two definitions. Write one sentence for each homonym.

1.
e. chimneys, monkeys, donkeys, candies, ponies, skies

f. suddenly, softly
   the suffix -ly

2.
a. poor - penniless or pitiful
   pore - to gaze intently or a small opening in the skin
   pour - to flow freely

✎ Teacher's Note: Depending on the regional accent, these words may sound slightly different.

2.
b. a comma

b. Note the dashes (–) in paragraphs two, three, and four. What other punctuation mark could be used instead to tell the reader to pause in these places? While a dash can be used to indicate a pause or break in thought, it also is used to emphasize and set apart a word or phrase. Sometimes a dash is used to indicate an interruption in speech by another person.

Ex: There is something – actually many things – that we need to accomplish this afternoon. (break in thought)

At this meeting – this private meeting – we will discuss our future plans. (emphasis)

Hello – no, I'm sorry – I'm afraid we won't be.

c. Look at the last sentence in the literature passage. Since both a dash and a comma causes the reader to pause, a comma could replace the dash following *Oh*. Words like *oh* used at the beginning of a sentence to express strong emotion or a sudden feeling are called **interjections**. Usually a comma or an exclamation point follows an interjection. If a comma is used, do not capitalize the next word; if an exclamation point is used, remember to capitalize the next word.

Ex: Well, I hope my cousins come to visit this year.
Oh! What a pretty dress!

Write two sentences; one using an interjection followed by a comma and another using an exclamation point.

d. Look at the word *can* in the first sentence of the last paragraph in the literature passage. It is printed in a different type for emphasis. Try reading the literature passage aloud using good expression.

e. The way we emphasize words can change the entire meaning of a sentence. Try reading the literature passage again, emphasizing different words. For extra fun, try taping your reading on an audio tape.

3. a. What do you think about Peter's attitude? Let your
imagination take you to the scene depicted in the literature
passage. What would you tell Peter?

b. Write what you think happened next. Be sure to write it in
conversational form (dialogue) and remember to use
quotation marks around all direct quotations. Everytime
someone different is speaking make sure you indent. You
can review the quotation rules in Lesson 7.

c. Quotation marks are also used around the titles of songs,
short stories, chapters of a book, magazine articles, and short
poems. Capitalize the first word and every other important
word.

Ex: "The Eagle" (short poem)
     "A Mighty Fortress" (song)
     "The Gift of the Magi" (short story)

d. Add quotation marks and punctuation to the following
sentences.

Ex: You must go with us to the museum said James
     "You must go with us to the museum," said James.

1) Which dog is best for a pet in an apartment asked Jim
2) If you will come with me pleaded Myra we will ask Mrs.
   Jimson together
3) There are many ways to solve the problem said Kelly
4) Run quickly or they will catch you exclaimed Janice
5) The teacher assigned the poem The Charge of the Light
   Brigade to read for discussion in class tomorrow

e. Review your spelling words.

3.
d. 1) "Which dog is best for
a pet in an apartment?"
asked Jim.
2) "If you will come with
me," pleaded Myra, "we
will ask Mrs. Jimson
together."
3) "There are many ways
to solve the problem,"
said Kelly.
4) "Run quickly or they
will catch you!"
exclaimed Janice.
5) The teacher assigned
the poem, "The Charge of
the Light Brigade" to
read for discussion in
class tomorrow.

4. a. Pretend you are a television reporter sent to get the "scoop" on a fire. Write out your report being sure to include the four essential information points of any news article.

   1) Who is the story about?
   2) What is the story about?
   3) When did the story take place?
   4) Where did the story take place?

   b. Once you have completed your report, practice saying it aloud. Use a cassette recorder or video camera to record your version of the news report.

   c. Take an oral or written spelling pretest.

5. a. Choose one of the following activities.

   1) Write the literature passage from dictation. Proofread and make any corrections. If you still have questions about the use of quotation marks, ask your teacher to explain.

   2) Try acting out the literature passage plus the part you added in **3b**.

   3) Choose skills from the *Review Activities* on the next page.

Review Activities

Choose only the skills your student needs to review.

1. *Homonyms (Pore, Pour and Poor)*
   Underline the correct homonym in each of the following sentences.

   a. He used (*pore, pour, poor*) judgment in choosing a fishing spot.
   b. Please (*pore, pour, poor*) yourself some lemonade.
   c. The sweat flowed from every (*pore, pour, poor*) of his body.
   d. He will often (*pore, pour, poor*) over old documents at night trying to unlocked their secrets.
   e. The (*pore, pour, poor*) cat looked terrible after falling into the puddle.

2. *Interjections*
   Underline the interjections and add punctuation.

   a. Oh What a lovely dress
   b. Well so you did decide to come
   c. Hurrah We won the championship
   d. My what a lovely daughter you have
   e. Behold I stand at the door and knock

1. a. poor
   b. pour
   c. pore
   d. pore
   e. poor

2. a. Oh! What a lovely dress!
   b. Well, so you did decide to come.
   c. Hurrah! We won the championship!
   d. My, what a lovely daughter you have.
   e. Behold, I stand at the door and knock.

3.

"Mary, it was a great concert last night!" exclaimed Ginger. "I wish you could have come."

"Well, it was hard to stay home and babysit last night, but I had already promised Mrs. Wilson I would watch her children while she went to a meeting," said Mary with a shrug. "How many in the youth group came?"

"Everyone came but Sam and John," answered Ginger. "The band sang my favorite song. It was great!"

"Oh well, I sat around and read an article in <u>Horses</u> magazine," sighed Mary, "but I know I made the right decision to be faithful to my promise."

3. *Dialogue and Quotation Marks*
Rewrite the following sentences of dialogue. Begin each new paragraph by indenting, and add quotation marks and punctuation where needed. Be sure to punctuate any interjections.

Mary it was a great concert last night exclaimed Ginger. I wish you could have come. Well it was hard to stay home and babysit last night, but I had already promised Mrs. Wilson I would watch her children while she went to a meeting said Mary with a shrug. How many in the youth group came? Everyone came but Sam and John answered Ginger. The band sang my favorite song. It was great! Oh well I sat around and read in Horses magazine sighed Mary but I know I made the right decision to be faithful to my promise.

4. *News Report*
Write a news report about something that has happened in your life. It could be about a sport, a trip, a concert, an accomplishment, etc. Be sure to include the who, what, when and where points in your story.

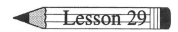

Give thanks to the Lord, for He is good;
For His lovingkindness is everlasting.
Give thanks to the God of gods,
For His lovingkindness is everlasting.
Give thanks to the Lord of lords,
For His lovingkindness is everlasting.
To Him who alone does great wonders,
For His lovingkindness is everlasting;
To Him who made the heavens with skill,
For His lovingkindness is everlasting;
To Him who spread out the earth above the
*   waters,*
For His lovingkindness is everlasting;
To Him who made the great lights,
For His lovingkindness is everlasting:
The sun to rule by day,
For His lovingkindness is everlasting,
The moon and stars to rule by night,
For His lovingkindness is everlasting.

To Him who smote the Egyptians in their
*   first-born,*
For His lovingkindness is everlasting,
And brought Israel out from their midst,
For His lovingkindness is everlasting,
With a strong hand and an outstretched arm
For His lovingkindness is everlasting;
To Him who divided the Red Sea asunder,
For His lovingkindness is everlasting,
And made Israel pass through the midst of
*   it,*
For His lovingkindness is everlasting;
But He overthrew Pharaoh and his army in
*   the Red Sea,*
For His lovingkindness is everlasting.
To Him who led His people through the
*   wilderness,*
For His lovingkindness is everlasting;

✐ **Teacher's Note:** As your student completes each lesson, choose skills from the Review Activities that he needs. The Review Activities follow each lesson.

To Him who smote great kings,
For His lovingkindness is everlasting,
And slew mighty kings,
For His lovingkindness is everlasting:
Sihon, king of the Amorites,
For His lovingkindness is everlasting,
And Og, king of Bashan,
For His lovingkindness is everlasting,
And gave their land as a heritage,
For His lovingkindness is everlasting,
Even a heritage to Israel His servant,
For His lovingkindness is everlasting.

Who remembered us in our low estate,
For His lovingkindness is everlasting,
And has rescued us from our adversaries,
For His lovingkindness is everlasting;
Who gives food to all flesh,
For His lovingkindness is everlasting,
Give thanks to the God of heaven,
For His lovingkindness is everlasting.

Psalm 136:1-5 (NASB)

1. a. Look over the literature passage. Read the literature passage aloud with your teacher. Alternate reading the lines with your teacher, saying the chorus together. This type of reading is called **choral reading.**

   b. This poem is from the book of Psalms in the Bible. Psalms is the songbook of the Bible; it contains poems that were sung. Some of the things they express are praise to God, confessions of fear or sin, and thanksgiving. Read a few psalms with your teacher and discuss the reason you think each psalm was written.

   c. Look at the bolded text of the literature passage and notice the punctuation and where it is indented. Write the bolded portion of the literature passage from dictation. Correct your copy.

d. Make a spelling list from any misspelled words or use the following suggested list:

      lovingkindness   everlasting

Both of the suggested spelling words are compound words. Divide them into the two words that make up each of the words.

e. Find the suffix **-ness** in the literature passage. This suffix means *state of.* Add this suffix to your list along with its definition and word examples.

> ### Spelling Tip
> When adding a suffix beginning with a consonant, such as **-ness** or **-ly**, do not drop or change any letters in the root word unless the word ends in **y**. If the last letter of the root word and the first letter of the suffix are the same, double letters will result. If a word ends in **y**, change the **y** to **i** before adding any suffix except **-ing**.

Ex: final + ly = finally
    happy + ness = happiness
    hurry + ing + hurrying

f. Add suffixes to the following words.

Ex: stubborn + ness = stubbornness

1) natural + ly
2) sudden + ness
3) date + less
4) rude + ly
5) weak + ness

2. a. Look at the first line of the literature passage. The verb is *give*. What is the subject? Identify the type of sentence: declarative, interrogatory, imperative, or exclamatory. Refer to Lesson 8 for information on the four types of sentences if you need help.

1.
d. loving/kindness
   ever/lasting

e. -ness - state of
   Possible examples:
   kindness, richness

f. 1) naturally
   2) suddenness
   3) dateless
   4) rudely
   5) weakness

2.
a. you
   imperative

b. 1. Imp
   2. Int
   3. Dec
   4. Dec
   5. Exc

c. Answers will vary.

3.
a. The line is repeated.

3.
b. Present -
    is everlasting
    gives
    give

  Past -
    slow
    gave
    remembered
    has rescued

b. Determine whether the following sentences are declarative (**Dec**), interrogatory (**Int**), imperative (**Imp**) or exclamatory (**Exc**).

Ex: <u>Dec</u> I like to read biographies.

_____ 1) Open a biography and look into the life of a famous person

_____ 2) What is the purpose of reading a biography?

_____ 3) A biography helps us to identify what character qualities helped to make that person great.

_____ 4) A biography helps us also to see a period of history through the viewpoint of a person who lived during that time.

_____ 5) It's a great way to study!

c. Just as God was good to Israel, He is good to you. List some ways He is good to you.

3. a. Not all poetry rhymes. The selection of the words and how they are placed in a line, or the pattern of sound and words are important. What do you notice about every other line of the poem? This is a technique called **repetition.**

b. Psalm 136 is a psalm of praise. Try writing a poem of praise to God using the technique of repetition. You can even use the same repetitive line used in Psalm 136. The alternate lines should state truths you know about God or tell of great deeds He has done. Use the list you wrote in **2c** about how God is good to you for some ideas.

c. Review your spelling words.

4. a. Verbs change their form in order to show the time of action. These forms of verbs are called **tenses.** A verb may be written in present, past, or future tense.

Ex: I stand here now. (present tense)
     I stood here yesterday. (past tense)
     I will stand here tomorrow. (future tense)

b. Find examples of verbs in the present tense and in the past tense in the literature passage.

c. Most verbs are changed to past tense by adding the suffix **-ed** to the verb. These are called **regular verbs.** If a verb changes in some other way or makes no change to form the past tense, then the verb is called an **irregular verb.**

Regular verb:
She *arrives* on time everyday. (present tense)
She *arrived* on time today. (past tense)

Irregular verb:
I *swim* often at the pool. (present tense)
I *swam* at the pool. (past tense)

d. Find seven examples of irregular verbs in the literature passage and underline them.

e. It is important to select one tense and use that tense consistently throughout your writing and not switch to another tense.

   Ex: Mary jumped up and hits the ball over the net.
      (Jumped is past tense; *hits* is present tense.)

   Mary jumps up and hits the ball over the net.
   (Both *jumps* and *hits* are in the present tense.)

f. Read the following paragraph. Change any necessary verbs so that the text reads consistently in the past tense.

   It was a beautiful morning, and Echo gallops for joy across the pasture. She stretches her long neck over the fence so she had a better view of the farmyard activities. The chickens clucked loudly from the henhouse as they lay their morning eggs. Bessie, the cow, moos from her barn stall as she waited to be milked. The barnyard cat chased a mouse around the corner and soon returns with it dangling by its tail. With his usual air of importance the proud rooster strutted into his position on the rickety fence post and crows as a signal to all that the day has begun.

4.
d. spread, smote, brought, overthrew, led, slew, gave

4.
f.   It was a beautiful morning, and Echo galloped for joy across the pasture. She stretched her long neck over the fence so she had a better view of the farmyard activities. The chickens clucked loudly from the henhouse as they laid their morning eggs. Bessie, the cow, mooed from her barn stall as she waited to be milked. The barnyard cat chased a mouse around the corner and soon returned with it dangling by its tail. With his usual air of importance, the proud rooster strutted into his position on the rickety fence post and crowed as a signal to all that the day had begun.

g. Take an oral or written spelling pretest.

5. a. Choose one of the following activities.

   1) Write the bold portion of the literature passage from dictation again, or have your teacher continue dictating the remaining verses from Psalm 136.

   2) Find the following words in the literature passage: *asunder*, *adversaries*, *heritage*, *smote*, and *slew*. Tell your teacher the meaning of each of the words. If you are unsure of their meanings, look them up in the dictionary. Write a sentence for each word using it correctly.

   3) Discuss with your teacher the difference in mood of Psalm 136 and Psalm 42.

   4) Choose skills from the *Review Activities* on the next page.

Review Activities

Choose only the skills your student needs to review.

1. *Suffixes*
Using your list of suffixes add a suffix that matches the definition given to the following words.

Ex: the state of being sad = sadness

    a. in the manner of the usual = usual____
    b. the state of being mean = mean_____
    c. without care = care_____
    d. the act of subtracting = subtract_____
    e. one who dives = div___

2. *Types of Sentences*
Write an example of each of the following types of sentences: **declarative**, **interrogatory**, **imperative**, and **exclamatory**.

3. *Poetry - Repetition*
Write a poem using the technique of repetition.

4. *Verb Tense*
Write the correct tense of the verb indicated in parentheses.

    a. I _____ the essay tomorrow. (*future tense of write*)
    b. The hummingbirds _____ quickly from flower to flower. (*present tense of fly*)
    c. The young boy _____ over the fence. (*past tense of jump*)

5. *Regular and Irregular Verbs*
Write the past tense of each of the following verbs and indicate whether the verb is regular (**R**) or irregular (**IR**).

Ex: freeze - froze (IR)

    a. blow   d. take
    b. lose   e. wave
    c. fill   f. draw

1. a. usually
   b. meanness
   c. careless
   d. subtraction
   e. diver

2. Answers will vary.

3. Answers will vary.

4. a. will write
   b. fly
   c. jumped

5. a. blew - IR
   b. lost - IR
   c. filled - R
   d. took - IR
   e. waved - R
   f. drew - IR

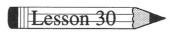

✏ **Teacher's Note: As your student completes each lesson, choose skills from the Review Activities that he needs. The Review Activities follow each lesson.**

Red took three uncertain steps forward and stopped again. Danny rushed angrily toward him. He reached down to grasp Red's collar, but the toes of his snowshoes crossed and he stumbled forward again. His bare hands plunged deeply into the snow. They hit something soft and yielding, something that gave before them. It was a man's trousered leg. Danny dug frantically, and lifted Ross Pickett from his snowy bed. His hand went under Ross's shirt. His father was warm and his heart still beat.

Big Red by Jim Kjelgaard.
Copyright 1945. Renewed 1973, Edna Kjelgaard.
Reprinted by permission Holiday House.

1. a. Look over the literature passage making note of punctuation and spelling, and then write the passage from dictation. Proofread your copy and correct any errors in punctuation and spelling.

   b. Make a spelling list of any misspelled words or use the following suggested list.

angrily	snowshoes
stopped	yielding
frantically	trousered

   c. What spelling rule applies to the word *angrily*?

   What spelling rule applies to the word *stopped*?

   d. Find the word *frantically* in the literature passage. When a word ending in **ic** is an adjective, the adverb is usually formed by adding **-ally** rather than just **-ly**.

   Ex: energetic - energetically

1.

c. When a word ending in y is preceded by a consonant, the y is changed to i before adding a suffix, except a suffix that begins with i such as -ing.

When a one-syllable word ends with a short vowel followed by a consonant, then the last consonant is doubled before adding a suffix beginning with a vowel.

e. Add the suffix **-ally** to the following words.

1) pathetic_____
2) realistic_____
3) enthusiastic_____

f. Underline the words in the literature passage that show ownership. What has been added to each of these words to show they are possessive?

2. a. Find and circle all the words in the literature passage that end with the suffix **-ly**. These words tell *how*, *when*, *where*, *how often* or *to what extent*. Note that although most words ending in **-ly** are adverbs, some are adjectives, such as *friendly* and *lovely*. If you need to review adverbs, refer to Lesson 5.

b. Draw an arrow from the adverbs you have circled to the verb it tells about. Tell your teacher what each adverb tells about the verb.

Ex: Danny rushed angrily toward him.
     (The adverb *angrily* tells how he rushed.)

c. Not all adverbs end in **-ly**. Adverbs modify not only verbs, but sometimes adjectives or other adverbs.

Ex: The car sped around the curb too rapidly.
     (The adverb *too* is modifying the adverb *rapidly*.)

     The players were very happy after winning the game.
     (The adverb *very* modifies the adjective *happy*.)

Look at the literature passage. Find four adverbs that do not end in **-ly** and indicate the verb being modified.

1.
e. 1) pathetically
    2) realistically
    3) enthusiastically

f. Red's collar
   man's trousered leg
   Ross's shirt

   an 's has been added

2.
a. angrily, deeply, frantically

b. angrily rushed; how
   deeply plunged; to what extent
   frantically dug; how

c. Any four of the following:
   forward took
   again stopped
   down reached
   forward again stumbled
   under went
   still beat

239

d. Write four sentences using adverbs to answer how, when, where, how often, or to what extent.

Ex: The rabbit hopped *merrily* through the field. (how)
     The plumber called *yesterday*. (when)
     The toddler fell *down*. (where)
     Mother is *very* happy. (to what extent or degree)

3. a. Every verb has four principal parts: the **present**, the **present participle**, the **past**, and the **past participle**.

Ex: present - look
     present participle - (is) looking
     past - looked
     past participle - (have) looked

Note that the present participle and past participle are used with helping verbs such as *is, are, am, have, has, had,* etc.

b. Regular verbs form the past and past participle by adding **-ed** to the present form. The present participle is formed by adding **-ing** to the present form. Write the principal parts of the following regular verbs. The first one is done for you.

Present	Present Participle	Past	Past Participle
1) change	changing	changed	(have) changed
2) ask			
3) fill			
4) love			
5) rush			
6) climb			

c. Irregular verbs form the past and past participle in different ways. Because there is no single rule that applies to irregular verbs, it is important to familiarize yourself with them. Look at the list on the next page for the most common irregular verbs. The present participle form has not been included in the list because it is always formed by adding **-ing** to the present form.

3.
b. 2) **ask, asking, asked, (have asked)**
3) **fill, filling, filled, (have) filled**
4) **love, loving, loved, (have) loved**
5) **rush, rushing, rushed, (have) rushed**
6) **climb, climbing, climbed, (have) climbed**

Irregular Verbs

Present	Past	Past Participle
beat	beat	(have) beaten or beat
become	became	(have) become
begin	began	(have) begun
bite	bit	(have) bitten
blow	blew	(have) blown
break	broke	(have) broken
bring	brought	(have) brought
burst	burst	(have) burst
catch	caught	(have) caught
choose	chose	(have) chosen
come	came	(have) come
creep	crept	(have) crept
do	did	(have) done
draw	drew	(have) drawn
drink	drank	(have) drunk
drive	drove	(have) driven
eat	ate	(have) eaten
fall	fell	(have) fallen
fight	fought	(have) fought
fly	flew	(have) flown
forget	forgot	(have) forgotten
freeze	froze	(have) frozen
get	got	(have) got or gotten
give	gave	(have) given
go	went	(have) gone
grow	grew	(have) grown
hang	hung	(have) hung
know	knew	(have) known
lay	laid	(have) laid
lead	led	(have) led
leave	left	(have) left
lie	lay	(have) lain
lose	lost	(have) lost
pay	paid	(have) paid
ride	rode	(have) ridden
ring	rang	(have) rung
rise	rose	(have) risen
run	ran	(have) run
say	said	(have) said

Present	Past	Past Participle
see	saw	(have) seen
set	set	(have) set
shake	shook	(have) shaken
shine	shone, shined	(have) shone, shined
shrink	shrank	(have) shrunk
sing	sang	(have) sung
sink	sank	(have) sunk
sit	sat	(have) sat
speak	spoke	(have) spoken
spring	sprang	(have) sprung
steal	stole	(have) stolen
swear	swore	(have) sworn
swim	swam	(have) swum
swing	swung	(have) swung
take	took	(have) taken
tear	tore	(have) torn
think	thought	(have) thought
throw	threw	(have) thrown
wear	wore	(have) worn
weep	wept	(have) wept
win	won	(have) won
weave	wove	(have) woven
write	wrote	(have) written

3.

d. took, stopped, rushed, reached, crossed, stumbled, plunged, hit, gave, was, dug, lifted, went, was, beat.

All the verbs are in the past tense.

Irregular verbs: hit, gave, wave, dug, went, beat.

You can tell they are irregular verbs because the past is formed by some other change than the addition of the suffix -ed.

d. Underline the verbs in the literature passage. What is the tense of each verb? Remember to watch for helping verbs that indicate past participle. Also indicate which of the verbs are irregular. How can you tell?

e. Complete the following sentences with the correct verb form.

Ex: *come* She <u>came</u> from India to study in our country.

1) We have _____ *(do)* the majority of the work for this project.
2) I _____ *(choose)* this subject for my experiment because it was interesting.
3) They ____ *(leave)* church early because Joshua did not feel well.
4) Jeremiah had _____ *(think)* over his plans for the future carefully.
5) They _____ *(build)* the house for a family whose house had burned down.
6) Have we _____ *(buy)* enough supplies for the trip?
7) Only a few people have _____ *(swim)* that distance.
8) We have _____ *(speak)* to Hannah about becoming a member of our Bible Quiz Team.
9) The garden _____ *(grow)* quickly in the summer heat.
10) She _____ *(take)* the letter to the post office to purchase a stamp.

f. Review your spelling words.

4. a. Imagine you work for your local newspaper. You have been assigned to report what happened to Danny and his father. A news story should be written in a short, crisp, direct form. Use your imagination and make up your own details to create a newspaper account of this story. Follow these guidelines:

1) The first paragraph of a story usually has very important information in it. It answers the questions *who, what, when,* and *where*.

2) The other paragraphs in the story usually tell why something has happened and how it happened. These paragraphs usually have details about the event. Sometimes quotes from the people involved are included.

3.
e. 1) done
   2) chose
   3) left
   4) thought
   5) built
   6) bought
   7) swum
   8) spoken
   9) grew
   10) took

Read some newspaper articles to see how they organize their information. Read the following example.

Snowy Town - On Saturday, Ross Pickett, his son, Danny, and their dog, Red, went on a cross country trek across the Snowy Mountain Banks. Little did they know that by Sunday afternoon, Danny and Red would be heroes.

Authorities say circumstances are still unclear as to what took place. However, it is known that Ross and Danny became separated just as an unexpected blizzard came upon them. Danny told authorities that as he searched for his father, Red insistently nudged him in the opposite direction. Danny tried to pull Red the other way, but he lost his footing and fell down. As his hands reached down into the snow, he felt a man's trousered leg. Frantically, Danny dug and lifted his father from the snowy bed. "I put my hand under his shirt, and he was warm and his heart still beat," Ross said with joyful tears, as he lay recuperating in his bed.

Father and son are in good condition at Hope Hospital. Red is in excellent health, enjoying his new found attention.

b. Create a headline for your story that will catch the attention of the reader.

c. Take an oral or written spelling pretest.

5. a. Choose one of the following activities.

   1) Write the literature passage from dictation. Proofread and correct any errors in punctuation and spelling.

   2) Use your thesaurus to revise your news story. Edit carefully. Be sure to use good descriptive words. Rewrite it neatly and give it to your teacher.

   3) Choose skills from the *Review Activities* on the next page.

Review Activities

Choose only the skills your student needs to review.

1. *Suffix*
   Look at the following words and decide if you add the suffix
   -ly or **-ally** to form the adverb.

   a. basic
   b. serious
   c. sweet
   d. drastic
   e. eager

2. *Adverbs*
   Circle the adverbs in the following sentences. Write the
   question the adverb answers: *how, when, where, how often*, or
   to what extent.

   Ex: The German shepherd ran (swiftly) beside the bicycle. How

   a. The keys were found inside the car._____
   b. We will be attending the concert today. _____
   c. We often take a walk after dinner. _____
   d. Laura laughed cheerfully at the joke. _____
   e. He is very concerned about his test scores. _____

3. *Principal Parts of a Verb*
   Underline the correct verb form in the following sentences.
   Indicate whether the verb form is present (**Pr**), past (**Past**), or
   past participle (**PP**).

   a. Anne (*swimming, swam*) in the second race.
   b. Greg and Don have (*decide, decided*) to stay for dinner.
   c. I (*fills, filled*) the pool with water last night.
   d. Jenny and Mark (*draw, drawn*) very detailed drawings.

---

1. a. **basically**
   b. **seriously**
   c. **sweetly**
   d. **drastically**
   e. **eagerly**

2. a. (inside) - where
   b. (today) - when
   c. (often) - how often
   d. (cheerfully) - how
   e. (very) - to what extent

3. a. Past - swam
   b. PP - decided
   c. Past - filled
   d. Pr - draw

4. *Irregular Verbs*
Underline the correct form of the irregular verb in the following sentence.

a. She (*sang*, *sung*) beautifully in the recital.
b. The shirt was (*stole*, *stolen*) from the store.
c. The large ship (*sank*, *sunk*) when the torpedo hit it.
d. The bell has (*rang*, *rung*); please go to your class.
e. Martha (*sprang*, *sprung*) forward to catch the little boy who was falling.

5. *Writing a Newspaper Article*
Read an article in your local newspaper. Find the answers to the *who*, *what*, *when*, and *where* questions.

4. a. sang
  b. stolen
  c. sank
  d. rung
  e. sprang

5. Answers will vary.

Assessment 5
(Lessons 26 - 30)

1. Find and underline three prepositional phrases in the literature passage used in Lesson 16. Circle the object of each preposition.

2. Find and underline two helping verbs in the last paragraph of the literature passage in Lesson 26.

3. Adverbs describe verbs and tell us *how*, *when*, *where*, or *to what extent* or *degree*. Write sentences using adverbs illustrating each of these.

4. Find two adverbs in the literature passage in Lesson 4.

5. Write the following dialogue correctly.

I have been asked to lead the program next week and I am a little nervous. Are you ever afraid to do something new Mark asked. Sometimes replied his father.

1. with a dark (back)
   to the (top)
   of the (water)
   in the (air)
   For a (moment)
   to the (top)
   of the (water)
   at the (crew)
   of the (Swallow)
   at (it)
   with a (twist)
   of its (tail)
   in the (water)

2. had been camped, were leaving

3. Answers will vary.

4. quickly, carefully

5.   "I have been asked to lead the program next week and I am a little nervous. Are you ever afraid to do something new?" Mark asked.
   "Sometimes," replied his father.

BOOK STUDY

on

The Horse and His Boy

The Horse and His Boy by
C.S. Lewis
**Published by Macmillan
Publishing**

**Readability level: 7th - 8th
grade**

Introducing
The Horse and His Boy

This fifth book in the Chronicles of Narnia series by C.S. Lewis deals with some of the events that took place during the time of the first book, *The Lion, the Witch, and the Wardrobe*. Mr. Lewis once again weaves deep truths into the excitement and high adventure of the skillfully told story.

Summary

Narnia and the North! This becomes the cry of young Shasta's heart after overhearing the man who calls himself his father, telling a visiting nobleman the story of how Shasta came to live with him. It seems some years ago a boat had washed up on the shore containing only a small baby and a man who had obviously starved himself to death keeping the baby alive. Thinking this was a fortunate gift of free labor, the man took the baby as his own and named him Shasta. Over the years, Shasta was treated as a slave, not knowing his origin. After learning this, Shasta runs to the stable to plan what to do when Bree, the horse belonging to his "father's" guest, speaks to him and convinces him that he is not a Calormene. Because of his fair coloring, he must have come from the North, from either Narnian or Archenland. Bree had been kidnapped as a pony and had served the Tarkaan as a war horse, keeping his ability to speak a secret. So the two decide to set off for Narnia and for freedom.

On the way, they meet a young Tarkeena who is fleeing a forced marriage. She, too, is riding a talking horse, Hwin. Hwin has told Aravis about Narnia, where they do not force young ladies to marry. Aravis and Hwin decide to join Shasta and Bree. Their journey takes them through the great city of Tarkaan, where they become separated when Shasta is mistaken for the prince of Archenland. Meanwhile, Aravis, in trying to escape through the palace of the Tisroc, finds herself hiding behind a sofa listening to the Tisroc agree to Prince Rabadash's plan to lead a surprise attack on the country of Archenland.

Finally, Shasta and Aravis are reunited with Bree and Hwin, and push onward to Archenland in order to sound the alarm before Prince Rabadash's army attacks. Almost there, they feel they can not go on. A lion chases them and proves they have more strength than they thought. Happily, Shasta is in time to give the cry of alarm and the Narnians go to the aid of the Archelanders in a brief but fierce battle with the Calormenes. After a decisive victory, Shasta learns that he is indeed an Archenlander and a very special one. Prince Rabadash learns what it is to be judged for his foolishness and Aravis, Bree, and Hwin learn what it means to find freedom at last.

Vocabulary

Find each of the following words in the chapters indicated and use context clues to decide the meaning of each word. Then, look up each word in the dictionary and write a definition.

1. jostled - (Chapter 4)

2. queue - (Chapter 6) /kyoo/

3. council - (Chapter 8)

4. assurance - (Chapter 11)

5. intense - (Chapter 14)

1. jostled - pushed or shoved
2. queue - a group of people waiting in line
3. council - a group of people gathered for discussion
4. assurance - certainty
5. intense - extreme

Choose the correct word from the words listed above to complete the following sentences.

6. The theater manager asked the crowd to form a _____ to purchase tickets.

7. The _____ met on Friday night to make a decision.

8. Ryan was _____ in the crowd as he tried to reach his friend.

9. The waiting became _____ as the minutes ticked by.

10. I have the _____ that I will live with God forever.

6. queue

7. council

8. jostled

9. intense

10. assurance

Discussion Questions

1. Who was your favorite character in this book. Why?

2. What parts made you laugh? Cheer? Afraid for the characters?

3. Were the characters believable? Have you ever known anyone like them?

4. We see pride and humility contrasted in the four main characters. Which were proud? Which were humble? How did this change by the end of the story?

5. How did you feel about the arranged marriage Aravis' father had planned for her? What did it tell you about her father? Do you think arranged marriages are always wrong?

6. Would you describe Rabadash's punishment as "poetic justice" (getting what he deserved)? Why?

7. Shasta felt that he was a most unfortunate boy; that everything went right for everyone else but him. Have you ever felt like Shasta? When? How did you deal with these feelings?

---

1. Answers will vary.

2. Answers will vary.

3. Answers will vary.

4. Bree and Aravis are both full of pride, mainly because of the way others have treated them.
   Hwin and Shasta are very humble because of the way they have been viewed by others.
   At the end of the book, as Bree is lecturing in a rather superior tone, he encounters Aslan and sees himself as he really is. Aravis has learned to think more highly of others than she does herself, expecially of Shasta, who bravely rushed to defend her. Shasta, while still humble, has to start thinking of himself as a prince instead of a slave and Hwin remains her own sweet self.

5. Allow for discussion.

6. Allow for discussion.

7. Allow for discussion.

8. As Shasta walks through the darkness getting colder, feeling alone, and very sorry for himself, he begins to cry. What put a sudden stop to this? What emotions did Shasta experience as he walked though the mist with "The Thing" beside him? As the mist clears, how does Shasta feel?

9. When Aravis exclaims that being in the battle must have been wonderful, Cor replies that it wasn't at all like what he thought. Have you ever experienced anything that turned out to be very different than you thought? Explain.

8. **A sudden fright put a stop to his tears.**
He felt fear because someone or something was walking beside him in the darkness. He was shocked to realize that he didn't know how long the creature had been there. His fear intensified to terror as he remembered stories of giants living in those parts. He began to hope he only imagined it.

Then in desperation, he finally spoke to it. He was relieved to find that it was not a giant, but immediately was even more terrified to think that it might be a ghost. He was told that was not the case and encouraged to tell of his sorrows. This reassured him a little and he felt relief in telling of all he had suffered.

When Shasta found out who was walking by him he was no longer afraid of being eaten or being accompanied by a ghost. Then a new and different sort of trembling came over him, and along with this, gladness. The mist evaporated and revealed his companion. Shasta looked into the Lion's face, slipped out of the saddle, and fell at its feet.

9. **Answers will vary.**

Activities

The following activities are intended to expand your understanding and enjoyment of this wonderful book. Choose two or three activities from this list.

1. Since authors always bring part of themselves to their work, it is interesting to find out something about them when you read their books. Find some information about C.S. Lewis and his life.

2. Have you ever ridden a horse? If possible, visit a stable and go for a ride. Do you have to hold on with your knees like Bree told Shasta?

3. The Calormenes are known for their story-telling capabilities. Practice telling an exciting story by choosing an incident from the book, *The Horse and His Boy*.

   Suggestions:

   Shasta gets separated from the horses and Aravis in Tarkaan

   the battle scene where Prince Rabadash is defeated

4. *The Horse and His Boy* is a type of literature called *fantasy*. What makes it so?

5. The Calormenes love to quote their poets.

   Ex: Natural affection is stronger than soup and offspring more precious than carbuncles.

   This could also be called a proverb. The Bible has a book of Proverbs. Read some and try writing your own proverb.

6. The idea of mistaken identity is intriguing to authors. Some examples are found in books such as Charles Dickens' *The Prince and the Pauper* and Anthony Hope's *The Prisoner of Zenda*. Try writing a story about twins or look-alikes being mistaken for each other.

7. Mr. Lewis uses analogies throughout the Chronicles of Narnia series. An **analogy** is a comparison of two similar things. The main analogy is Aslan as a picture of Jesus. What other analogies did you notice in reading *The Horse and His Boy*?

8. Read the other books in this series:

   The Lion, the Witch, and the Wardrobe
   Prince Caspian
   The Voyage of the Dawn Treader
   The Magician's Nephew
   The Last Battle

I C.A.N. Assessment

for

The Horse and His Boy - Book Study D

After the *Book Study* is completed, check off
each I C.A.N. objective with your teacher.

C — I can **complete** my work.

— I can be **creative**.

A — I can be **accurate**.

— I can do my work with a good **attitude**.

N — I can do my work **neatly**.

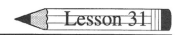

*Pooh was thoughtful when he heard this,
and then he murmured to himself:*

*But whatever his weight in pounds,
shillings, and ounces,
He always seems bigger because of bounces.*

*"And that's the whole poem," he said.
"Do you like it, Piglet?"*
*"All except the shillings," said Piglet.
"I don't think they ought to be there."*
*"They wanted to come in after the
pounds," explained Pooh, "so I let them. It
is the best way to write poetry, letting things
come."*
"Oh, I didn't know," said Piglet.

The House at Pooh Corner by A. A. Milne.
© 1956, A. A. Milne.

📝 **Teacher's Note:** As your student completes each lesson, choose skills from the Review Activities that he needs. The Review Activities follow each lesson.

1. a. Read the literature passage. Why do you think the shillings wanted to come into Pooh's poem? Look up *shilling* in the dictionary to find its meaning.

b. Look at the literature passage paying special attention to punctuation. This literature passage contains written conversation known as dialogue. In what ways does the writer let the reader know a new person is speaking?

c. Write the literature passage from dictation. Proofread and correct any mistakes. Make a spelling list of any misspelled words or use the following suggested list:

thoughtful	murmured	weight
pounds	shilling	ounces

d. Look at the words *pounds* and *ounces* in the suggested spelling list. Words with the /ow/ sound are usually spelled with **ow**. Some words are spelled **ou**, but **ou** will usually not end a word.

1.
a. Pounds is a unit of money as well as a unit of weight. Shillings is also a unit of money.

b. The writer begins a new paragraph by indenting each time a new person speaks.

Spelling Tip
Most words spell the *low/*
sound with **ow**. Some words
are spelled **ou**.

1.

e. thoughtful
thoughtful - full of
thought
part of speech - adjective
Possible word examples:
restful, beautiful

f. comparative form: bigger
superlative form: best

g. colon; to set off the poem
from the rest of the text

2.

a. Refer to Lesson 7,
Quotation Rules

b. "They wanted to come in
after the pounds,"
explained Pooh, "so I let
them.

e. Locate the word in the literature passage with the suffix **-ful**.
The suffix **-ful** means *full of*. This suffix usually changes a
word into an adjective. Add **-ful** to your suffix list. Also fill
in the definition, part of speech, and word examples.

f. Find an adjective in comparative form and an adjective in
superlative form in the literature passage. Refer to Lesson 7
if you need any review.

g. In the literature passage, what punctuation separates the text
from the poem which Pooh composed? Why do you think
the writer chose this punctuation?

2. a. Look at the literature passage. What do you notice about the
use of quotation marks? Write two rules about the use of 7
if you need help.

b. Underline the sentence in the literature passage which
contains a split quotation.

c. Add correct punctuation to the following direct quotations. Refer to the quotation rules in Lesson 7 if needed.

Ex: Come with us to the rally begged Alicia
"Come with us to the rally," begged Alicia.

1) We need to find a way for the whole group to take the canoe trip explained Jim
2) Janice replied I'm not sure I'll be able to afford the cost
3) One way to help cover the cost interjected Seth is to have a car wash
4) What a great idea exclaimed Jim That would help reduce everyone's cost.
5) Where would we have the car wash asked Ruth

3. a. Dialogue is used in a story to bring the characters to life. Good stories usually contain some element of dialogue. Look through some stories you have available. Do they all contain dialogue?

b. Write a short conversation between you and your teacher. Remember to indent each time the speaker changes. Be sure to identify the speaker when necessary so the reader is clear about who is speaking.

c. Check your punctuation. Did you use the quotation marks correctly?

d. Review your spelling words.

4. a. Pooh is very good at making up poetry. The poem he composes in the literature passage is a **couplet**, a two-lined stanza of poetry ending in words that rhyme. What two words in Pooh's poem rhyme?

b. In Pooh's poem he is describing his friend, Tigger. Write a list of words that describe someone you know or an animal. Write two or three couplets about this person or animal. Make sure the ending words of each stanza rhyme.

c. Take an oral or written spelling pretest.

2.

c. 1) "We need to find a way for the whole group to take the canoe trip," explained Jim.
2) Janice replied, "I'm not sure I'll be able to afford the cost."
3) "One way to help cover the cost," interjected Seth, "is to have a car wash."
4) "What a great idea!" exclaimed Jim. "That would help reduce everyone's cost."
5) "Where would we have the car wash?" asked Ruth.

4.
a. ounces, bounces

5. a. Choose one of the following activities.

  1) Write the literature passage from dictation. Compare your copy with the passage and correct any errors. Were you able to correctly punctuate all the direct quotations?

  2) A play is similar to a short story with dialogue. You can write dialogue in the form of a one-act play. This form of a mini-play is called a **duolog**. Plan your basic plot and decide on your characters. Most stories have a problem of some kind which the characters must overcome. Try to provide the reader with some insight into the personalities of your characters. When writing in play form, quotation marks are not used. When your play is complete, find someone to act it out with you. Look at the following example:

SETTING: A hiking trail that follows a creek in a forest wilderness

NANCY: I don't know how you talked me into this hiking experience. You know how I hate bugs!

JOANNA: Come on Nancy! The bugs aren't that bad. Look at the beauty around you. Enjoy God's wonderful creation.

Review Activities

Choose only the skills your student needs to review.

1. *Punctuation (Dialogue)*
Rewrite the following dialogue adding punctuation.

> Do you feel the judging team is ready for the competition asked Martha. I really don't think we are. We need to spend some more time practicing and studying answered Mike. Well, the competition is only two weeks away said Martha and everyone's schedule is full. Then we will have to practice the best we can individually and hope we can still do well as a team at the competition said Mike with a shrug.

2. *Poetry - Couplet*
Write a couplet describing an animal.

1.

    "Do you feel the judging team is ready for the competition?" asked Martha.

    "I really don't think we are. We need to spend some more time practicing and studying," answered Mike.

    "Well, the competition is only two weeks away," said Martha, "and everyone's schedule is full."

    "Then we will have to practice the best we can individually and hope we can still do well as a team at the competition," said Mike with a shrug.

2. Answers will vary.

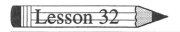

Marilla was a tall, thin woman, with angles and without curves; her dark hair showed some gray streaks and was always twisted up in a hard little knot behind with two wire hairpins stuck aggressively through it. She looked like a woman of narrow experience and rigid conscience, which she was; but there was a saving something about her mouth which, if it had been ever so slightly developed, might have been considered indicative of a sense of humour.

Matthew dreaded all women except Marilla and Mrs. Rachel; he had an uncomfortable feeling that the mysterious creatures were secretly laughing at him. He may have been quite right in thinking so, for he was an odd-looking personage, with an ungainly figure and long iron-gray hair that touched his stooping shoulders, and a full, soft brown beard which he had worn ever since he was twenty. In fact, he had looked at twenty very much as he looked at sixty, lacking a little of the grayness.

A child of about eleven, garbed in a very short, very tight, very ugly dress of yellowish gray wincey. She wore a faded brown sailor hat and beneath the hat, extending down her back, were two braids of very thick, decidedly red hair. Her face was small, white and thin, also much freckled; her mouth was large and so were her eyes, that looked green in some lights and moods and gray in others.

Anne of Green Gables by L. M. Montgomery.
Used by permission. David R. Godine Publishers Inc.

1. a. Read the three character descriptions. Can you visualize these people? An author tells about a character by describing him physically, but he also describes his personality. Some description is usually given when a character is first introduced to the reader, as in these paragraphs. This is commonly referred to as a **character sketch**. Look through some books on your shelf and find other character sketches. How does the author make you "see" the person?

   b. Write the third paragraph of the literature passage from dictation. Compare your copy with the passage and correct any errors in spelling and punctuation. Make a spelling list of any misspelled words or use the following suggested list:

garbed	wincey	freckled
decidedly	yellowish	sailor

   c. The word yellowish contains the suffix **-ish**, meaning *origin, nature*, or *resembling*. Add this to your list of suffixes along with the definition and word examples.

   d. Locate the word *uncomfortable* in the literature passage. This word contains the suffix **-able** which means *able* or *can do*. This suffix can also be spelled **-ible** in words such as *invisible* and *sensible*. Add these suffixes to your list along with the definition and word examples.

   e. Spelling words with the suffixes **-able** and **-ible** are often confused with one another. Because the suffix **-able** is used more often, the suffix **-ible** is often misspelled. Copy the following words and underline the suffix noting which suffix is used. Say each word aloud as you write them. Listen for the short /a/ sound or the short /i/ sound in the suffix.

eligible	indispensable
legible	edible
flexible	reversible
predictable	dependable
acceptable	irritable

1.
a. The author use descriptive adjectives to help you picture each of the characters.

c. -ish; origin, nature, resembling
Possible examples: childish, fiendish

d. -able, -ible; can do, able
Possible examples: fashionable, capable, eligible

265

1.

f. The article *an* is used
with a word beginning
with a vowel sound.

2.

a. short, tight, ugly dress

yellowish, gray wincey

faded, brown, sailor hat

two braids

thick, red hair

small, white, thin face

much freckled

large mouth

✏ **Teacher's Note:**
Of about eleven is a
prepositional phrase;
eleven is therefore the
object of the preposition
making it a noun. *Freckled*
is a noun. *Green* and *gray*
are nouns.

c. Predicate adjective - large
Linking verb - was

2.
d. odd-looking, iron-gray

f. Locate the phrase *with an ungainly figure* in the second
paragraph of the literature passage. Why is the article *an*
used in this phrase instead of the article *a*? If you are unsure,
refer to Lesson 16.

2. a. An adjective is a word that modifies or describes a noun or
pronoun and answers the questions *what kind, how much,* or
which one. Circle the adjectives in the third paragraph of the
literature passage.

b. Look at this simplified sentence from the literature passage.

Her face was small.

Adjectives usually come before the noun or pronoun they are
describing, but in this sentence the adjective, *small,* comes
after the noun, *face.* These are called predicate adjectives.
Predicate adjectives follow a verb and describes the subject.
The verb that links the subject to the predicate adjective is
called a **linking verb**.

Ex: The rising sun is *beautiful.*

Beautiful is the predicate adjective; it follows the linking verb
is.

c. Find the predicate adjective in this simplified sentence from
the literature passage.

Her mouth was large.

What linking verb does it follow? Draw an arrow from the
predicate adjective to the noun or pronoun it describes.

d. Sometimes a noun is described by an adjective of two
or more words. When two or more words act together
as a single adjective, it is called a **compound adjective.**
Sometimes these adjectives are compound words (two words
joined together) or hyphenated words.

Find the two compound adjectives in the second paragraph of
the literature passage that are joined together by a hyphen.

e. Add hyphens to compound adjectives where needed in the following sentences. Underline any predicate adjectives.

1) She looked beautiful in her floor length dress.
2) The new student was well liked.
3) He had a soft spoken manner and a gentle smile.
4) The theater had a good supply of chocolate covered raisins.
5) The idea you expressed in class was mind boggling.

3. a. Think of a person you know or create a fictitious character that you would like write to describe in a character sketch. Write down words that you feel would be descriptive of him. Remember, don't just describe the physical features; also describe the person's personality. You can include details about how the person speaks, moves, or dresses. In order to give more insight into his personality you can include details about the person's surroundings, hobbies, plans for the future, viewpoint, and background.

b. Once you have completed your list, write a character sketch about the person you have chosen. Be sure to make use of adjectives in your description. Read the following example of a character sketch.

She looked up expectantly at the entrance way to the college. Her wavy blonde hair encircled her youthful freckled face as her blue eyes glimmered with the spark of determination. A faded flowered dress caressed her slender frame in the breeze as she stood momentarily with her one suitcase of possessions. She knew she must succeed; she had worked too hard for this day.

c. Review your spelling words.

✏ **Teacher's Note:** Dictionaries will vary in hyphen use of compound words.

e. 1) <u>beautiful</u>, floor-length
   2) <u>well-liked</u>
   3) soft-spoken
   4) chocolate-covered
   5) <u>mind-boggling</u>

Predicate adjectives follow being verbs and modify the subject of the sentence. Predicate adjectives can also follow linking verbs. Since *had* is not a linking verb, examples 3 and 4 in 2(e) do not have predicate adjectives. *Gentle* is an adjective modifying the noun *smile* and *good* is an adjective that modifies the noun *supply*.

4.

b. *very* short - modifies
adjective, short

very tight - modifies
adjective, tight

very ugly - modifies
adjective, ugly

extending *down* -
modifies verb, extending

very thick - modifies
adjective, very

decidedly red - modifies
adjective, red

c. garbed - clothed;
Answers will vary.

4. a. To tell the difference between an adjective from an adverb, remember that an adjective always describes a noun or pronoun. An adverb can describe a verb, adjective, or another adverb. It answers the questions *how, where, how often, when,* and *to what extent.* When an adverb describes an adjective it usually appears just before the adjective and tells *how* or *to what extent.* If the adverb is describing an adverb, it usually appears just before the adverb and usually tells *how.*

b. List the six adverbs found in the third paragraph of the literature passage. One adverb is used four times. Beside each adverb listed, write the word it describes and indicate whether it is describing a verb, adjective, or another adverb.

c. Look up the word *garbed* in the dictionary to find the definition. Use the word correctly in a sentence.

d. Take an oral or written spelling pretest.

5. a. Choose one of the following activities.

1) Write the third paragraph of the literature passage from dictation. Correct any errors in spelling and punctuation.

2) Using the three descriptive paragraphs of the literature passage, draw a picture of one or more of the characters. Pay attention to details.

3) Choose skills from the *Review Activities* on the next page.

Review Activities

Choose only the skills your student needs to review.

1. *Suffixes*
   Add suffixes from your list that match the definition of the following words.

   a. fool + (*having the nature of a fool*) =
   b. sneak + (*inclined to sneak*) =
   c. like + (*able to like*) =
   d. life + (*without life*) =

2. *Adjectives and Adverbs*
   Underline the adjectives and circle the adverbs in the following sentences. Draw an arrow to the word each is modifying.

   a. The sun rose quickly over the steep mountaintops and chased the dark shadows from the lush meadows.
   b. The fierce waves break against the rugged shore before the storm.
   c. The very agitated boy struck the hard ground with his small fist.
   d. Yesterday we decided we can never know which team will win the game.
   e. The orange frisbee was expertly caught by the clever dog as the wide-eyed group of children watched.

1. a. foolish
   b. sneaky
   c. likeable
   d. lifeless

✎ Teacher's Note: Assist your student if he confuses adverbs with prepositions.

2. a. The sun rose (quickly) over the steep mountaintops and chased the dark shadows from the lush meadows.

   b. The fierce waves break against the rugged shore before the storm.

   c. The (very) agitated boy struck the hard ground with his small fist.

   d. (Yesterday) we decided we can (never) know which team will win the game.

   e. The orange frisbee was (expertly) caught by the clever dog as the wide-eyed group of children watched.

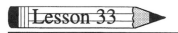
✎ **Teacher's Note:** As your student completes each lesson, choose skills from the Review Activities that he needs. The Review Activities follow each lesson.

The Crow and the Pitcher

A crow perishing with thirst saw a pitcher, and hoping to find water, flew to it with delight. When he reached it, he discovered to his grief that it contained so little water that he could not possibly get at it. He tried everything he could think of to reach the water, but all his efforts were in vain. At last he collected as many stones as he could carry and dropped them one by one with his beak into the pitcher, until he brought the water within his reach and thus saved his life.

Aesop's Fables

1.

a. Capitalize the first word and every other important word in a title.

1. a. Before writing this literature passage, look at the title. Why are certain words in the title capitalized and others not? Write the literature passage from dictation, then compare with the model. Correct any errors you find.

   b. Make a list of any misspelled words or use the following suggested spelling list:

perishing	delight	discovered
possibly	contained	grief

c. i before e except after c, and in words that say /ā/ as in *neighbor* and *weigh*.

   c. What spelling rule will help you remember how to spell *grief*?

   d. Look at the word *discovered* from your suggested spelling list. Note how the suffix **-ed** is added to the word. The last consonant, **r**, is not doubled because it is preceded by a vowel.

Spelling Tip
Words with more than one syllable that end with a consonant preceded by a vowel do not double the final consonant when adding a suffix beginning with a vowel unless the last syllable is accented.

Ex: travel - traveled (The last syllable is not accented.)
    commit - committed (The last syllable is accented.)

e. Add suffixes to the following words applying this *Spelling Tip*. Also remember that one-syllable words ending with the one vowel and one consonant doubles the last consonant before adding a suffix beginning with a vowel.

1) begin + ing   6) benefit + ed
2) refer + ed   7) ship + ing
3) recoil + ed   8) marvel + ed
4) admit + ing   9) transfer + ing
5) trap + ed   10) shop + ing

f. The suggested spelling list contains the prefixes **dis-**, **con-**, and **de-**. Refer to your list of prefixes for the meaning of each. Use the correct prefix to complete each of the following words.

1) The members of the club _____verged on the small town for the annual meeting. (*together*, *with*)
2) I am afraid Mary has become _____couraged after she did poorly on the test. (*take away*)
3) The team will ____part at 2:00 P.M. in order to be on time for the track meet. (*down*, *from*)

g. How does the crow in the literature passage exhibit the character quality of resourcefulness?

2. a. Look at the simplified sentence from the literature passage, and underline the subject once and the verb twice.

A crow saw a pitcher.

1.
e. 1) beginning
   2) referred
   3) recoiled
   4) admitting
   5) trapped
   6) benefited
   7) shipping
   8) marveled
   9) transferring
  10) shopping

f. dis- reverse, apart
   con- together, with
   de- down, from

   1) converged
   2) discouraged
   3) depart

g. The crow used what he had on hand to meet the need of his situation effectively.

2.
a. A <u>crow</u> <u>saw</u> a pitcher.

2.
b. pitcher

b. Now ask the question "A crow saw what?" Circle the noun that answers that question. The noun you circled is called the **direct object**. Direct objects receive the action from the verb and answer the questions *what* or *whom* after an action verb. A direct object must be a noun or pronoun.

Look at the following examples. Find the verb and ask the questions *what* or *whom*.

The boy threw the ball. (Threw what? *Ball* is the direct object.)
Mom baked a cake. (Baked what? *Cake* is the direct object.)
Ginger held it tightly. (Held what? *It* is the direct object.)

c. A sentence may have more than one direct object. Sometimes you have a compound direct object.

Ex: Dan chose Mike and Lisa to be on his team.
(Chose whom? *Mike* and *Lisa* are the direct objects.)

d. A direct object is never part of a prepositional phrase.

Ex: David lifted the rock over his head.
(Rock is the direct object. *Over his head* is a prepositional phrase. *Head* is the object of the preposition, *over*.)

2.
e. collected, could carry, dropped, brought, saved

f. collected - no direct object
could carry - no direct object
dropped - *them* is the direct object
brought - *water* is the direct object
saved - *life* is the direct object

e. Underline the action verbs in the last sentence of the literature passage.

f. Read the action verbs you have underlined and ask the question "What?" If there is a noun or pronoun that answers the question, circle it. Not all action verbs have a direct object.

Ex: collected what?

g. Underline the action verbs and circle the direct objects in the following sentences.

1) The pilot flew his plane into enemy territory.
2) The horse jumped the fence.
3) Jenny baked chocolate chip cookies and peanut butter candies for the party.
4) The Pilgrims signed the Mayflower Compact before leaving the ship.
5) Galileo developed a working telescope.

3. a. *Aesop's Fables* were written to teach lessons or morals. What do you think is the moral of this fable?

b. Try an experiment filling a cup half full of water. Drop pebbles or marbles into the cup. What happens to the water level?

c. Read the following two morals which Aesop wrote about.

   Whatever you do, do with all your might.

   Those who seek to please everybody please nobody.

   List three other morals that could be written as a fable. If you have trouble thinking of three, read over the book of Proverbs in the Bible for ideas.

d. Review your spelling words.

4. a. Choose one of the morals you listed in **3c** and write a fable about it. Fables usually use animals that talk and act like human beings. They are simply written, usually involving only two or three characters. One character faces a problem or situation and tries to overcome it. The ending will always teach us a lesson, or moral.

b. Take an oral or written spelling pretest.

g. 1) <u>flew</u> - (plane)
   2) <u>jumped</u> - (fence)
   3) <u>baked</u> - (cookies), (candies)
   4) <u>signed</u> - (Mayflower Compact)
   5) <u>developed</u> - (telescope)

3.
a. **Possible answers: Little by little does the trick. OR Necessity is the mother of invention.**

b. **It climbs higher.**

5. a. Choose one of the following activities.

   1) Rewrite the literature passage from dictation.

   2) Read about the history of *Aesop's Fables* in a reference book or read two or three fables and explain their morals.

   3) Choose skills from the *Review Activities* on the next page.

Review Activities

Choose only the skills your student needs to review.

1. *Direct Objects*
   Underline the action verbs and circle the direct objects in the following sentences.

   a. At night many bats eat insects which they locate with their high-pitched radar.
   b. Spiders capture moths and flies in their intricate webs.
   c. In early hours of dusk dragonflies chase mosquitoes throughout the sky.
   d. Birds devour many insects during the daytime hours.
   e. Insects encounter many enemies everyday.

2. *Fable*
   Write a fable that depicts a moral message.

---

1. a. <u>eat</u> - (insects)
   b. <u>capture</u> - (moths, flies)
   c. <u>chase</u> - (mosquitoes)
   d. <u>devour</u> - (insects)
   e. <u>encounter</u> - (enemies)

2. **Answers will vary.**

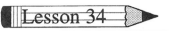

Laurie had vanished round the bend, Jo was just at the turn, and Amy, far behind, striking out toward the smoother ice in the middle of the river. For a minute Jo stood still with a strange feeling at her heart; then she resolved to go on, but something held and turned her round, just in time to see Amy throw up her hands and go down, with the sudden crash of rotten ice, the splash of water, and a cry that made Jo's heart stand still with fear.

Little Women by Louisa May Alcott.

1. a. Read the literature passage. Write it from dictation. Compare your copy to the passage. Did you place the commas in the right places?

   b. Make a spelling list from any misspelled words from your dictation or use the following suggested list.

vanished	smoother	strange
resolved	sudden	rotten

   Divide the words into syllables. Use your dictionary if you are unsure. This will help you remember the spelling. What do you notice about the division of syllables in the words *sudden* and *rotten*?

   c. Divide the following words into syllables.

   Ex: supper - sup/per

   1) butter
   2) master
   3) fiddle
   4) invite
   5) cotton

1.

b. They are divided between the double consonants.

c. 1) but/ter
   2) mas/ter
   3) fid/dle
   4) in/vite
   5) cot/ton

d. To form the plural of words ending in **o**, first look at the word. If the **o** is preceded by a consonant, add **es**; otherwise, just add **s**. Music related words are exceptions; just add **s** regardless of how the word ends.

Ex: hero - heroes (**o** preceded by a consonant)
banjo - banjos (music related word)
studio - studios (**o** preceded by a vowel)

> ### Spelling Tip
> To form the plural of words ending in **o** preceded by a consonant, add **es**; otherwise, just add **s**. **Exception**: Music related words - just add **s**.

e. Write the following words in plural form.

1) piano
2) tomato
3) video
4) alto
5) potato

2. a. Find the adjective *smoother* in the literature passage. Is *smoother* a positive, comparative, or superlative adjective? If you are not sure, refer to Lesson 7. What things are being compared?

b. Find the possessive noun in the literature passage. What punctuation identifies the word as a possessive noun? What object does the possessive noun own?

c. Possessive pronouns such as *her, his, my, our*, and *their* show ownership without the use of an apostrophe and **s**. Circle the possessive pronouns in the literature passage. Substitute a possessive noun for each of the possessive pronouns. Read the literature passage for Lesson 34 with the substitutions. Which version sounds better?

1.
e. 1) pianos
   2) tomatoes
   3) videos
   4) altos
   5) potatoes

2.
a. comparative: The ice in the middle of the river is compared to the ice on the edges of the river.

b. Jo's; an apostrophe; heart

c. her heart - Jo's heart; her hands - Amy's hands

Answers will vary.

Laurie had vanished round the bend, Jo was just at the turn, and Amy, far behind, striking out toward the smoother ice in the middle of the river. For a minute Jo stood still with a strange feeling at Jo's heart; then Jo resolved to go on, but something held and turned Jo around, just in time to see Amy throw up Amy's hands and go down, with the sudden crash of rotten ice, the splash of water, and a cry that made Jo's heart stand still with fear.

d. Amy, Jo, and Laurie

d. Who are the characters in the passage? Imagine Amy is your sister and you are at the scene depicted in the literature passage. Write a few sentences explaining what you think may have happened next in the story. Choose descriptive adjectives to express how you feel.

3. a. A **semicolon** separates two independent clauses that are joined together without a conjunction. Circle the semicolon (;) and underline the two independent clauses in the following simplified sentence.

For a minute Jo stood still with a strange feeling at her heart; then she resolved to go on.

3.
a. <u>For a minute Jo stood still with a strange feeling at her heart</u>(;)<u>then she resolved to go on.</u>

b. Look at this simplified sentence from the literature passage.

She resolved to go on, but something held and turned her round.

A comma is used before the conjunction because it joins two complete sentences. This is called a **compound sentence**.

Rewrite the following sentences as compound sentences by using the conjunctions *and, but*, or *or*. Remember the comma.

3.
b. Possible answers:
1) Jason plays baseball, and Lynn plays basketball.
2) Sue likes ice cream, but I like frozen yogurt.
3) We tried to be on time, but we were late.

1) Jason plays baseball. Lynn plays basketball.
2) Sue likes ice cream. I like frozen yogurt.
3) We tried to be on time. We were late.

c. Review your spelling words. Be sure to sound them out by syllables as you write them.

4. a. Find and circle the action verbs in the paragraph. You learned in Lesson 29 that verbs change their form in order to show the time of an action. These forms of verbs are called **tenses**. A verb may be written in present, past, or future tense (time). In what tense is this paragraph written?

   b. The literature passage was written by the author in past tense. Rewrite the literature passage as if you were Jo telling it as it is happening. (first person, present tense). The first two sentences are done for you.

   Ex: Laurie vanishes round the bend. I am just at the turn, and Amy, far behind, is striking out toward the smoother ice in the middle of the river...

   c. Take a practice test of your spelling words.

5. a. Choose one of the following activities.

   1) Write the literature passage once again from dictation. Pay close attention to your punctuation and spelling.

   2) Write a short story describing an exciting event in your life.

   3) Choose skills from the *Review Activities* on the next page.

4.
a. had vanished, was, striking, stood, resolved, held, turned, see, throw, go, stand

past tense

Review Activities

Choose only the skills your student needs to review.

1. *Syllables*
   Divide the following words into syllables:

   a. riddle   d. blanket
   b. tablet   e. bottom
   c. confess   f. hobby

2. *Spelling*
   Circle the correct spelling of the following words.

   a. echos, echoes   d. cellos, celloes
   b. tornados, tornadoes e. stereos, stereoes
   c. sopranos, sopranoes f. potatos, potatoes

3. *Possessive Pronouns*
   Underline the possessive nouns in the following sentences and change them to possessive pronouns.

   Ex: Please turn down the volume on <u>Mike's</u> radio. __his__

   a. We will be attending Laurie's graduation ceremony. _____

   b. Lane's fishing spot is the best one on the lake. _____
   c. Will the youth group's skit be done soon? _____
   d. Did you know the Smith family's vacation was canceled? _____

   e. Anne's horse completed all the jumps. _____

4. *Regular and Irregular Verbs*
   Write the past tense form of the following verbs.

   a. freeze   d. catch
   b. spring   e. twirl
   c. splash   f. weep

5. *Verb Tenses*
   Find a paragraph in a book. Change the tense to past or present tense.

---

1. a. rid-dle
   b. tab-let
   c. con-fess
   d. blan-ket
   e. bot-tom
   f. hob-by

2. a. echoes
   b. tornadoes
   c. sopranos
   d. cellos
   e. stereos
   f. potatoes

3. a. <u>Laurie's</u> - his
   b. <u>Lane's</u> - His
   c. <u>group's</u> - their
   d. <u>family's</u> - their
   e. <u>Anne's</u> - Her

4. a. froze
   b. sprang
   c. splashed
   d. caught
   e. twirled
   f. wept

5. Answers will vary.

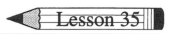

Here Louisa played on the grass, made friends with the passersby, or, plumping down to rest, would sit looking up at the tall elms with their high trunks and enormously long branches, so different from the round leafy beeches of the woods at her birthplace. The tall elderly houses of Beacon Hill looked down on her out of their many-paned windows, where the blue and purple glass was a sign of exceedingly aristocratic old age.

Invincible Louisa by Cornelia Meigs.
© 1933, © 1961, 1968 by Cornelia Meigs.
Used by permission, Little, Brown and Company.

✐ Teacher's Note: As your student completes each lesson, choose skills from the Review Activities that he needs. The Review Activities follow each lesson.

1. a. Write the literature passage from dictation. Compare your copy to the passage and correct any errors.

   b. Look up the word *aristocratic* in the dictionary. What does it mean?

   c. Make a spelling list of any misspelled words from your dictation or use the following suggested list:

passersby	enormously
birthplace	elderly
aristocratic	exceedingly

   d. Three of the words in the suggested spelling list have the same suffix. Identify the suffix. What part of speech are each of these words? Remember, most words ending in **-ly** are adverbs. Some are adjectives, such as *friendly* and *lovely.*

   e. What two words in the suggested spelling list are compound words? What words make up each compound?

   f. Find the word *different* in the literature passage. Usually words ending in **-ent** and **-ant** sound alike but are often misspelled. It is the same with words ending in **-ence** and **-ance**. When spelling a word with one of these endings, carefully enunciate each syllable.

1.
b. having the characteristic of nobility

d. -ly - adverb

e. passers-by
   birth-place

281

Spelling Tip
Do not confuse the spelling of words ending in **-ent** and **-ence** with words ending in **-ant** and **-ance**.

1.
g.
-ant: defiant, instant, relevant, resistant, abundant
-ent: confident, dependent, insistent, persistent, insolent
-ance: instance, defiance, relevance, resistance, abundance
-ence: confidence, insistence, persistence, dependence, existence

2.
a. beech - a type of tree

beach - a sandy place at the edge of a body of water

2.
c. branches
long
enormously

g. Copy the following words under the correct heading.

defiant   defiance   confidence
confident   instant   instance
dependence   dependent   insistent
insistence   relevant   relevance
resistant   resistance   abundant
abundance   sentence   persistent
persistence   existence   insolent

	-ant	**-ent**	**-ance**	**-ence**
Ex:	defiant	confident	instance	independence

2. a. Find the word *beech* in the literature passage. What is the meaning of this word? Can you think of a homonym for the word *beech*? What is the meaning of the homonym?

b. The first word of the literature passage is *here;* it is telling us where Louisa played. Words that answer the questions *where, how, when,* or *how much* are called adverbs.

c. Adverbs modify or describe verbs, but they also can describe adjectives or another adverb. Look at the phrase *enormously long branches.* What is the noun being described? What word describes the branches? What word describes *long*?

d. Look at the last phrase of the literature passage.

of exceedingly aristocratic old age

Underline the adjective and circle the adverb.

e. A good writer uses strong verbs and descriptive adverbs and adjectives to help the reader see and feel what is happening. Sometimes, a writer will give human qualities to animals or objects to bring the story alive. This is called **personification**.

Ex: Bright yellow daisies peeked over the hillside. Daisies do not really peek, but with the use of personification, the daisies come alive.

Find an example of personification in the literature passage.

f. Write a paragraph that tells about your home or neighborhood. Be sure to use descriptive adjectives and adverbs.

3. a. A **biography** is a nonfiction story of a person's life written by someone else. Biographies contain information about a person's life such as when they were born, their childhood, their interests, and more. Think of someone you know that you think would be interesting to interview; perhaps a grandparent, a missionary friend, or someone who has achieved goals you would also like to achieve. Make a list of questions you would like to ask them. Then ask permission for an interview and schedule an appointment. Be sure to take along a camera and take a picture if possible.

d. of exceedingly aristocratic old age

e. elderly houses of Beacon Hill looked down on her out of their many-paned windows

b. Below are some sample questions that could be used for the interview.

Sample Interview Questions

1) When and where were you born?
2) What did your parents do for a living?
3) Where did you grow up?
4) Where did you go to school?
5) What are some of your fondest childhood memories?
6) How many brothers and sisters did you have?
7) Where did you go to church?
8) What were your interests growing up?
9) What kind of jobs did you work as a teenager?
10) Did you go to college? If so, where?
11) Were you ever in the military?
12) What kind of job did you start with after finishing school?
13) Where did you first meet your husband/wife?
14) What attracted you to him/her?
15) When did you get married?
16) Where did you first live after getting married?
17) How many children did you have?
18) What was your family like?
19) What goals have you had in your life and have you reached them?
20) What is the most important advice you could give me?

---

c. Review your spelling words.

4. a. Interview the person using the questions as a guideline. Ask the person if you may use a tape recorder to record the interview. Take careful notes of what they say.

b. Compare the recorded interview with your notes. Did you miss anything important?

c. Begin your biography by following these guidelines.

   1) Read through your notes and determine the main idea.
   2) Decide on your opening sentence. Try to capture your audience's attention by presenting your topic in an interesting way.
   3) Biographies are usually written in chronological order, so write your sentences accordingly.

d. Take an oral or written spelling pretest.

5. a. Choose one of the following activities.

   1) Write the literature passage from dictation. Check your copy for spelling and punctuation.

   2) Complete writing the biography. Edit carefully for mistakes and make a final copy for your teacher. If possible include a picture of the person you interviewed.

   3) Choose skills from the *Review Activities* on the next page.

Review Activities

Choose only the skills your student needs to review.

1. *Adjectives and Adverbs:*
   Circle the adjectives and underline the adverbs in the following paragraph.

   The sun shone brillantly in the clear blue sky. Majestic oaks gently spread their strong limbs to shade the little creatures from the scorching sun. The babbling brook gingerly wound its way through the tiny crevices in the rocky hillside. The quiet woodlands patiently waited for the coolness of dusk.

2. *Personification*
   Find at least one example of personification in the paragraph above.

3. *Bibliography*
   Read a short biography of a famous person. Compare the biography you wrote in Lesson 35 with the one you read. Does it contain some of the same elements? Is there anything you would like to add to your next biography?

1.
Adjectives: clear, blue, majestic, strong, little, scorching, babbling, tiny, rocky, quiet
Adverbs: brillantly, gently, gingerly, patiently

2. trees gently spread their strong limbs

babbling brook gingerly wound

woodlands patiently waited

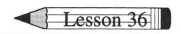

You are the salt of the earth; but if the salt has become tasteless, how will it be made salty again? It is good for nothing anymore, except to be thrown out and trampled under foot by men. You are the light of the world. A city set on a hill cannot be hidden. Nor do men light a lamp, and put it under the peck measure, but on the lampstand; and it gives light to all who are in the house. Let your light shine before men in such a way that they may see your good works, and glorify your Father who is in heaven.

Matthew 5:13-16 (NASB)

1. a. Read the literature passage. Write it from dictation. Compare your copy with the passage and correct all spelling and punctuation errors. Why is the word *Father* capitalized?

   b. What is the suffix in the word *tasteless*? How does this suffix change the meaning of the root word *taste*?

   c. The suffix **-fy** appears in the word *glorify* in the literature passage. This suffix means *make*. Add it to your list of suffixes. Can you think of any other words that have this suffix? How was the spelling of the root word *glory* changed before this suffix was added?

   d. Make a spelling list of any misspelled words or use the following suggested list.

tasteless	trampled	lampstand
measure	glorify	works

   e. Find two verbs from the suggested spelling list that is written in the past tense. Are they regular verbs (**R**) or irregular verbs (**IR**)?

1.
a. **Names referring to God are capitalized.**

b. **-less; changes the meaning to *without taste***

c. **-fy; to make**
   Possible examples: fortify, liquefy, amplify;

   the y was changed to i

e. **trampled -R; hidden - IR**

f. Look at the word *works* from the suggested spelling list. When spelling a word with a **/w/** sound followed by the **/er/** sound, the word is usually spelled **wor**.

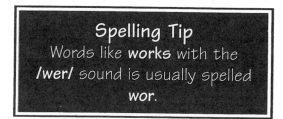

Spelling Tip
Words like **works** with the
/wer/ sound is usually spelled
wor.

g. Copy these words and underline **wor**. Say the words aloud as you write them.

word	worth	world
worm	worse	worry

2.
a. Second person - use of the pronoun *you, your*

2. a. In what person is the literature passage written? First, second, or third? What pronoun used throughout the literature passage helps you determine in what person the passage is written?

b. to exalt and honor Answers will vary.

b. Look up the word *glorify* in the dictionary. What does it mean? How can God be glorified by your good works? Memorize the last sentence of the literature passage. Practice until you can say it and write it from memory.

c. You are the light of the world. It compares you with light.

c. Read the first sentence of the literature passage again. It compares *you* with *salt*. When a comparison of two unlike things is made <u>without</u> using *like* or *as* it is called a **metaphor**. Find another metaphor in the literature passage. Tell your teacher what two things are being compared.

d. Write two metaphors. Be sure not to use *like* or *as* in your comparison.

Ex: This situation is a thorn in my side.

3. a. Find some information about salt and light in an
      encyclopedia, science book, or library book. What are some
      uses for salt and light? What are some of their
      characteristics? Write down what you find.

   b. The literature passage is filled with comparisons. One way
      to compare words is to look at a word that means the
      opposite of the word. This is the **antonym** of the word.
      For example, the antonym of *light* is *dark*.

   c. Choose the word from the word group that is the best
      antonym for each word.

      1) tall   little, small, short
      2) slow   fast, accelerate, sluggish
      3) sunny   windy, hot, cloudy
      4) loud   shrill, quiet, peaceful
      5) near   beside, removed, far

3.
c. 1) short
**   2) fast**
**   3) cloudy**
**   4) quiet**
**   5) far**

4. a. Find the word *cannot* in the literature passage. The word
      cannot contains the negative word *not*. Do not use two
      negative words in the same sentence. Some negative words
      are *no, not, (n't), nothing, none, never, no one, hardly,* and
      scarcely.

      Ex: I *don't hardly* ever go there.
           (Incorrect - contains two negative words.)

      I *don't* ever go there. (Correct)
      I *hardly* ever go there. (Correct)

4.
b. 1) ever
   2) any
   3) any
   4) anything
   5) can

b. Choose the correct word. Avoid double negatives.

Ex: We couldn't see (*anything*, *nothing*) in the darkness.

1) I don't (*never*, *ever*) run in the hallway.
2) We couldn't see (*any*, *none*) of the boats that were crossing the river.
3) She didn't receive (*any*, *no*) donations for the mission fund.
4) I never found (*anything*, *nothing*) in the refrigerator to snack on.
5) We (*can*, *cannot*) scarcely do anything without someone changing the plans.

c. In the verses that make up the literature passage Jesus says that His followers are like salt and light. What do you think Jesus is encouraging us to do? Write a paragraph explaining how people can be salt and light. Use the information you found in your research in **3a** to help you.

d. Take an oral or written spelling pretest.

5. a. Choose one of the following activities.

1) Write the literature passage from dictation. Be sure to correct any spelling errors.

2) Write a thank you note to someone who has been a *light* in your life.

3) Choose skills from the *Review Activities* on the next page.

Review Activities

Choose only the skills your student needs to review.

1. *Suffixes*
Knowing that the suffix **-fy** means *to make*, try to define the following words. Then look them up in the dictionary to see if you are correct.

   a. liquefy
   b. fortify
   c. simplify

2. *Metaphor*
Underline the metaphors in the following paragraph. There is also one simile contained in the paragraph. Identify the simile and be sure not to confuse it with the metaphors.

     The sound of her voice was a summer breeze that brought warmth to everything it touched. Her eyes were blue sapphires that sparkled from under thick, long lashes and glowed with happy thoughts. Her laugh was like a thousand tinkling bells awakening the world with a cheerful sound.

3. *Antonyms*
Write an antonym for each of the following words. If you have trouble thinking of an antonym, use a thesaurus. Antonyms are usually listed at the end of the list of synonyms.

   a. divide
   b. guilty
   c. eagerly
   d. trust
   e. fact

---

1. a. to make into a liquid
   b. to make strong
   c. to make simple

2. Metaphors: her voice was a summer breeze
her eyes were blue sapphires

   Simile: her laugh was like a thousand tinkling bells

3. Possible answers:
   a. combine, unite
   b. innocent, blameless
   c. unwillingly, slowly
   d. doubt, disbelieve
   e. fiction, imagination

4. Possible answers:
We hardly ever go to the store without first making a list of the items we need to purchase. I can scarcely understand how anyone remembers everything they need without making a list. Mary didn't need any help in getting all the necessary items together at the store, and I didn't find anything missing when we arrived home.

4. *Double Negative*
Rewrite the following paragraph correcting any double negatives.

We don't hardly ever go to the store without first making a list of the items we need to purchase. I cannot scarcely understand how anyone remembers everything they need without making a list. Mary didn't need no help in getting all the necessary items together at the store, and I didn't find nothing missing when we arrived home.

Assessment 6
(Lessons 31 - 36)

1. Write three sentences describing yourself. Circle the adjectives you used.

2. Adjectives describe nouns answering the questions *what kind, how much,* or *which ones.* Write three sentences using adjectives that answer each of these questions.

3. Write the title of a book you've read.

4. How are adjectives and adverbs different?

5. Circle the direct object in the following sentence.

   Sharon played the piano beautifully.

6. Circle the pronouns in the literature passage used in Lesson 34. Tell what the antecedent of each pronoun is.

7. Look at the first three sentences in the literature passage in Lesson 16. Make a list of the verbs. Write the present and past tense for each verb.

8. Looking at your list of verbs from question above, which of them are regular verbs (**R**)? Which are irregular (**IR**)?

9. What is a biography?

10. Read the following sentences and write **CS** if it is a complete sentence or **F** if it is a fragment.

    a. I was tired after running the race.
    b. Gloria's sweet face.
    c. The walls were painted blue.
    d. Very fast moving ship.
    e. Running the race.

---

1. Answers will vary.

2. Answers will vary.

3. Answers will vary.

4. Adjectives modify (tell about) nouns and pronouns while adverbs modify (tell about) verbs, adjectives, or other adverbs.

5. piano

6. (her) - Jo
   (she) - Jo
   (her) - Jo
   (her) - Amy

7.
Present - come, lift, open, shake, fly
Past - came, lifted, opened, shook, flew

8. Regular - lift, open
   Irregular - come, shake, fly

9. A nonfiction story of a person's life written by someone else.

10.
a. Sentence
b. Fragment
c. Sentence
d. Fragment
e. Fragment

Enrichment Activities

The Enrichment Activities answers are listed below. Since the Enrichment Activities are not numbered, you can easily locate them by the lesson number that proceeds them in the *Student Activity Book.* Some of the Enrichment Activities do not have a specific answer. For those, please read the directions in your student's book and evaluate the activity accordingly.

Carry On, Mr. Bowditch Book Study
1. chronometer
2. ship log
3. sextant
4. compass
5. spyglass

Lesson 1, 3a - Answers will vary.

Lesson 1, 4c
1. big - large
2. tiny - small
3. make - build
4. rough - bumpy
5. carve - slice
6. grin - smile

Lesson 2, 4c - Answers will vary.

Lesson 3, 2c - Answers will vary.

Lesson 3, 4d
1. circle, triangle, circle
2. circle, circle, triangle
3. dot, rectangle, rectangle, rectangle, dot

Lesson 4, 3d
1. a rectangle on a triangle
2. a circle on a circle
3. a circle on a square
4. a square on a circle
5. a triangle on a rectangle
6. a circle on a rectangle

Lesson 5, 4d - Answers will vary.

Lesson 6, 3d
1. Q
2. C
3. S

Lesson 6, 4f - Answers will vary.

The Bronze Bow Book Study

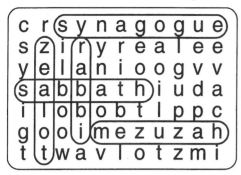

Lesson 7, 3d - Answers will vary.

Lesson 8, 3e
1. table   5. paper
2. cow   6. book
3. broccoli   7. oven
4. shark

Lesson 8, 4c
Sky - clouds, moon,stars   Land Vehicles - truck, car, bus
Ground - flowers, rocks, dirt   Water Vehicles - submarine, ship, sailboat

Hot - radiator, flame, summer   Hot Drinks - hot chocolate, coffee, hot tea
Cold - freezer, snowflake, ice cream   Cold Drinks - soda, milk, Orange Juice

Forest Animals - raccoon, squirrel, woodchuck   Nouns - building, car, shelf
Farm Animals - cow, goat, chicken   Verbs - stand, believe, whisper

Lesson 9, 3g
1. flour, dough, bread   4. food, vegetables, beans
2. vehicle, car, race car   5. clothes, shirt, sweatshirt
3. sport, baseball, Little League 6. book, novel, "Carry on, Mr. Bowditch"

Lesson 9, 4e - Answers will vary.

Lesson 10, 3e
1. antonym   6. antonym
2. category   7. category
3. synonym   8. synonym
4. part/whole   9. characterisitic
5. characteristic   10. part/whole

Lesson 10, 4d
1. degree   5. homonym
2. homonym   6. degree
3. function   7. function
4. sequence   8. sequence

Enrichment Activities

Lesson 11, 3e
1. category
2. synonym
3. sequence
4. homonym
5. antonym
6. function
7. part/whole
8. characteristic
9. degree
10. homonym
11. function
12. part/whole
13. characteristic
14. category
15. synonym

Lesson 11, 4d
1. fish
2. dull
3. cold
4. winter
5. bag
6. tired
7. jar
8. build
9. knot
10. run

Lesson 12, 3
1. hit
2. finish
3. rainbow
4. army
5. relax
6. fair
7. green
8. forget
9. soak
10. shape

Lesson 13, 5
Possible answers:
1. ship
2. state
3. hair
4. playful/cute
5. peace
6. cut
7. hour
8. baby
9. afternoon
10. whole
11. see
12. upset/stormy
13. soft
14. sky
15. disease
16. quick
17. learn
18. tail
19. sentence/paragraph
20. young

Lesson 15, 2d

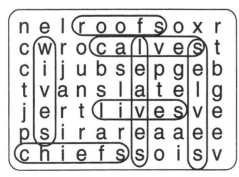

Lesson 15, 4e Answers will vary.

Lesson 16, 2c
1. hot dog   hitter   peach pit   pin prick   pancake
2. hot dog   an archaeological dig   pig sty   pumpkin pie lie down

Lesson 16, 4d
1. cat nap   car chase   chin up bar   baseball bat   bit and bridle
2. cat nap   cat nip   tip over   tin can   suntan

Lesson 17, 2c   Answers will vary.

Lesson 17, 4b   Answers will vary.

Lesson 18, 2c

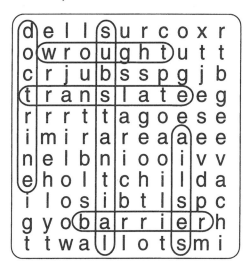

Big Red Book Study
1. careening   4. profoundly
2. ravenous   5. indispensable
3. hypodermic

Lesson 22, 2c   Possible Answers:
1. mean/keen   4. book   7. frown
2. rain   5. frantic   8. wake
3. toy   6. meek   9. fright

Lesson 22, 3c
I did not come to bring peace, but a sword.

Lesson 23, 3d
14

Lesson 23, 4d
1. a square on a square   4. a square on a triangle
2. a triangle on a triangle   5. a circle on a circle
3. a triangle on a rectangle   6. a circle on a square

Lesson 24, 4b Answers will vary.

Lesson 25, 1b
If at first you don't succeed, try, try again.
Suzy and her friends have the most books.

Lesson 26, 3d Answers will vary.

Lesson 26, 4c
1. a blue circle on a yellow square
2. a green rectangle on a red circle
3. a yellow square on a blue circle
4. a red triangle on a green triangle

Lesson 28, 4c Answers will vary.

Lesson 29, 2c
It is better to give than to receive.

Lesson 29, 3c Answers will vary.

Lesson 30, 4c
John, Melissa, Sally, Albert

Lesson 31,1e thoughtful
thoughtful - full of thought
part of speech - adjective
Possible word examples: restful, beautiful

Lesson 31, 2c and 3d Answers will vary.

Lesson 32, 3c Answers will vary.

Lesson 32 - 4d
1. noun
2. adverb
3. adjective
4. verb
5. adverb
6. adjective - verb
7. noun - adverb
8. adjective - noun - verb - adverb

Lesson 33, 3d and 4b Answers will vary.

Lesson 34, 3c Answers will vary.

Lesson 35, 4d
1. a red circle on a yellow square on a green rectaqngle
2. a green square on a blue circle on a red triangle
3. a blue triangle on a green triangle on a yellow circle
4. a green rectangle on a red square on a blue circle

Lesson 36, 2d Answers will vary.

Lesson 36, 3c
Kelly

Prefixes

A prefix is a letter or group of letters which come before the base or root word, changing the meaning of the word.

Commonly Used Prefixes

a, an - not, without (*anew, anonymous, apathy*)
ab - away, from (*abomination, absent, absolve*)
al - to or towards (*alarm, alcove*)
ante - before (*antecedent, antemeridian*)
anti - against (*antibiotic, anticlimactic, antifreeze*)
be - on, away (*beguile, behind, betray*)
bene - well (*benediction, benevolence, beneficiary*)
bi - both (*biathlon, biannual, bicycle*)
bio - living (*biology, biopsy, biography*)
by - near, side (*bylaw, bygone, bystander*)
circ - around (*circumstance, circumstantial, circulation*)
co, con - together, with (*cohabitant, coheir, copilot*)
contra - against (*contraband, contradict, contrary*)
de - down, from (*deprivation, depression, denounce*)
di - twice, two (*diameter, dialect, dialogue*)
dis - reverse, apart (*disarray, disappoint, disintegrate*)
dys - bad (*dyspepsia, dystrophy, dyslexia*)
en - in, into (*envelope, endow, enforce*)
ex - out, forth(*extol, excitement, exchange*)
extra - beyond (*extracurricular, extraneous, extragalactic*)
fore - before in time (*forego, foremost, forefather*)
il, im, in - into (*illumine, implant, inside*)
il, im, in, ir - not (*illegal, impartial, indivisible, irrelevant*)
inter - between (*intermission, interrupt, intercept*)
mal - poorly, badly (*malady, malpractice, maladjusted*)
mis - incorrect (*misspell, misinterpret, misconduct*)
mono - one (*monogamous, monotone, monocle*)
multi - many (*multiplication, multipurpose, multitude*)
neo - new (*neolithic, neonatal, neophyte*)
non - not (*nonfiction, nonsense, nonexistent*)
para - almost, beside (*paragraph, paraphrase, parachute*)
per - complete, through (*perambulate, perceptible, percolator*)
poly - many (*polygamy, polyunsaturated, polyurethane*)
post - after (*postwar, postgraduate, postglacial*)
pre - before (*preview, prevent, precursor*)

pro - in favor of, forward (*pro-life, prolific, prologue*)
pseudo - false (*pseudonym, pseudoclassic*)
quad - four (*quadruplets, quadrant, quadriplegic*)
quint - five (*quintuplets, quintet, quintile*)
re - back, again (*return, remember, revive*)
retro - backwards (*retrospect, retroactive*)
self - by oneself (*self-serve, self-indulgent, self-employed*)
sub - under (*submarine, subway, substitute*)
super - over, more (*superhuman, supernatural, supervise*)
trans - across (*transcontinental, translate, transfusion*)
tri - three (*tricycle, tripod, trimester*)
ultra - beyond (*ultraviolet, ultramodern, ultraconservative*)
un - not, release (*undress, untie, undo*)
under - beneath (*underline, underground*)
uni - one (*universe, unity, unicycle*)

Suffixes

A suffix is a letter or group of letters which come after the base or root word, changing the meaning of the word. The suffix is usually helpful in determining the part of speech (noun, verb, adjective, etc.)

Commonly Used Suffixes

able, ible - able to do (*sensible, possible, pliable*)
age - act or state of (*manage, salvage, bandage*)
al - relating to (*final, natural, remedial*)
an, ian, ese, ish - native of (*American, Japanese, Spanish*)
ance, ence - action, state of (*abstinence, reluctance, alliance*)
ant - agent, performing (*reactant, servant*)
ar, er, or - one who, that which (*operator, manager, beggar*)
ary, ery, ory - relating to, connected with, place where (*category, supervisory, infirmary, stationery*)
asis - process, condition (*hypothesis, neurosis, catharsis*)
ate - make, cause (*compassionate, suffocate, generate*)
cian - having a certain skill (*physician, musician, technician*)
cide - kill (*infanticide, suicide, homicide*)
cule - very small (*minuscule, molecule, ridicule*)
cy - action, function (*vagrancy, truancy, leniency*)
dom - quality, realm, office (*freedom, wisdom, kingdom*)
ee - one who receives the action (*emcee, employee, refugee*)

er - one who or that which (*singer, mocker*)

en - make, made of (*flatten, lighten, wooden*)

ess - female (*princess, goddess, actress*)

et, ette - group, a small one (*majorette, midget*)

ful - full of (*beautiful, joyful, plentiful*)

fy - make (*multiply, unify, amplify*)

hood - condition, order, quality (*neighborhood, brotherhood, womanhood*)

ic - nature of, like (*fantastic, poetic, heroic*)

ice - condition, state (*justice, poultice, novice*)

ile - relating to, capable of (*senile, revile, penile*)

ine - nature of (*clandestine, morphine, chlorine*)

ion, sion, tion - act of, state of, result of (*intrusion, salutation, opinion*)

ish - origin, resembling (*childish, fiendish, reddish*)

ism - system, characteristic (*Buddhism, Communism, monotheism*)

ist - one who, that which (*pianist, philanthropist, dentist*)

ite - nature or quality of (*stalagmite, infinite*)

ity, ty - state or quality of (*university, clarity, unity*)

ive - causing, making (*captive, active, submissive*)

ize - make (*victimize, scrutinize, penalize*)

less - without (*thoughtless, helpless, homeless*)

ly - like, manner of (*lovely, quickly, softly*)

ment - act or state of (*bewilderment, sentiment, advertisement*)

ness - state of (*happiness, holiness, sleeplessness*)

oid - like (*android, spheroid, steroid*)

ology - study, science (*theology, sociology, biology*)

ous, ious, eous - full of, having (*spacious, superfluous, fabulous*)

ship - office, state, quality (*fellowship, friendship*)

sis - process, condition (*hypothesis, neurosis, catharsis*)

some - like, tending to (*meddlesome, twosome, lonesome*)

tude - state or condition of (*solitude, altitude, multitude*)

ure - state of, act, rank (*seizure, rapture, culture*)

ward - in the direction of (*forward, backward, wayward*)

y - inclined to, tend to (*bumpy, silky, scary*)

Skills Index

The numbers and letters listed after each skill refer to the Lesson number and Book Study.

Book Studies

Carry On, Mr. Bowditch - A
The Bronze Bow - B

Big Red - C
The Horse and His Boy - D

Composition

advertisement - 22
bibliography - 19
biography - 2,35
business letter - 27
caricature - 6
character sketch - 32
circle word picture - 6
closing paragraph - 19,20
closing sentence - 5
creative writing - 2,6,7,8,9,10,11,15,16,22,23,27,32,34,35,36
dialogue - 7,28,31
duolog - 31
essay - 18,19,20
expressive verbs - 23
figurative language - 3,4
first draft - 19,20
first person - 16
friendly letter - 5,26
irony - 22
journal - A,16,21
main idea - 18,20
mood - 3,10
news story - 28,30

opening paragraph - 19
outline - 19,20
paragraph - 5,27
paraphrase - 1,25
personification - 3
plagiarism - 18
poetry - 4,14,31
prose - 4
research - 12,13,18,19,20
simile - 3,8
summary - 2
supporting detail - 20
supporting sentence - 5
thesis statement - 18,19,20
titles - 4
topic - 18
topic sentence - 5,9
types of sentences - 8,11,29
writing a fable - 33
writing dialogue - 7
writing instructions - 5

Grammar

adjective - 3,6,7,8,16,30,31,32,34,35
adverb - 5,6,16,27,30,32,35
antecedent - 4,16,23,25
antonym - 36
apostrophe - 6,9,11,20,30
articles - 16,32
being verb - 2
capitalization - 6,14,15,16,18,26,27,28,33,36
colon - 27
comma - 5,9,10,11,20,22,23,27,34
common noun - 2
comparative adjective - 7,31,32,34
complete predicate - 8
complete sentence - 8
complete subject - 8
compound sentence - 9,27,34
compound subject - 9,27
compound verb - 9,27
compound word - 5,6,29,32,35
conjunction - 2,9,10,26,34
contraction - 6,11,22,25,26
declarative sentence - 8,11,29
dependent clause - 23
direct address - 11
direct object - 33
direct quotation - 7,22,31
double negative - 36
exclamation mark - 8,22
exclamatory sentence - 8,11,29
fragment - 8
helping verb - 2,30
homonym - 10,15,24,25,28
hyphen - 6,32
imperative sentence - 8,11,29
independent clause - 10,23,34
interjection - 22,28
interrogative sentence - 8,11,29
irregular noun - 15
irregular verb - 29,30,34,36
its / it's - 16,23

linking verb - 32
noun - 2,8
object of the preposition - 26
parenthetical expression - 22
parts of speech - 2
period - 8
pore / pour / poor - 28
possessive noun - 6,11,30,34
possessive pronoun - 16,20,23,25,26,34
predicate adjective - 32
prefix - 1
preposition - 21,23,26
prepositional phrase - 21,23,33
principal parts of verb - 30
pronoun - 4,14,15,16,20,25,27,34,36
proper noun - 2,16
question mark - 8
lay / lie - 15
quotation marks - 7,8,11,22,28,31
quotation rules - 7,11,28
semicolon - 10,26,34
simple predicate - 9
simple subject - 9
sit / set - 21
speech tag - 7
split quotation - 11,22
subject/verb agreement - 27
suffix - 21,26
superlative adjective - 7,31,34
syllables - 3,34
synonym - 1,7,16
there / they're / their - 24
titles - 16,27,28,33
to / too / two - 15
transitional words - 5
underlining - 27
verb - 2,6,9,23,27,33,34,36
verb phrase - 2
verb tense - 29,30,34

Reading

alliteration - 14
antonym - 36
autobiography - 17
biography - 2,17,35
bound base - 7
character study - 32,34
choral reading - 29
climax - 10
comprehension - 1,20,28,A,B,C,D
conclusion - 10,11
conflict - B,11
context clues - 4
couplet - 31
dialect - 14
dialogue - 7,28,31
duolog - 31
end rhyme - 4,14
etymology - 1,22
exposition - 10
fable - 33
falling action - 10
fiction - 17
first person - 10,15,27,34
foreshadowing - 26
free base - 7
homonym - 10,28
internal rhyme - 14
irony - 22
metaphor - 36
mood - 3,10,11,20
narrator - 10,15,20
news story - 28,30
personification - 3,4,7,35
plot - 10
plot line - 10
poetry - 3,4,14,29,31
point of view - 10,15,18
prefix
    al- 7,
    be- 4,23
    con- 24,33
    de- 15,33
    dis- 27,33
    en- 24
    ex- 5
    fore- 9
    im- 3,
    in- 6,7,27

    pre- 1
    re- 8,15
    pro- 15
    un- 1,27
    under- 16
    sub- 18
prose - 4
reciting poetry - 14
repetition - 14,29
research - 17
resolution - 10,11
rhyme scheme - 14
rising action - 10
second person - 15
simile - 3,4,8
speech - 24
stanza - 4
suffix
    -ally 30
    -ed 3,4,9,33
    -er 7
    -es 11
    -est 7
    -fy 36
    -ing 3,9
    -ion 21
    -ish 32
    -less 27,36
    -ness 29
    -ous 21
    -ful 5,31
    -ly 5,16,29,30,35
    -sion / -tion 21,24
    -ious / -eous 21
    -able / -ible 32
    -ent / -ant 35
    -ence / -ance 35
syllables - 3,10
synonym - 1,7,16
third person - 10,15,27
topic sentence - 5
triplet - 4
vocabulary - 4,A,B,C,D
word analogy - 11

Spelling

-able / -ible - 32
-ent,-ant / -ence,-ance - 35
-sion/-tion /shun/ - 24
adding prefix- 27
adding suffix - 26,29,30,33
c and **k** make **/k/** sound - 2
c before **a** or **u** - 2
change **f** to **v** - 15
change **y** to **i** - 9,11,15,28
compound words - 5
contractions - 6
dg/dge - 21
double consonants - 20
double last consonant before adding suffix - 7,9,30,33

drop silent **e** and add suffix - 4,9,25
er/ir/ur/ear - 23,33
i before **e** - 8
-igh - 10
kn / gn - 20
ou /ow/ - 31
ough /o/ - 22
plural of words ending in **o** - 34
plural rules - 15
plurals - 11,15,28,34
plural of irregular words - 15
sh,ch,x,s,z - 11, 15
wor - 36
wr - 18

Study Skills

alphabetical order - 17
Bible translation - 1
Caldecott Award - 17
checklist - 19
context clues - 4
Dewey Decimal System - 17,18
dictionary - 1,22,24,31,32,35,36
encyclopedia - 17,24,36,B
essay - 18,20
etymology - 1,22
illustration - 4,7,9
interview - 35
library - 17
map skills - A
memorization - 24,25,36

moral - 33
Newbery Award - 17
news story - 28,30
note cards - 18,25
note-taking - 21
oral presentation - 25
organizing information - 13
organizing thought - 4
reference materials - 12,13
research - 2,12,13,17,18,19,36,B
research story - 13
sequence - 5,23,35
thesaurus - 1,16,20
timeline - 1
word analogy - 11

Bibliography

Aesop's Fables.

Alcott, Louisa May. *Little Women*, 1868.

Aldrich, Thomas Bailey. *The Story of a Bad Boy*. 1870.

Beechick, Ruth. *You Can Teach Your Child Successfully*. Arrow Press, 1988.

Brink, Carol Ryrie. *Caddie Woodlawn*. Macmillian Publishing Company, (1935) 1973.

Defoe, Daniel. *Robinson Crusoe*. 1719.

DeJong, Meindert. *The Wheel on the School*. Harper and Row, 1954.

Field, Eugene. "Jest 'Fore Christmas."

Grahame, Kenneth. *The Wind in the Willows*. 1907.

Henry, Marguerite. *King of the Wind*. Rand McNally & Company, 1948.

Kjelgaard, Jim. *Big Red*. Random House.

Latham, Jean Lee. *Carry On, Mr. Bowditch*. Houghton Mifflin, 1955.

Lewis, C.S. *The Horse and His Boy*. Macmillan Publishing, 1954.

Lewis, C.S. *Prince Caspian*. William Collins and Sons, Ltd., 1951.

Meigs, Cornelia. *Invincible Louisa*. Little, Brown and Company, 1933.

Milne, A. A. *The House at Pooh Corner*.

Montgomery, L.M. *Anne of Green Gables*. 1908.

Nesbit, E. *The Railway Children*. 1906.

Ransome, Arthur. *Swallow and Amazons*. David Godine, Publisher, Inc., 1931.

Rawls, Wilson. *Where the Red Fern Grows*. Doubleday, 1961. 1974.

Salten, Felix. *Bambi*. Simon & Schuster, Inc., 1928.

Speare, Elizabeth George. *The Bronze Bow*. Houghton Mifflin, 1861.

Stevenson, Robert Louis. *Kidnapped*. 1886.

Ten Boom, Corrie. *The Hiding Place*. Chosen Books, 1971.

Tennyson, Lord Alfred. "The Eagle."

Wilder, Laura Ingalls. *Little House in the Big Woods*. Harper and
  Row Publishers, 1932.

Wyss, Johann. *The Swiss Family Robinson*. 1818.

See where learning takes you.

www.commonsensepress.com

Congratulations,

You Are Part Of The *Common Sense Press* Family.

Now you can receive our FREE e-mail newsletter, containing:
- Teaching Tips
- Product Announcements
- Helpful Hints from Veteran Homeschoolers
- & Much More!

Please take a moment to register with us.

Common Sense Press
Product Registration
8786 Highway 21
Melrose, FL 32666

Or online at
www.commonsensepress.com/register

After registering, search our site for teaching tips, product information, and ways to get more from your *Common Sense Press* purchase.

Your Name _____

Your E-Mail Address _____

Your Address _____

City _____ State _____ Zip _____

Product Purchased _____

From What Company Did You Purchase This Product? _____

Get involved with the *Common Sense Press* community.
Visit our web site to contribute your ideas, read how others
are teaching their children, see new teaching tips, and more.